2 √4

P9-BZK-050

GIVE ME A BREAK

Give Me

a Break

How I Exposed Hucksters,
Cheats, and Scam Artists
and Became the Scourge
of the Liberal Media . . .

John
Stossel

HarperCollins*Publishers*

HarperCollins books may be purchased for educational, business, or sales promotional use. For information, please write: Special Markets Department, HarperCollins Publishers Inc., 10 East 53rd Street, New York, NY 10022.

FIRST EDITION

Designed by Amy Hill

Printed on acid-free paper

Library of Congress Cataloging-in-Publication Data is available upon request.

ISBN 0-06-052914-8

04 05 06 07 08 ❖/RRD 10 9 8 7 6 5 4 3 2 1

I dedicate this book to Aaron Wildavsky. His work taught me how risk taking makes life safer, and gave me the courage to report against the grain. He died before I could interview him.

CONTENTS

GIVE ME A BREAK

CHAPTER ONE

What Happened to Stossel?

*Journalism without a moral
position is impossible.*

— M a r g u e r i t e   D u r a s

I was once a heroic consumer reporter; now I'm a threat to journalism.

As a consumer reporter, I exposed con men and thieves, confronting them with hidden camera footage that unmasked their lies, put some out of business, and helped send the worst of them to jail. The *Dallas Morning News* called me the "bravest and best of television's consumer reporters." Marvin Kitman of *Newsday* said I was "the man who makes 'em squirm," whose "investigations of the unjust and wicked . . . are models." Jonathan Mandell of the *New York Daily News* quoted a WCBS official who "proudly" said, "No one's offended more people than John Stossel."

Ah, "proudly." Those were the days. My colleagues *liked* it when I offended people. They called my reporting "hard-hitting," "a public service." I won 18 Emmys, and lots of other journalism awards. One year

I got so many Emmys, another winner thanked me in his acceptance speech "for not having an entry in this category."

Then I did a terrible thing. Instead of just applying my skepticism to business, I applied it to government and "public interest" groups. This apparently violated a religious tenet of journalism. Suddenly I was no longer "objective."

Ralph Nader said I "used to be on the cutting edge," but had become "lazy and dishonest." According to *Brill's Content*, "Nader was a fan during Stossel's consumer advocate days," but "now talks about him as if he'd been afflicted with a mysterious disease."

These days, I rarely get awards from my peers. Some of my ABC colleagues look away when they see me in the halls. Web sites call my reporting "hurtful, biased, absurd." "What happened to Stossel?" they ask. CNN invited me to be a guest on a journalism show; when I arrived at the studio, I discovered they'd titled it "Objectivity and Journalism—Does John Stossel Practice Either?" People now e-mail me, calling me "a corporate whore" and a "sellout."

How did I get from there to here? This book is the story of my professional and intellectual journey.

THE MAKING OF A CONTRARIAN

I never planned to be a reporter. In college, when I tried to write a story for the school newspaper, the editors sneered and said, "Leave the writing to us." I was never much of a public speaker. I'm kind of shy, and I stutter.

It all happened because I wanted to postpone graduate school. I'd been accepted by the University of Chicago's School of Hospital

Management, but I was sick of school. I was an indifferent student. I daydreamed through half my classes at Princeton, and applied to grad school only because I was ambitious, and grad school seemed like the right path for a 21-year-old who wanted to get ahead. Hospital management sounded like a useful and interesting career. But before I headed for the University of Chicago, I took a job. I thought the stress of a real job would make me appreciate school, and then I would embrace graduate studies with renewed vigor.

Every time a company sent a recruiter to Princeton, I volunteered for an interview. I got a dozen job offers and took the one that offered me a free flight that would take me the farthest: *Seattle Magazine*. They said they'd teach me how to sell advertising or do bookkeeping. But by the time I graduated, *Seattle Magazine* had gone out of business. I was lucky, though: Ancil Payne, the boss of the parent company, King Broadcasting, called me to say, "We have a job available at KGW, our Portland, Oregon, TV station. Want to try that?"

I said yes, although I had never thought about a career in TV news. I'd never even watched much of it. I had no journalism training.

In Portland I started as a newsroom gofer and worked my way up. I researched stories for others. Then, after studying how the anchormen spoke, I started writing stories for them. A few years later the news director told me to go on the air and read what I wrote. I reluctantly tried, but I was horrible at it—nervous, awkward, scared. When I watched a tape of my performance, I was embarrassed.

But I persisted because I *had* to succeed. When I was growing up, my mother had repeatedly warned me that if I didn't study hard, get into a good college, and succeed in a profession, I would "freeze in the dark." I believed it.

I was also determined to keep pace with my brother Tom, who was the superstar of the family. While I partied and played poker, he studied hard, got top grades, and went to Harvard Medical School. Since I knew there was no way I could compete with Tom in his field, I tried to become a success in the profession I'd stumbled into.

In retrospect, I see that it probably helped me that I had taken no journalism courses. Television news was still inventing itself then, and I was open to new ideas. I learned through *fear*. My fear of failure made me desperate to do the job well, to try to figure out what people *really* needed to know and how I could say it in a way that would work well on TV. I stayed late at night to experiment with different ways of editing film. I watched NBC's David Brinkley and Jack Perkins and shamelessly copied them.

But I couldn't talk as well as they could. Since childhood, my stuttering had come and gone. Sometimes I was sure the problem had disappeared forever. Then it would return with such a vengeance, I'd fear saying anything at all. I'd sit silent in class, and miss out on dates because I was afraid to talk to girls. When I went to work for the TV station in Portland, I didn't worry much about my stuttering because I never thought I'd have to speak on television. Then, when they actually asked me to go on the air, I thought I could pull it off because many of us stutterers (James Earl Jones, for example) are fluent when we read out loud or act.

At first, reading the news on TV felt a lot like acting and I could read what I wrote without stuttering. But as I got better—as my on-air work became more like my normal speech—I started having problems getting words out. Since I wasn't on the air live, however, I was able to conceal my stuttering. The film editor would simply snip out the repetitions. As I started doing live TV, I would hide my problem by substituting synonyms for words I thought would be trouble (mostly those beginning with the plosive sounds, *d, g,* and *b*). That became more awkward when I started consumer reporting because the words "good," "better," and "different" are so basic to product comparisons, but I tried to glide around that problem by using phrases like "works well" and "it's superior to."

One day, however, my boss told me to announce the local election expenditure totals on a five-minute midday newscast. It was a stomach-turning shock when, on the air, I realized there's no workable synonym for "dollar." (There's "bucks," but that wasn't dignified enough for a newscast, and anyway, it begins with a plosive, too.) I was still in mid-sentence, saying that some politician had "spent ninety-five thousand d-d-d-," struggling to get the word out, when time ran out and they cut me off the air.

Even though my stuttering usually wasn't that bad, the fear tortured me. On days when live work was scheduled, I'd wake in a cold sweat, anticipating the humiliation that might come eight hours later, when thousands of people would watch my mouth lock. That all-day anxiety often made me want to quit.

But it was a cool job. I was learning a lot, and amazingly, unlike school, they paid me. Seven thousand dollars per year wasn't great money, even in 1970, but the work felt *important*. Sometimes I came up with information I thought really helped people. And being on TV was a great way to meet women. So I kept postponing grad school.

THE BIG TIME

After a few years, I was ready to try to test the waters in a bigger city. I looked for a job on the West Coast, sending videotapes of my work to news directors at KGO and KPIX in San Francisco. Both said no. KTVU Oakland turned me down; KNBC, KABC, and KCBS, too. Then out of the blue I got a job offer from WCBS-TV in New York. I thought, "Wow, New York City—the biggest market—now I'll really learn what journalism is about."

But WCBS was a disappointment. The journalism at KGW in Portland was better. We did more research and tried harder to find creative ways to use the film. We'd work together, filling in for each other so some of us could pursue stories for days, or weeks. At WCBS, there were many hardworking people, but union work rules discouraged extra work and creativity.

We'd show up for work at 10 A.M., and the assignment editor would tell us what we'd cover that day. I sometimes suggested we ought to report on something else, and he'd tell me, "Do what you're told." Each correspondent would then grab one of the three-man union crews and drive to the scene of the fire, murder, news conference, or whatever the assignment editor wanted us to cover. We'd arrive like a lumbering army. It was remarkable how much time a cameraman, a soundman, and an electrician could take just getting out of the car. Every move was deliberate.

They had no reason to hurry because no one ever got fired. There was no reason to work harder because union rules demanded everyone be paid the same. Many union workers were masters not just at killing time but at killing innovation. "Can't be done." "Against the rules." "Equipment won't do that." It stunned me that so many of them could be indifferent to what I thought was important work. They cared about overtime. And lunch. They had endless discussions over where to eat.

"Can't we keep shooting? This is just getting interesting!"

"No—it's time for our break. It's in our union contract."

Once, for a story on sleep disorders, we needed footage of someone snoring. The only snoring person we could find was our own union electrician, who had so little to do that he dozed off on the job. We got great footage of *him* snoring, but didn't use it, after he begged us not to. WCBS's "union shop" was my first real introduction to the deals made by special interests.

RATINGS SUCCESS

The man who hired me at WCBS was Ed Joyce. At the time, he was news director at the local station; later, he became president of CBS News. Joyce worked with a man who traveled the country, watching local news from motel rooms and sending back videotapes of reporters whose work he liked. Joyce had a good eye for TV journalists—he hired Arnold Diaz, Linda Ellerbee, Dave Marash, Joel Siegel, and Lynn Sherr, all of whom soon became network correspondents. He plucked me out of faraway Portland, Oregon. I'm grateful for that, but I hated Joyce. He was cold and critical. Colleagues told me he thought he'd get more out of people if they were scared. I don't think that's the best way to manage people, but he sure scared me, and I worked hard to avoid his wrath.

Although I hated Joyce, he did three great things for me: He hired me, he freed me to pursue my own story ideas, and he fixed my stuttering.

Well, he didn't fix it personally, but when I heard about a promising three-week stuttering clinic in Roanoke, Virginia, he gave me time off and encouraged me to give it a try. This clinic is called the Hollins Communications Research Institute, and it has a novel approach to stuttering; it has stutterers relearn how to make every sound. Apparently we stutterers, even when we don't block on words, articulate the sounds harder than necessary, and that often leads to word blocks. In Roanoke, they had us sit in little rooms, reading words into a microphone, concentrating on beginning each sound gently. Every time we hit a word too hard, a red light came on. The therapy was tedious, but it worked for me; it changed the way I spoke. Three weeks later, I was back in New York, eager to try out what I had learned. It was liberating. For the first time in my life, I felt I could approach any sound without fear of a humiliating mouth lock. It was as if a cork had been removed from my throat and 20 years of speech were pouring out. People couldn't shut me up. I'm not "cured"—I still stutter sometimes—but stuttering is no longer the obstacle it was.

At WCBS I was steadily growing more frustrated with following the assignment editor's vision of what was "news." Perhaps because of my stuttering, I'd always avoided covering what the pack covered. I didn't think I could succeed if I had to compete by shouting out questions at news conferences, so I seldom volunteered to report the day's "big news." That turned out to have an unexpected benefit. It helped me realize that the most important news happens slowly. The assignment editor at WCBS was focused only on that day's events: government pronouncements, election results, grisly fires and murders. But the world's real life-changing developments were things like the women's movement, the shrinking of computers, the invention of the birth control pill. They mattered more but happened quietly, well off the radar screen of my assignment editor, because they weren't in that day's news releases, the AP daybook, or that morning's paper. I decided I wanted to search out those trends and cover health and science news, the environment, sociology, psychology. The assignment editor wasn't interested.

One day, with great trepidation, I went over his head. I brought Ed Joyce a list of the stories the assignment editor had rejected. I said I thought my ideas were better. I feared Joyce would fire me, or tell me to shut up and do what the assignment editor had told me. Instead he said, "You're right—yours are better. Do them."

FREEDOM

That changed my career. From then on I was mostly free of the assignment desk. I still did a report every night, but it wasn't *that day's* news. I worked on a dozen stories at a time. While others went out to cover news conferences and crimes, I covered longer-term trends. These "slower" stories required more investigation, and I soon realized I couldn't do all the investigating work myself. When I asked WCBS to hire a researcher, my bosses smiled and said no. Since they wouldn't pay, I started calling colleges to ask if they had students who wanted internships. Many did. From then on, I got much of my best help from unpaid college students.

Still do. Many interns later moved on to paying jobs at the networks, and some became network TV producers—Janet Klein of CBS, and Abby Rockmore, Tom Nagorski, Kathleen Friery, Kristina Kendall, and Joy Levy of ABC.

At first I felt guilty asking students to work for no pay. I stopped feeling bad about it after most told me they'd learned more in our newsroom than they'd learned on their campuses. Their schools charged them money, while I taught them for free. Periodically, unions try to kill the internship programs, so the networks are careful to limit how many interns we hire and insist that every one gets college credit. Somehow that satisfies the lawyers.

With the interns' help, I could do more investigative work. We reported what was being dumped into the Hudson River, and what that meant for the fish and for us. I told viewers which new drugs scientists thought worked best for colds or upset stomachs, explained why high-octane gas was a waste of money for most drivers, and pointed out sales pitches that were scams. This turned out to be a ratings success for WCBS—and good for me: I got raises and two three-year contract extensions.

Then in 1981, the mysterious Roone Arledge offered me a job at ABC. I say mysterious because he was invisible. I rarely met with him in the 20 years he was my boss. He tended to hide in his office, not returning phone calls and avoiding many of the people who worked for him. I didn't mind, because he left me alone to do my contrarian work, but some correspondents and producers camped outside his office, hoping for an audience. I'm just grateful that Arledge hired me and built up ABC, partly by paying big salaries.

Moving to ABC was an exciting opportunity, but I hesitated to take it. By then I had a good deal at WCBS: great pay, my own producer and researcher, and freedom to report on whatever I wanted. It seemed foolish to leave that just for a network job, and I'd heard worrisome things about ABC. "Don't come," *20/20* correspondent Dave Marash told me, "unless you get your own editing room." He said he'd be in the midst of editing a piece when Geraldo Rivera—an ABC star at the time—would "bigfoot" him out because Geraldo had the lead story that week. Others complained about not getting enough research help.

So I told Roone I wouldn't go to ABC unless ABC also hired my two producers and researcher (I sneakily gave my staff promotions) and assigned me my own editing room. (Actually, I didn't talk to Roone; I told my agent, Richard Leibner, who told Roone's assistant—that's how things are done in this business.) "Forget it!" was the response from Roone's office. So I did, sort of. I told Leibner I'd sign with WCBS. But as usual, the lawyers were slow with the paperwork. Two months later, when it was ready, Leibner was on vacation; then Neil Derrough, the general manager of WCBS, was on vacation.

Finally, when everyone was ready for me to sign, Roone Arledge suddenly called and agreed to my terms: ABC would hire my staff and give me the edit room.

NETWORK NEWS

I was thrilled. Finally, I'd made it. The network! I'd be a correspondent for *20/20* and do consumer reports for *Good Morning America*. I thought this would bring me everlasting happiness and job satisfaction, but of course it didn't. Part of my dissatisfaction was caused by my own psychological deficiency. When I achieve something, it feels good for about a week. Then I go back to worrying. I always have to do more.

But it wasn't just my personality that was the problem. The step up to "big-time network" had its drawbacks, too. There were plenty of fine journalists whose courage and resourcefulness were remarkable. But there were also plenty of people who thought the news was whatever was in that day's *New York Times*. A lot of people were afraid to try anything new.

My first battle came within weeks, when I tried to do my first consumer report on *Good Morning America*. I prepared a story on Alka-Seltzer. For years, its manufacturer had run ads featuring a character named Speedy Alka-Seltzer whose catchphrase was "What do you take for an upset stomach?—Alka Seltzer!" It was a great ad but bad medical advice. We called 20 gastroenterologists and asked if they would recommend Alka-Seltzer for an upset stomach. All 20 said, "Never. It's got aspirin in it. Aspirin makes your stomach *bleed*." The doctors suggested magnesium-aluminum products like Di-Gel, Mylanta, and Maalox.

The morning I was to air this, I brought in bottles of Maalox and Alka-Seltzer to use as props. One of the lawyers shouted, "You can't hold up brand names on TV!"

The lawyers were worried about what they called "product disparagement." Bose Corporation had just sued *Consumer Reports* over a critical article, so the executives were nervous. It put me in a ridiculous position. Here I was, ABC's first consumer reporter, on a program that took pride in telling the truth about politicians and movies, but products—which probably had a greater impact on people's lives—would be off limits?

I said, "Okay, I quit."

The lawyers conferred and decided that since I had been hired by the news department, I was in a special category and *could* mention brand names.

I went on to do a thousand stories on high-pressure car salesmen, rip-offs by various businesses, medical breakthroughs, and other assorted scams. Consumer reporting thrived. In the end, I merged it with another form of TV reporting—the on-camera confrontation.

CHAPTER TWO

Confrontations

Confrontation [is] the best kind of journalism as long you don't confront people just for the sake of a confrontation.

—Don Hewitt

I was the first in-your-face TV consumer reporter. I confronted people because if I ask you to give up your valuable time to watch me on TV, I should be both concise and informative. Nothing does this like confrontation. It lets you listen to both sides under pressure and decide what's credible.

I'd approach the con men with the cameras rolling and ask them why they were cheating people. I was always hoping for that Perry Mason moment, for the villain to fall to his knees, confess he'd been caught, and beg forgiveness. That never happened. Usually, they'd just lie.

Some of the best liars were the quacks, the doctors who were (and still are) hawking miracle cures to thicken your hair, slim your thighs, and enlarge your breasts. I guess some weren't exactly lying, because they'd convinced themselves their treatments had merit. (It's easy to delude yourself when you're making money.) Often, gullible patients believed, too. They'd think their hair *was* thicker or their breasts were larger—it was rare that anyone took objective measurements.

But we did. For example, we investigated a doctor in Oregon who made money promising to enlarge women's breasts through hypnosis—a service you can still find on the Internet. We took before-and-after measurements of his "patients" (TV news directors are always eager to broadcast stories about breasts). They showed the expensive eight-week treatment had no effect.

When I confronted the doctor on camera, he just kept repeating, "No, my research shows hypnosis *does* increase breast size."

Here's what he *didn't* do: He didn't raise his voice; he didn't run out of the room; he didn't hit me. I was asking rude, hostile questions, calling him a liar, threatening his livelihood—and he was just weirdly polite about it.

That was the norm. I was constantly amazed at how blasé people seemed when they were having their career exposed as a fraud. I'd call them crooks, they'd calmly lie; I'd pull out tape recordings to prove they were liars, and they'd lie again. Usually, after the camera stopped rolling, they'd *thank* me for the interview.

I worried that someone would slug me or shoot me, but the explosion never came. It's as if the presence of the camera suggested that Mom might be watching and people didn't want to misbehave. Or maybe they were just slow to react. Often, a few days later, after they'd thought about it, I'd get nasty threats from their lawyers—but nobody ever hit me.

Well, once. I was doing a story explaining that professional wrestling is fake. We took a poll that found one-third of the fans in the audience believed "pro wrassling" was real. I had wrestled in high school and it annoyed me that promoters were distorting a real sport, so I'd been looking for an opportunity to expose the fakery. We found Eddie Mansfield, a disgruntled ex-pro who would admit to it.

Eddie showed us how it's done. We rented a wrestling ring and he taught me how to throw him. As I lifted, Eddie jumped; the "throwee" did most of the work.

To cap off the segment, I went to Madison Square Garden to confront the "real" fake wrestlers. WWF boss Vince McMahon offered me an interview with 6-foot-8-inch, 280-pound Dave Schultz, aka Dr. D. Here's how it went:

John Stossel: Is this a good business?
Dave Schultz: Yeah, it's a good business. I wouldn't be in it if it wasn't.
John Stossel: Why is it a good business?
Dave Schultz: Because only the tough survive. That's the reason *you* ain't in it.
John Stossel: I think this is fake.
Dave Schultz: You think it's fake?

Then he slugged me in the ear. I didn't think guys that big could move so fast. Next thing I knew, I was on the ground looking up, and he was shouting, "What's that? Is that fake?"

Stunned, I got up. That was dumb. He hit me in the other ear and knocked me down again. This time I stayed down until he stopped yelling and stalked off.

It's ironic. I confront people all the time—expose them as con men, and they shake my hand. The one time I confront someone we all *know* is a fake, I get slugged for it.

THE AMBUSH

My other confrontations were less violent but often made for compelling TV. My first *20/20* story was on envelope-stuffing scams. You've seen the ads: "Work in the comfort of your own home. Earn $500, even

$1,000, a week!" We answered dozens of these ads. No one sent me any envelopes to stuff. Instead, they sent more hyped-up letters inviting us to send in $25 for a "starter kit." When we paid for that, all we got was brochures that told us to run ads in the local paper saying, "Envelope stuffers wanted." In other words, we should rip off other people the way we just got ripped off.

Do people really fall for these scams? Sure. The con artists wouldn't keep running them if they didn't. Most of the victims are poor and can't afford to lose the small amounts of money they've "invested." I thought it would be interesting to see what happened if I brought a few of these victims with me when I confronted the con artist. My cameraman and I loaded four elderly victims into a van and went to the office of the man who had conned them.

I asked him why he was cheating people. He hemmed and hawed and tried not to answer me. I asked him again and he stalled some more. Just as I started to call him a crook, something dumb happened: The cameraman ran out of tape. This should have been a minor setback; ordinarily the cameraman would grunt to let me know he had a problem, and I would stall while he slipped in a new cassette. But instead, he announced out loud, "Hey! We're out of tape!" That gave the crook a chance to kick us out.

Getting kicked out in front of the camera is often the next best thing to that elusive Perry Mason moment; it at least shows that the bad guy may have something to hide. But if it doesn't happen on tape, it might as well have never happened. Here I had a story about poor people being victimized by a man who, when I confronted him, said, well, nothing. I'd blown my chance—I had no ending to my story.

I couldn't go back into his office and ask again. That would be trespassing; once he kicked us out, we had to stay out.

Today I would write the experience off as bad luck. But this was my first network assignment and I was desperate not to fail. So I asked my cameraman and the elderly victims if they'd be willing to do an "ambush": We'd stake out the con artist. When he came outside, we'd ask him about ripping people off.

We hid behind a billboard next to the guy's parking lot and waited. I hate ambushes. While waiting, I feel foolish and scared. Here we were, seven adults crouching behind a billboard in the California sun, waiting until . . . I had no idea. Maybe he'd *never* come out; maybe he lived there. Maybe he'd come out with a gun.

After an hour, he did come out. We ran out from behind our billboard and before I could ask him anything, the elderly victims surprised me by chasing him around the parking lot yelling, "You ripped me off!" It was perfect television: little old ladies, like a posse of Keystone Kops, running after the bad guy. He still wouldn't talk; he just got into his car and drove away. But this time we had it on tape.

No one who watched that show will ever fall for an envelope-stuffing scheme.

CONSUMER REPORTING

Day after day, I chased such small-time crooks, but before I went after them I had to prove they were ripping people off.

Sometimes my researcher and I could do that with phone calls and paperwork, but it was best when we caught the rip-off on camera. To expose crooked diamond merchants I borrowed a $5,000 diamond ring, disguised myself with a fake beard, and went from store to store asking dealers to appraise the ring, saying I wanted to sell it. One of them offered just $700. A week later, I came back as John Stossel, consumer reporter, and asked that dealer to demonstrate the appraisal process for our viewers. Suddenly the ring was worth three times as much. I asked why he'd offered only $700 the week before, and he flat-out denied it. Then I played him the tape. "Oh," he said. "That was *you*? Last week the diamond must have been dusty."

That's how it went, time after time. I'd confront the crooks, and they'd lie. *How* they lied was often interesting.

When I got a tip that a real estate office discriminated against blacks, I sent in a black woman to ask for an apartment. Sorry, said the real estate agent, no vacancies. Then I sent in a white woman, who asked for the same kind of apartment—same neighborhood, same price range and number of rooms. Now there were plenty of vacancies. We tried it again with another pair of women, and it happened again. So I returned with all four women and a film crew and asked the agent why there were no apartments for blacks. He picked up a magazine and held it over his face for almost 15 seconds. Finally he said, "I don't care if people are black, red, or yellow. I will rent to anybody."

Newsday's television critic, Marvin Kitman, wrote that the scene was "like the Marines landing in the old Hollywood movies to save the American way of life." Ambushing the bad guys with a camera often felt that way. These bullies were taking advantage of people and I had a unique chance to call them on it. We weren't "saving the American way of life," but at least we could catch them in the act and let everyone know what they were doing.

Our investigations didn't always pan out. I read a newspaper article that claimed veterinarians routinely made extra money by billing pet owners for nonexistent diseases. So I had my assistant take my cat to 17 different vets for a checkup. Not one vet ripped me off. All said the cat was healthy, and billed us reasonable amounts for the checkup. I told the story on TV and said, "Three cheers for the vets." My cat never forgave me.

Sometimes the investigations bore fruit but the confrontations failed. Grace Ziem, a doctor in Maryland who called herself a "clinical ecologist," treated patients she claimed had "multiple chemical sensitivity." Many doctors say there's no such disease and when we tried to replicate some of the tests she prescribed, scientists at top laboratories told us the tests were meaningless.

I wanted to confront Dr. Ziem about all this, but when I showed up for our scheduled interview she wasn't there. An "environmental illness" activist who worked in a lab we'd consulted had warned Ziem that we were skeptical of her tests. Before I could react, someone confronted *me*. Ziem had brought in a reporter from the *Baltimore Sun*, who accused us of secretly videotaping the doctor when we sent in patients to test her clinic. Maryland is one of 12 states with laws against hidden taping. The state attorney promptly filed criminal charges against me. He later dropped them, since there was no evidence of illegal taping, but the accusation cost ABC $10,000 in legal fees.

It's good hidden taping is legal in most states because some deceit is hard to believe unless you see and hear it.

I had heard some doctors were so greedy they'd perform abortions on women who weren't pregnant. In the era before home pregnancy tests, crooked doctors could take advantage of women whose periods were late. They would simply test the women's urine, tell them they were pregnant, and pretend to give them abortions.

To catch them, I sent two female researchers to six abortion doctors with samples of *my* urine. Two of the six clinics told the women they were pregnant and tried to abort them. They only escaped by jumping off the tables and shouting, "No! I've changed my mind!" We got the conversations on tape and broadcast them. Both doctors closed their clinics and disappeared.

Today we probably couldn't do that story that way. The lawyers would say using a hidden camera in a private doctor's office is an invasion of privacy. There's a sense that many viewers don't like the sneakiness of hidden taping—they consider it underhanded. We might get sued over such a story—even if it were true.

Today we confine our hidden taping to more public places, and we do it sparingly.

RIP-OFFS

When I started, there were few rules. We made it up as we went along. To catch the bad guys, we resorted to elaborate deceptions. I got a tip that some expensive cosmetics sold by companies like Lancôme, Calvin Klein, and Stagelight were no different from one another and the cheap knockoffs you could buy in drugstores. But how do you prove that on TV?

Here's how: Producer Bob Lange posed as an entrepreneur who wanted to start a cosmetics line. Secretly wired, he visited a cosmetics factory, where a salesman told him exactly what we'd heard: Their inexpensive products were sold, in different packaging, by Calvin Klein, Stagelight, and others. They offered to sell him eye shadow at $1 per half ounce. We found the same product selling under the name Adrian Arpel for $33, Diane von Furstenberg for $35, Calvin Klein for $45, and Stagelight for $50. The label on Calvin Klein's product claimed it was an "exclusive formula."

We called the companies, telling them we wanted to ask them why their products were so expensive. Von Furstenberg, Klein, and others wouldn't talk to us, but Stagelight president Mark Genauer agreed to an interview. I suppose he thought it would be good publicity for his company.

"Our colors are special!" he beamed. "*Nobody* has colors like that!"

Well, of course, lots of people had colors like that—in fact, *exactly* like that, and I pulled out the cheap lipstick to prove it.

Mark Genauer: Does this really look like it comes from the same place?
John Stossel: No. But it *does.*
Mark Genauer: Well, depending on . . . how do you *know* that it does?
John Stossel: Because we went to the factory and they told us.
Mark Genauer: But, but our customers don't *believe* that.

That was an unusually candid answer. Maybe he was too stunned to lie.

Another factory in New Jersey showed us a single vat where they made cheap discount lipsticks and the much more expensive Lancôme lipsticks. When I interviewed the head of Lancôme, Joe Augeri, he insisted his lipstick was "special."

Joe Augeri: These are our *special formulas.*
John Stossel: They are not. It isn't Lancôme of *Paris.* It's Lancôme of *New Jersey!* I can buy it for 75 cents and sell Stossel Lipstick!
Joe Augeri: That formula is ours.

The next day, Augeri called and admitted he didn't own the formula. Maybe his lawyer told him he shouldn't lie on television.

But once again, no Perry Mason moment. Just stonewalling, or lying, and weird politeness.

The cosmetics exposé is another story we probably wouldn't do today. The lawyers are nervous about reporters pretending to be someone else. If there were a lawsuit, jurors might not like our dissembling. The lawyers might approve deception for a terrorist investigation, but they'd probably say a consumer report on cosmetics isn't worth the risk.

"THAT'S NOT ME!"

My worst nightmare was that I'd call someone a crook on the air and be wrong. It hasn't happened yet, but once I thought it had.

In 1980 I was doing a report on price-fixing. Wholesalers who supplied New York City with milk had colluded to keep prices high, dividing the city into Mafia-like territories and agreeing not to undercut one another's profits by offering milk for less. If a supermarket put milk on sale, someone from the local dairy would come around to say, "That low price is unacceptable. Raise it or we'll cut off your supply."

The dairies denied they were price-fixing, of course. But a store manager called me to complain about the threats and we persuaded him to let us put a hidden camera in his store. The camera caught a dairy president named Martin Frum threatening to cut off that store's milk supply. When I confronted Frum about it, he denied it again and again:

Martin Frum: The retail price is set by the storekeeper.
John Stossel: You never go in and say you've got to keep your price up?
Martin Frum: No.
John Stossel: You don't go over there and tell him to raise his prices?
Martin Frum: No.
John Stossel: Yes, you did. It's right here.

Then I triumphantly went for the Perry Mason moment, playing the videotape, expecting him to crumble. Instead, he said, "That's not me."

That was a shock. Then Frum's public relations man, Howard Tisch, spoke up. "Look at their lips," he said. "The man on the tape has thin lips. Frum has big fat lips." Frum nodded eagerly.

I started to sweat. Videotape isn't DNA. What if this *wasn't* the right guy? What if I had made a horribly wrong accusation? We rushed back to the office and reviewed the tape. After Frum made his threats, our camera followed him to his car, where the license plate was visible. A quick check found that the car was registered to Frum's wife. What a relief. He *was* the guy on the tape.

New York's attorney general then investigated the dairy industry, discovered price-fixing was routine, and got them to refund $6.7 million to consumers.

COMMONSENSE SKEPTICISM?

I often wonder why such confrontational reporting isn't more common. Once we'd determined that someone was cheating people, it seemed like confronting them was the logical thing to do. Yet few reporters do it. Maybe they're more polite than I am. Some people consider ambushes and confrontational questions to be rude. They *are* rude, but I think they have to be asked.

Sometimes they have to be asked several times to cut through the evasions.

"Haven't you been cheating people?"

"No, I'm a nice guy. My family loves me."

"That may be true, but I think you've been cheating people."

"No, actually my lawyer says that what I'm doing is perfectly legal."

"That may be true, but haven't you been cheating people?"

"No, let me explain. . . ."

That last response is the one worth waiting for; usually it takes several rounds to get there. I just keep asking. Not that I look forward to it—I dread the confrontation almost as much as I dread ambushes. I sweat, worry I'll say something wrong, worry about stuttering, worry that the person I'm confronting might kill me. But I do it because the con man *is* cheating people, and somebody *ought* to get in his face about it.

"NOBODY TALKS TO ME THAT WAY!"

Also, we learn from confrontation. It cuts through the clutter. Still, so few reporters do it that I often find rich and powerful people—even those who are interviewed often—are shocked when I confront them directly.

When the U.S. Department of the Interior *couldn't find* $2 billion that taxpayers had given it, I went to ask Bruce Babbitt, President Clinton's secretary of the interior, about it. Babbitt's press secretary agreed to the interview. She directed us to a Department of the Interior office, where we spent three hours setting up our equipment. Then Babbitt came in, sat down, took one look at me, and, before I could ask a question, announced: "I'm gonna fire whoever scheduled this interview." Then he walked out. Apparently, he doesn't talk to reporters who are likely to ask confrontational questions.

I'm told the Department of the Interior now uses video of my interview with Babbitt as a lesson in how not to deal with the media.

Then there was Richard Gephardt, the Democratic leader of the House of Representatives. We'd discovered that Gephardt was part-owner of a luxurious beach house. I asked him why affluent people like him should get a government handout, like federal flood insurance, that protects million-dollar vacation homes. He wouldn't answer—he just kept saying Congress would "look into the program." I kept asking whether he thought it was wrong, but he would never answer. I must have asked him six times. After the interview, his assistant told me Gephardt said I was rude. I thought, "Jeez. He's the most powerful Democrat in Congress. He's been interviewed by a million people. Am I the only rude one?"

I suppose beat reporters who cover people like Babbitt and Gephardt are reluctant to offend because they may need the powerful people's cooperation tomorrow. I didn't worry about cooperation tomorrow, so I kept offending people today.

And I was mad. I'd been bullied as a kid, and was always angry that the bullies got away with terrorizing me. I was small and helpless and couldn't do anything about it. Now I had a camera. A million viewers gave me power to embarrass the bullies and expose their tricks. I was eager to make the most of the opportunity.

Donald Trump was offended when I called him a bully for trying to force an old lady out of her house to make more room for his Atlantic City casino. After the interview, the producer stayed behind to pack up our equipment. Trump came back into the room, puffed himself up, and started blustering, "Nobody talks to me that way!"

Well, someone should.

CHAPTER THREE

Confusion

*Trade and commerce, if they were
not made of India-rubber, would never
manage to bounce over the obstacles
which legislators are continually
putting in their way.*

—Henry David Thoreau

It was satisfying to confront bad guys, but it wasn't enough. I'd expose them, and a month later, they'd be back at it. I wanted the government to do something to stop the crooks, to compensate the victims. After I spent time with the victims listening to their sad stories, I was angry. I wanted someone to help those people. What was the purpose of government if it couldn't protect them?

Occasionally the government *did* act, but its actions rarely worked out well.

Every regulation seemed to have an unintended consequence. Taxpayers' dollars wound up in the pockets of the rich instead of the poor. Well-meaning regulations designed to protect consumers often hurt them by narrowing their choices and raising prices.

I did a story on how some repair shops overcharged. The TV-repair department at a local community college helped me rig a TV set with a burned-out picture tube—an obvious fix. Some shops replaced the tube and charged us a few bucks. Others claimed more was wrong and charged much more.

So I put the results on TV, including caught-in-the-act confrontations with the cheaters—"Whaddya mean you never said the whatchamacallit needed replacing? Here you are on tape!"

Local politicians would quickly leap to the rescue. They'd create a new "Bureau of TV Repair," or maybe it was the "Consumer Electronics Supervisory Board" or the "Electronics Repair Consumer Protection Agency." Politicians were always eager to create "solutions" in the form of new consumer protection agencies. There were endless permutations, all based on the best of intentions.

Okay, not entirely—some players had ulterior motives. Politicians were eager to get their faces on TV. And certainly Consumer Reporter John Stossel, having exposed this problem on TV with sweeps-week promotion, would like to put the important politician on TV? Yes, I admit, Stossel would do that. After all, the politician would praise me for my investigation, flattering me by implying I was powerful. And I must have been powerful—my exposé led to the creation of an entire consumer protection department!

Within a year, the consumer protection department would be in business, issuing regulations. Within five years its staff would be even bigger, but it would have done little that benefited consumers. The department usually began by announcing that all repair shops had to be licensed. That sounded good. Dogs have licenses. Drivers have licenses. It seems safe and orderly. The department would set standards for TV and car repairs, appraisers, travel agents, whatever.

Today, there are thousands of licensing boards. Some states even license astrologers. But as I kept doing consumer reports, I began to notice that licensing didn't make life better. The richer, better-plugged-in businesses paid lawyers to file the paperwork and passed the cost on to consumers. The rest of the businesses weren't even aware of the law, or couldn't afford the lawyers to show them how to deal with it. They just ignored the law.

I don't blame them. There are so many consumer protection laws, it's impossible to keep track of them all. Some even contradict one another. Occasionally, licensing boards would be as aggressive as ambitious TV reporters, sending in undercover agents to test the repair shops. That caught some cheaters and might deter others. But this was rare. Usually the boards would kill time doing what most government bureaucracies do: shuffle papers.

Sometimes licensing boards would hold a news conference where the bureaucrat in charge got TV face time, announcing that he had "protected you" by finding out that "47 percent of repair shops lack consumer licenses!" Then they'd announce they were shutting down those unlicensed vendors. But rarely were the unlicensed vendors the genuine bad guys. They were usually just the fringe businesses—the places most likely to give affordable service to people in poor neighborhoods. These "crackdowns" never did anything for consumers.

Once I became known as a consumer reporter, I got regular calls from viewers who said they'd been ripped off by vocational schools. They'd signed up for computer training, truck-driving school, or beautician training, lured by promises of work, only to find that the training was lousy or nonexistent. After working hard and graduating, even the best students couldn't get jobs. Many students called me in tears. When I'd ask the state agency charged with policing the schools what it was doing about the situation, someone would say it was "investigating." Yet the complaints kept coming. I'd call again and again I'd be told the state was still "investigating." This went on for years; nothing ever changed. What made this even more remarkable was that most students were given government scholarships to attend the scam schools. The state was paying the rip-off artists $5,000 for every student they ripped off.

Wouldn't the regulators act even when the state's own money was at stake? No.

BUSINESS CAPTURES
THE REGULATORS

In fact, the more I watched the regulators work, the more it seemed the real beneficiaries of the regulations were entrenched businesses, unions, and the regulators themselves. Once my eyes were open, I saw the evidence everywhere.

We visited Cornrows & Company, a thriving African hair-braiding business in Washington, D.C. A married couple, Taalib-Din Uqdah and Pamela Farrell, had done exactly what politicians say needs to be done in inner cities—they built a business. They soon had 20,000 customers, employed 10 people, taking in half a million dollars a year. Women came from as far away as Connecticut, a six-hour trip, to have their hair braided by Cornrows & Company.

I thought a success story like this would thrill local politicians. Instead, the bureaucrats ordered Uqdah and Farrell to cease and desist or be "subject to criminal prosecution." Why? Because they didn't have a license. "It's a safety issue," said the regulators. The chemicals they use to dye or perm hair might hurt someone.

Hair dye is hardly a serious safety threat, but even if it were, Cornrows & Company didn't dye or perm hair. They only braided it. That didn't matter, said the cosmetology board—they still had to get a license.

What would it take to get one? Uqdah and Farrell would have to pay about $5,000 to take more than a thousand hours of courses at beauty school.

It's unclear what beauty school would have taught them. Beauty schools didn't even teach the service Cornrows & Company provided. They taught things like pin curls and gelatinized hairstyles that hadn't been popular for 40 years. One rule required students to spend 125 hours studying *shampooing*.

Uqdah thought he understood why the cosmetology board wanted to shut his salon: "Money—other salons don't like the competition."

I think he was right. Even if licensing boards mean well at first—intending to protect the public—in time they are captured by the people who care most. And who cares most? Not consumers—you don't get your hair done that often, and even if you did, you wouldn't care enough about it to want to join a regulatory bureaucracy. Innovators don't join the board either; they're busy innovating. Scientists, economists, doctors, and others with genuine expertise in safety and commerce don't get involved. They're busy doing more important things. So boards are usually captured by the established businesses. William Jackson, a former member of the Washington, D.C., Cosmetology Board, admitted, "The board, ninety percent of the time, are salon owners."

Once established players capture a licensing board, they tend to use their power to stifle competition and keep newcomers out. Every day businesses are killed by "consumer protection" regulators.

In Charlotte, North Carolina, we interviewed two "criminals," Thelma Connell and Louise Koller, elderly ladies who liked to stay home and knit mittens and sweaters. They sold what they made at a local market, until one day authorities told them, "No businesses are allowed in the home. It might disrupt the neighborhood."

It was the law. Given their first names (one reason we interviewed them), you might think Thelma and Louise would ignore the authorities. But they wanted to be known as law-abiding citizens. They quit selling what they knit.

One more little business killed.

Another "criminal" was Linda Fisher of Baltimore. After she lost her job, Fisher was determined to stay off welfare. So every morning before dawn, she baked six dozen muffins and sold them door-to-door near her home. The neighbors loved Fisher and her muffins, but when the local health department learned about her "food business," it shut her down. She didn't have a "commercial kitchen."

It would be nice if everyone who cooked for others had a "commercial" kitchen located in an area zoned for commercial use, with state-of-the-art environmental controls, handicapped-accessible doorways, fire-marshal-approved wiring, emergency exits, and sign language interpreters for deaf customers. But the perfect is the enemy of the good. Such well-intended regulation just discourages entrepreneurs—and makes everything cost more.

Even death. In America these days, the *average* funeral costs $5,000. Some people want to pay $5,000, but many spend that much only because they don't know there is a cheaper alternative. When a loved one dies, few people have the heart to shop around. A casket alone often costs $3,000. That's a lot of money for what is essentially a large wooden box.

Pastor Nathaniel Craigmiles, of Chattanooga, Tennessee, thought grieving families were getting ripped off, so he opened a store and started selling caskets for less. This did not endear him to funeral directors.

Tennessee's state funeral board soon told Craigmiles that he had to stop selling caskets because he was not "licensed." To get a license, he would have to apprentice for two years, embalm bodies, and master vast amounts of utterly irrelevant information. The funeral board said this was necessary "to improve sanitary conditions."

Funeral boards, cosmetology laws, and zoning rules are designed to create order and safety, but they end up becoming tools of established businesses that want to limit competition. Funeral directors don't want anyone selling cheaper caskets, bakeries don't want other people selling muffins, and hair salons resent a successful hair braider.

It's natural to resent competition, but established companies shouldn't get to use the power of government to kill it. I began to see that some businesses get so comfortable with government regulators they come to depend on special deals. The milk business, for example, has grown accustomed to rigged prices. Its political action committees give millions of dollars to politicians. In return, the politicians give them price supports that force everyone to pay more for milk.

Recently the milk producers demanded even more. They asked the Food and Drug Administration to take immediate action against makers of soy milk for "misuse" of the term "milk." They demanded soy milk be renamed soy *beverage.*

Soy milk comes from soybeans instead of cows. It looks like milk but has a slightly different flavor. With as much calcium as milk but less saturated fat, it may also be better for you and it tastes pretty good. In fact, we did a taste test with 50 people and most liked soy milk; some even preferred it. I understand why the dairy industry doesn't want the competition.

Too bad. Competition is good.

Maybe the soy farmers should argue that *they* own the name, because soy milk was made in China 2,000 years ago. They might get the regulators to force the milk industry to rename its product "cow juice."

The spokesman for the National Milk Producers Federation didn't find that funny.

Rob Byrne, National Milk Producers Federation: We're just asking for a level playing field here.

John Stossel: You don't want a level playing field. You want to stack the deck.

Rob Byrne: We don't want to stack the deck. We actually are looking for fairness in labeling, accurate information for consumers, and a protection from these beverages that aren't milk.

They're worried about *consumers?* Give me a break. They're worried about themselves.

That time, the government wisely ignored the dairy industry, but business often succeeds in manipulating consumer protection so that it becomes business protection. I was starting to see that agencies that were supposed to help consumers often hurt them by blocking new ideas and limiting competition. If businesses can use government to rig the system to suppress competition, they will.

FAIR PAY?

Unions will, too. The result is the same: higher costs and fewer choices.

In fact, there is a law, the Davis-Bacon Act, passed in 1931, that sets wages on government construction jobs. Under Davis-Bacon, the bureaucrats issue wage edicts for every government construction job. Prices are different in every town. Carpenters in Washington, D.C., must be paid $19.40 an hour. In Chicago, though, they get $31.97; in Cleveland, $20.30. Everyone must be paid "the prevailing wage."

President Clinton's assistant secretary of labor, Bernie Anderson, explained it to me: "What the American people want is for their government to protect the wage level of American workers." In theory this sounds as if it would keep workers from getting short-changed by employers. But in practice, it means that some union workers benefit at everyone else's expense. High fixed wages means the work goes to expensive union contractors rather than hungry young entrepreneurs. Beginning construction workers lose out—as do consumers.

I taped people working on a bridge spanning from New York to

Pennsylvania. Workers got $31 an hour on the New York side, $22 on the Pennsylvania side. The wage rates are based on a complicated formula that supposedly averages previous union and nonunion wages in a given town. But of course the union contractors, because they're organized, are more likely to get their wage data to the government, so the averages are skewed. The Davis-Bacon paperwork alone costs millions.

Have you noticed those guys waving flags near road construction projects, the ones who redirect traffic? It's not highly skilled work, but on government jobs in my town, they had to be paid $22 an hour.

I asked one of the flag wavers how much he's paid when he does normal construction.

Bill Colhop: I get, like, twelve dollars an hour.

John Stossel: The private job you get paid twelve bucks an hour; a government job, twenty-two bucks an hour. Do you have to work twice as hard on the government job?

Bill Colhop: Not really, no.

It might be funny, if it weren't so harmful. Construction had long been the kind of work where young people could break in by helping, watching, working cheap until they acquired skills. Davis-Bacon eliminates that.

When Chicago decided to repair the Cabrini Green housing project, people who lived in the project assumed such a big job would provide work for the unemployed young men who grew up there. These were the desperately poor, unskilled young men government always professes to help. But because of Davis-Bacon, every contractor had to pay high salaries—even for the simplest jobs. Locked into paying high salaries, contractors were not about to take a chance on beginners. Instead they hired the most experienced union workers they could find.

They used workers who would "normally never come near our neighborhood," said aspiring construction worker John King. "I think it's wrong that they do that. We want to provide. We're not just derelicts and drug dealers and thugs." Davis-Bacon meant he couldn't even work on his own building. Community activist Bertha Gilke told us Davis-Bacon "will not let him in. We have residents who want to go to work, who want to come off of welfare."

Why does government care so much about helping some workers that it's willing to exclude the needy, and make taxpayers pay more to boot? "It's the union thugs who care about this," says lawyer Clint Bolick of the Institute for Justice, a libertarian public interest law firm. "This law protects union jobs. It screws the taxpayers."

Davis-Bacon was passed partly because white construction workers feared losing jobs to black workers who had cut into the white monopoly on government construction by having the gall to work for less. Now Davis-Bacon is used to protect unions, and as a result, government buildings cost taxpayers millions more and deserving nonunion workers are denied opportunity.

Unions claim Davis-Bacon is necessary "to make sure government buildings are well built." Without first-class union labor, unions say, the buildings might not be safe. That might sound reasonable if you didn't stop to consider that most buildings are *not* government buildings, and they're safe.

In most of American life, we do quite well without government setting wages. Wages are best set by competition—by supply and demand. When there's more demand for workers, wages rise. When business slows, wages drop. Some wage rates change every day. It keeps things flexible, efficient. It allows more people to keep working. Prices are valuable information. They tell workers where it might be better to work, and contractors where it might be better to hire. Supply and demand lets every individual earn in proportion to what he or she contributes. Contractors who want the best carpenters and electricians bid up the wages for the most outstanding workers; beginners or goof-offs get less.

There are some in Congress who realize this and want to repeal Davis-Bacon. There is almost no chance they will succeed. The people who like the law make good money from it and lobby well. Davis-Bacon hurts the less organized. Congress's most potent defender of Davis-Bacon, Senator Edward Kennedy, declined our request to talk about it.

20/20 once assigned me to another "hard-hitting exposé," this time on unsanitary conditions in chicken-processing plants. A union, Government Workers Local 2357, persuaded us and several other TV programs to go in with hidden cameras to document its claim that conditions in the plants were deplorable and the chickens contaminated with bacteria.

Inside the plants, with bird intestines strung all over the place, it was easy to see why the chickens we buy are often crawling with germs. We had a lab perform tests and found four kinds of bacteria—*Yersinia*, salmonella, *Listeria*, and campylobacter. The union argued that this proved the government must hire more union chicken inspectors.

The Agriculture Department already has inspectors inside every plant. It's tiresome work. Each inspector is required to examine each bird visually as it slides by on the assembly line. Hiring more inspectors would make that work easier, but I wondered, would it really make chicken safer?

Almost a decade prior to my exposé, epidemiologist Dr. Glenn Morris had been asked by the National Academy of Sciences to evaluate the inspection system. He and the other scientists on the panel concluded that it made little sense. Bacteria make people sick and without a microscope you can't see bacteria. What inspectors can see usually isn't what makes people sick. A chicken could be covered with its own feces and not make us sick. And "birds that have no evidence of feces whatsoever may be covered with campylobacter and salmonella," said Dr. Morris.

When the inspection program began, the government assumed that visible signs of disease and discolorations in the skin were the danger. But by the time we did the show, everyone had known for years that microbes are the real problem. Microbes are invisible to inspectors. It would make much more sense to take samples off the line and put them in petri dishes to see what kind of bacteria grows. Had the inspection system been changed? No, government rarely changes anything.

As Carol Tucker Foreman, who ran the inspection program in the Carter administration, told us, "parts of the industry have come to rely on the inspectors doing a certain portion of their work." The chicken industry likes things the way they are because it gets free employees. Instead of having to hire more quality-control people, chicken plants have taxpayer-funded inspectors to make sure all the birds look good; they even stamp the bacteria-laden birds with a government label that promises they're wholesome. Today the government does do some microbial testing, but basically the USDA still pays inspectors to stare at the chickens.

If the government had implemented what the National Academy of Sciences recommended 20 years ago, chickens would cost less, because you'd need fewer inspectors to do the random sampling. But that's not what the union wanted reported. It wanted more inspectors. The scientists told us the best protection would be to forget the inspectors and treat poultry with cobalt irradiation, which kills virtually all disease-causing organisms. Then we'd have safer chicken at less cost. But Government Workers Local 2357 certainly wasn't about to promote that!

SORRY, YOU MUST WAIT FOR THE BUS

A few years ago, in my town, I noticed groups of people who seemed to be waiting for a bus, but who instead were picked up by mini-vans. What was this, a company's private transport service? No. It was a new venture, run by immigrants, the start of their American dream. It was a hit with customers, too. Without the vans, they'd have to take city buses, which followed rigid routes and charged $1.50. The vans were a better deal. They only cost a dollar, and got you there faster because they often went exactly where you wanted to go.

Did city politicians stand up and cheer—thank the van drivers for making the city a better place? No. They declared the vans illegal.

Why outlaw a cheaper way to get to work? Because the bus drivers' union complained. They said the vans shouldn't be allowed to compete on "their streets" since their bus service "was good enough."

Excuse me, but the success of the vans proved that the union's bus service was not "good enough." Customers freely chose the vans over the buses. In addition, the vans were self-supporting, while the bus service needed taxpayer subsidies to survive. Maybe if there were competition, the city bus service would operate more efficiently, buy more cost-effective buses, run more routes, give people better service.

It's not likely to happen, because in New York City, unions often get to decide what's "good enough." The city council decided that the "unregulated" vans must stop picking up passengers on bus routes. I wonder if its decision had anything to do with the fact that council members' biggest source of political contributions was the bus drivers' union.

I asked Willie James and Bill Pelletier, the heads of the union, "Isn't competition good?"

Willie James: Competition is fine if it's done legally.

John Stossel: But you make the competition illegal.

Willie James: No. The law is the law.

Bill Pelletier: You're going to have to wait for the bus. That's what the law says. Why are we going to let these entrepreneurs come onto the streets and take away from this service?

John Stossel: Because the customer wants it.

Bill Pelletier: Well, because a customer wants it, that doesn't mean it's right.

It *should* mean it's right. Why can't we customers decide who will drive us to work? Why is this government's business?

Safety is one reason the bureaucrats cite, but we already require motor vehicles to be licensed and drivers to be licensed. Too much "safety" regulation deprives us of good choices.

"EXPLOITING" CHILDREN

Child labor law is an example of that. American law now says no child under 14 may hold a job, and there are strict rules for 16-year-olds.

Everyone wants children protected, and those who passed the laws meant well. I used to think these were good rules. We don't want to return to Charles Dickens's time, when young children labored long hours under harsh conditions in coal mines and mills. But when I had a chance as a reporter to watch the bureaucrats enforce the laws, I never saw victims wanting rescue.

I've accompanied Labor Department cops as they barged into "sweatshops that illegally employ kids." But what the cops call "sweatshop," I simply call "employer." No teens ABC interviewed after the raids said they were being abused. They wanted the work. As the employers sullenly filled out Labor Department paperwork, the teens would slip out the back door and find another illegal job. The Labor Department's rules didn't help kids. The unintended consequence of the laws is to hurt kids by taking away some of their options.

In Snowmass, Colorado, we visited a local market that once hired students to bag groceries—never more than a few hours a week. It was a great entry-level job, but when someone asked about child labor laws, the kids were immediately fired. One disappointed bag boy told us, "I was really sad because they're not ... *making* us work. I mean, we *wanted* to do this."

In Georgia, 12-year-old Tommy McCoy was having the time of his life working as a batboy for a minor-league baseball team. Then the *Savannah Morning News* published a story about him. "The next day, the Labor Department was at my front door," said Rick Sisler, general manager of the Savannah Cardinals. He was told he was breaking the law and had to fire Tommy.

The crime? A child under 16 may not work on school nights. The law is supposed to make sure kids have time for schoolwork, but the stadium was filled with kids. If it's okay for them to watch the game, why is it terrible for the batboy to work the game?

Tommy McCoy said, "I was disappointed that somebody would take somebody's dream away like this."

Fortunately, there was enough publicity about Tommy's firing that Robert Reich, then U.S. Secretary of Labor, intervened. So Tommy lucked out. Child actors luck out, too—the Labor Department gives them a special exemption. Farmworkers also get one, and so—for some reason—do wreath makers. Is that how regulation should work? Special breaks for some, often those who lobby best? Aren't we all supposed to be equal under the law?

Why does America even need a Department of Labor? Today's workers have plenty of choices. There are 14 million businesses in America and they compete hard for workers. People change jobs frequently. That marketplace competition protects workers better than job-killing Labor Department rules. If Burger King treats a kid badly, he can get a job at McDonald's.

The Labor Department regulations are so onerous that some businesses that could legally employ teens don't. Wendy's won't even consider hiring anyone younger than 16 because the regulations require so much time-consuming record keeping and carry the risk of a big fine if anyone makes a mistake. Wendy's decided it's safer just not to hire young people.

How does this help kids?

When I argued this on *20/20,* Barbara Walters defended the Labor Department. "Laws are made to protect the majority. There are still sweatshops in this country. So how do you protect those kids?"

I say, let parents make these decisions. Some will make bad decisions, but clumsy and rigid regulation is worse. Child labor laws passed to protect children from dangerous factories now keep strapping teenagers out of air-conditioned offices.

WHAT ABOUT THE SELLERS OF SNAKE OIL?

I always assumed that when our health and safety were clearly on the line—for example, when we put medicine inside our bodies—we absolutely needed government to protect us. Without regulation we'd be victims of greedy capitalists peddling snake oil. They'd sell dangerous products and pills "Guaranteed to make you lose weight!" Individuals can't be expected to make informed judgments about such things, right? That's where the "experts" in government come in.

We need the Occupational Safety and Health Administration, the Food and Drug Administration, the Drug Enforcement Administration, the Consumer Product Safety Commission, and so on—the entire alphabet soup of agencies—"protecting" us. I cheered them on when they led "crackdowns" on industry. But after watching them work, I now think the protection often does more harm than good.

It was easy to see how they protected us. It took me longer to see the unintended consequences. Every regulation turned out to have many: Lawyers had to be hired to police the regulators and punish corrupt ones; reams of paperwork were required to notify the regulated about the rules; more lawyers had to be hired to interpret the rules. Many businesses responded to these complications by ignoring the regulations or, worse, avoiding the regulated activity. It meant that regulation, by protecting us from bad things, also "protected" us from good things.

WHO'S WATCHING OUT FOR YOU?

Covering the FDA was an eye-opener. This is an agency universally regarded as absolutely necessary. It protects us from any drug not shown to be "safe and effective." Who could argue with that?

In 1962, the FDA protected American women from the tranquilizer thalidomide. It was the agency's first big success. The FDA's stringent rules delayed thalidomide's introduction in America, while in Europe, women who took it sometimes gave birth to children with severe birth defects.

While the FDA's power to forbid the use of thalidomide seemed to be an unequivocally good thing, after watching the FDA grow in size and power, I see the downside. The regulators, seeking to screen out trouble, also screen out benefits.

After the thalidomide tragedy, the FDA grew like a malignant tumor. It quintupled the number of regulations and became a bureaucratic obstacle to innovation. Getting a new drug approved now costs hundreds of millions of dollars and takes 12 to 15 years. It takes that long because the FDA wants to be extra sure every drug is safe and effective. But this vigilant pursuit of safety also kills people.

For example, every year thousands of Americans die because they are too fat. Drug and food companies have invented fat substitutes—food ingredients that taste as good as fat, but are not absorbed by your body. These fat substitutes would let you eat chocolate cake without getting fat. The chemicals wait for approval in the FDA's 12-to-15-year pipeline because there's a tiny chance that something about them might hurt you.

But what about the thousands of lives that would be saved by the fat substitute? Don't those lives count? No. When the FDA debates what should be approved, it focuses on who might be hurt.

It's easy to understand why. The victims of a bad drug are very visible. The lawsuits over the Fen-Phen deaths were on the front pages of most every newspaper. The media put pictures of armless and legless thalidomide babies on the covers of magazines. But whom would we photograph for the story on the fat substitute? We don't know which thousand fat people might be saved.

Some years ago, the FDA held a news conference and proudly announced, "This new heart drug we're approving will save fourteen thousand American lives a year!" No one stood up at the press conference to ask, "Excuse me, doesn't this mean you *killed* fourteen thousand people last year—by delaying its approval?" No one asked that because reporters don't think that way, but that's what the FDA's announcement meant. If the drug saves 14,000 lives a year, then 14,000 people died each year while the drug awaited approval. Thousands will die this year while cancer therapies and fat substitutes wait for approval. Some of us may *want* to wait. Many of us wait to be absolutely certain a drug is safe before we take it. Why isn't the choice left to us? In a "free" country, why do we meekly allow the FDA to act as a police agency that can tell us, "You may not"? Why does it get to use force?

I interviewed Janet Cheadle, a young girl suffering from neuroblastoma, a form of cancer that, if left untreated, would kill her before she became an adult. Her parents wanted to take her to a clinic in Texas run by a doctor who said he had a treatment that might help. But the FDA decides who may be treated and the agency turned Janet down, saying "it's not safe" for her to pursue medical treatments the government hasn't sanctioned. Later, when the FDA tried to shut the clinic down and put the doctor in jail, desperate parents and their children went to Congress to protest. Then the FDA agreed to let Janet have the treatment. But why did her parents have to beg?

What's the alternative? Have no oversight? Let any company peddle every dubious medicine to an unsuspecting public? That's not going to happen. It sounds terrifying. Snake oil sellers might sell all kinds of harmful stuff. That's why we created the FDA in the first place.

But wait a second. Snake oil sellers sell it anyway. I'd been reporting on snake oil sellers for years. I did it while the FDA was supposedly in charge. Crooks and deluded optimists sold useless baldness remedies, breast enlargers, and diet products regardless of what the law said. The FDA didn't matter—government was too incompetent to stop crooks. What it mostly stopped or delayed was the serious drug companies' attempts at genuine innovations.

But without the FDA, how would doctors and patients know which drugs were safe and effective? The same way we know which computers and restaurants are good—through newspapers, magazines, and word of mouth. I was coming to see that in a free, open society, competition gets the information out, and letting that process flow protects consumers better than government command and control.

I don't claim to have all the answers, but let's imagine, as a thought experiment. Let's say FDA scrutiny was voluntary. Companies that want government blessing would pay the $500 million, wait 10 or 15 years, and get the FDA's seal of approval. Those of us who are cautious would take only those FDA-approved drugs. But if you had a terminal illness, you could *try* something that might save your life without having to wait 15 years—or without having to break your country's laws by importing it illegally from Europe or sneaking into Mexico to some dubious clinic. If I'm *dying*, shouldn't my government allow me the right to try whatever I want?

If FDA scrutiny were voluntary, the government testing agency would soon have competition. Private groups like *Consumer Reports* and Underwriters Laboratories would step in to compete with the FDA. The UL symbol is already on more than 17,000 electrical appliances, automotive products, and other equipment and material. No government force was required. Yet even though UL certification is voluntary, its safety standards are so highly respected that many stores won't carry products without the UL symbol.

In fact, knowing what we know about the incompetence of government monopolies, there's little doubt that competing private groups would do the testing better—cheaper and quicker.

Not having a big and mandatory FDA to protect us from bad things sounded scary, but only until I considered the alternatives, and the good things we lose by being "protected." Not only do thousands die because they don't have access to drugs that might have saved them, but we cripple the *self*-regulation that might protect us, without stifling innovation. In a free market, customers spread the word about good things and warn people about the bad. But under FDA rule, consumers assume "government takes care of all that," so we become less vigilant. The consumer is encouraged to fall asleep: Don't ask questions; just take what Big Brother approves.

I acknowledge that if innovation were freer and easier, some people might die because they took bad drugs, but in the Internet age, word would get out immediately. In the long run, if the FDA let go a little, more would live.

It made me wonder if there might also be alternatives to OSHA, the CPSC, and the rest of the regulatory behemoth. Did we really need licensing boards to protect us from hair braiders, Labor Department rules that keep kids from bagging groceries, an FDA that outlaws fat substitutes?

What else was I missing? The more reporting I did, the more it dawned on me that government is often the problem rather than the solution. Free markets, not coercive governments, are the consumer's best friend. The people who are *really* ripping us off are the lawyers, the politicians, and the regulators. The evidence was in the stories I'd been reporting all along. It had just taken me 15 years to see it.

CHAPTER FOUR

Epiphany

*An expert is a man who has made
all the mistakes which can be made
in a very narrow field.*

—Niels Bohr

For years I bought the stereotypes that serve as conventional wisdom in the news business: Corporations are evil; all risk is intolerable; consumers need more government to protect us.

It's embarrassing how long it took me to see the damage regulators do. The taxes that pay their salaries and build their offices are the least of it. The bigger harm is the indirect cost, all the money businesses spend trying to wade through the red tape (lobbying, filling out forms, hiring lawyers), plus the damage the regulation does to the American spirit. So much creativity now goes not into inventing things, but into gaming the system, manipulating the regulatory leviathan.

It took me too long to understand that. If you leave people alone, they will, without planning or intervention, create the system that benefits everyone most. This is because in a free market, every exchange is voluntary:

You're always trading something you have for something you want more. It's a win-win proposition. Otherwise, why would anyone trade?

When you go to the store and trade your dollar for an ice cream cone, it's because you want the snack more than you want the money. If you don't like it or you feel it's a bad trade, you won't buy it again. But if the store gives you what you want, you'll return. That repeat business will benefit not just the store owner but a huge network of other people as well—the ice-cream maker, the delivery-truck driver, the maker of the truck he drives, the oil company, and so on.

If at any point in the web, one of the parties stops benefiting from the trade or feels he's being coerced, he'll call the deal off, creating a demand that will be filled by someone else who wants the business. This simple principle makes possible everything from a mom-and-pop store to a network of ATMs spanning the globe; it rewards people who dream up goods and services that make life better, and punishes those who disappoint.

In a free market, adults are free to make their own decisions as long as they respect the equal rights of others. Such a market requires a legal framework to enforce the rules of property and contract, but the rules are pretty simple. They boil down to what you learned in kindergarten: Don't hit other people, don't take their stuff, and keep your promises. To enforce those rules, we have contracts, police, and courts. Government accomplishes this through force. You obey, or you will be jailed, or at least fined. Societies need some of this force. Taxes must be collected, environmental standards set, criminals punished.

But voluntary is better than forced. Free is better than coerced. It's why, whenever possible, we are better off if the private sector is bigger and government smaller. Government can never hope to attend to people's needs and wants as well as the market, simply because it's not as fast or efficient. The government makes big adjustments every two or four or six years; the market, driven by countless trades like your ice-cream purchase can adjust thousand of times a second.

NECESSARY EVIL?

I had moved from seeing regulation as a good thing to seeing it as a necessary evil. More years of reporting led me to conclude that much of it is also an *un*necessary evil. We don't need a million rules because *free markets police themselves.* Institutions that serve customers well are rewarded with more customers. Bad guys who cheat get a reputation for cheating. They lose customers, lose investors, and go out of business. Think of how eBay works. The selling price of each item is determined by auction, so buyers and sellers both get the best possible deal. Sellers are rated by their customers, so the "community" quickly identifies cheaters.

Some things can only be done by governments: waging war, guarding borders, policing cities, and enforcing pollution rules, for example. I see no practical way for the private sector to do any of that. But we'd be better off if almost everything else were left to the private sector. The free market is not perfect—there will always be fraud on eBay and, on a larger scale, Enron-like scams. But the more I watched the markets work, the more impressed I was with how competition solved problems with speed and flexibility rarely seen in government-imposed solutions.

Enron and the other recent business disasters are evidence of the market *working.* Government regulators didn't discover the deceit. Enron's lies were revealed when private security analysts raised questions and private investors started dumping the stock. The cheaters have been caught, and the cheating stopped. The bad guys can't do it anymore. No one is laughing all the way to the bank.

By contrast, government almost never polices itself. When government agencies lose money, or fail at their missions, they ask Congress for more money. They usually get it, citing their failure to achieve their goals as proof that they need more funds.

THE PRIVATE SECTOR
DOES IT BETTER

The market solves problems even in areas where I never antici-
pated market forces would help consumers. Consider the behavior of the
greedy, profit-driven companies that have employed me.

I've worked for ABC, CBS, and NBC. Since they get nearly all their
revenue from advertising, I assumed they'd allow advertisers to say *anything*—to exaggerate, lie, manipulate. But they don't. They have "standards" departments that demand changes in advertising copy to make
ads more accurate. Sometimes they reject ads outright, turn the money
away. Why would they do that when they're as hungry for profit as any
other company?

Government doesn't make them do it. The Federal Communications
Commission regulates TV stations, but rarely has the commission
revoked a license or expressed any interest in TV advertising. Stations
police themselves because it *increases* their profit. Okay, they have moral
reasons, too—few people want to be party to deceit. But the main reason
they do it is because it's good for business. Honest advertisers want their
products advertised in credible forums. By policing their own airwaves,
networks attract *more* ads.

The fact that TV stations hired me to do consumer reporting is
another bizarre example of the markets working in counterintuitive
ways to protect consumers. Thirty years ago Ralph Nader proclaimed
that consumer reporting would never appear on commercial TV. It
would only thrive on public TV, he said, because commercial TV stations
would defer to advertisers. It made sense. But Nader was totally wrong
(as he is so often). PBS carries almost no consumer reporting, probably
because the bureaucrats who run it are too nervous about offending

*any*one. By contrast, there is plenty of consumer reporting on commercial TV. I criticized my employers' most valued customers for years: I questioned their research, their promotion, their products, even their motives. For heaping such abuse on the people who paid us, I was given promotions and extravagant paychecks.

How can this be? Advertisers pay for everything. The networks court them; media buyers are favored with fine food, lavish parties, and hard-to-get tickets. Why would a business undermine this courtship by criticizing the people they were courting? Why pay me to bite the hands that feed them?

BITING THE HAND

Before I answer, let me give two examples. Appropriately, since these incidents were painful to my employers, both involved painkillers.

While working for WCBS-TV in New York City, I reported that the Federal Trade Commission had charged the makers of aspirin-based painkillers with deceptive advertising. Each company claimed its brand worked best—was faster, or killed more pain. This was bunk—they were all about the same. Their only active painkilling ingredient was aspirin. The makers of Anacin even had the nerve to call Anacin a "tension reliever" although Anacin is just aspirin and, of all things, caffeine.

The government wanted the aspirin sellers to run "corrective" advertising, something like "Contrary to our prior ads, Bufferin will *not* work twice as fast" or "Excedrin will *not* relieve more pain."

Remember those ads? No? It's because they never ran. What usually happens, happened. The lawyers fought in court for six years, eating up your aspirin-buying dollars, until the companies agreed to sign "consent orders." By signing the orders, the companies effectively said, "We don't admit doing anything wrong . . . but we won't do it anymore."

My report on this event inspired Bristol-Myers, maker of Bufferin and Excedrin, to sue me and CBS for $25 million. That was a chilling experience: I'm 25 years old, opening my mail one day, and I see an important-looking legal document that says I violated all kinds of rules and "injured" Bristol-Myers with "malice." Therefore, I (and my employer—they weren't going to get big bucks from a young reporter) must pay them $25 million.

Why did they sue? My reporting wasn't groundbreaking; I just told people what the government had said. I think Bristol-Myers sued because of the way I said it. The wire services carried similar stories but used government—lawyer—press release language, like, "The FTC filed a deceptive-trade-practices action against the manufacturers of analgesics." That's not clear to people.

I just said, "Look, the ads are hogwash." And instead of saying the "makers of analgesics," I said, "Anacin, Bufferin, Excedrin, Cope, Vanquish, and Arthritis Pain Formula." They didn't like that.

It was my first lawsuit, and if its purpose was to terrorize me, it worked. I thought my career was over. I waited for CBS to disown consumer reporting and fire me. To my surprise, the network merely issued a statement saying it considered its consumer reporting a "valuable public service" and told me to carry on.

Years later, it happened again; on ABC's *Good Morning America*, I explained that Sterling Drug's heavily advertised new "discovery," Panadol, was just an expensive brand of acetaminophen, the same painkiller that's in Tylenol. I suggested that people ignore the Panadol ads because they could buy store-brand acetaminophen for half as much. Sterling Drugs then pulled all its advertising from ABC.

In both cases, you would think a commercial television network would say, "Who needs this? Let's get rid of Stossel." Instead, CBS defended me. Bristol-Myers eventually dropped its lawsuit. ABC never even told me that Sterling pulled its ads. I only learned of the cancellation months later, when someone at an advertising agency told me it had cost the network $550,000.

Why did CBS and ABC stand by me? Why would network executives go out of their way to protect reporting that criticizes the people who pay the bills? Everyone talks about that "wall" between sales and news, but who would think that when big money was at stake, the wall would be respected?

My bosses in the News Division say it happens because news is special, an important public service that deserves insulation from crude market forces. There is truth to that, but there is a second factor that is usually overlooked. Consumer reporting is broadcast by commercial media because the market, working in its infinitely bizarre and unexpected ways, encourages it.

To a commercial broadcaster, the business cliché "be customer driven" has two meanings because he has two sets of customers: advertisers and viewers. Okay, viewers don't pay, but if viewers stop watching, advertisers won't pay either. Hence the obsession with ratings.

The ratings wars inspire some schlock TV but they also represent democracy at its best. Viewers vote with their dials. If they don't like what we do, we're gone. American television programming is miles ahead of Europe's and Asia's government-driven broadcasters simply because our ratings-obsessed system creates better competition.

This competition also benefits the consumer reporter because, although his reporting may initially cost his bosses money, viewers want consumer information. A broadcaster could protect some ad revenue by killing the consumer beat, but if that loses viewers, it's not worth it. By contrast, if he promotes consumer reporting and more people watch, he can charge the remaining advertisers *more*. Weirdly, pursuit of profit encourages consumer reporting—usually, at least.

There is the rare exception. *Good Morning America* once killed a story I did on "premium" beers. I did a taste test in a bar that showed that people who claim they like only more expensive brands like Bud or Michelob really cannot tell the difference. In a blind test they often don't even like their "favorite" brand. It was hilarious watching loyal drinkers sneer at "their" beer, while favoring (much cheaper) Schlitz.

I thought it was a good story, but it never ran. ABC insiders told me the story was killed because a *Monday Night Football* Budweiser sales deal was in the works and the network was afraid of offending the brewery. The censorship was infuriating. I thought about quitting but chickened out. I imagined my colleagues' comments: "He left *Good Morning America* over killing a beer-tasting test? Who cares? *GMA* isn't even part of ABC News, it's ABC Entertainment."

And that was a key point. At the time, *Good Morning America* was not run, as it is now, by the News Division. "I can't defend your test," ABC News vice president Dick Wald told me. "You didn't do it under the auspices of the News Division. Anyway, some of the tasters looked drunk." He had a point. We'd taped for three hours, and by the end of it, some of the tasters were, indeed, pretty tanked. Two years later, I repeated the beer story using sober tasters and *Good Morning America* broadcast it.

My point is this: despite Ralph Nader's predictions, sponsors *don't* control news content. And although some nervous executives may try to protect advertisers, only one in 30 years of TV reporting was I unable to get my story broadcast. My successor at *Good Morning America* says she was never censored.

The capitalism-hating pooh-bahs of the journalism community constantly wail about "sponsor censorship," implying that it happens all the time. *Investigative Reporters and Editors Journal* published an article titled "Terrifying Trend" claiming that executives were running a "clampdown on advertiser-sensitive reporting." Yet even though hundreds of

TV stations are doing millions of news stories, the article could cite only a few examples of self-censorship, admitting at the end that even those stations "allowed their reporters to go after other sponsors." Ralph Nader later repeated the *IRE*'s complaints, conveniently omitting the "other sponsors" qualification. According to Nader, consumer reporting had been "decimated."

Nonsense. Sponsor censorship is rare. The system works. When companies make inferior or harmful products, the news gets out. What I learned from nearly two decades of consumer reporting is that the market delivers more to the consumer than our government "protectors" ever can. The "public" stations were supposed to be the ones that would carry the "sensitive" consumer news. They do not. Profit-seeking, advertiser-beholden private businesses do a much better job.

RELAXING THE RULES

Reporters' focus on problems and the need for regulation to "solve" them makes us miss the good things that happen when regulation stops and markets take over. It's easier to report on rule making—just go to Washington, D.C. But to report on constantly innovating markets, you'd have to go everywhere. Every second, millions of Americans respond to the markets' signals by making little improvements. That's hard to cover.

In 1989, the cumulative effect of the little improvements hit me in the face. I realized how much better off we were because government and other authorities did something unusual—they *let go* a little. A decade before, economists in the Carter administration argued that some regulation had become counterproductive. They were right. At the time, government was smothering the airline business with a thousand "consumer protection" rules. The Civil Aeronautics Board decided who could fly where, when, and for how much. Airfreight companies had to ship packages by checking them with ordinary baggage. Get it there overnight? Only if you flew it there yourself.

Then government got out of the way. Suddenly, Federal Express could offer better service. The abolition of the CAB's rule-making power allowed airfreight companies to fly their own planes and implement new technologies that revolutionized the shipping business. For years the post office had claimed it was not reliably possible to "get it there overnight." Now we take airfreight for granted. Until government relaxed the rules, however, no one imagined such a service could exist.

In the 1970s, the government believed that the only way to prevent "overcharging" by shippers was to have something called the Interstate Commerce Commission tell them what routes they could take and how much they could charge. The rules became so byzantine that trucks that carried carrots from a farm made return trips empty—because it was too difficult to get permission to carry, say, furniture back to the farm in the same truck.

When abolishing the ICC was proposed, critics said shippers could charge anything they wanted—they'd rip us off. Prices would skyrocket. Yet when the ICC was abolished, the opposite happened. Left to make their own decisions, shippers found more efficient ways to do things and competition lowered prices. A few years after deregulation, one study found shipping things cost, on average, 2 percent less. You saved $200 on lumber for your house, a penny on paper towels. It didn't make the news, because those individual savings were not exciting—but the gain to the economy was in billions.

Until the '80s, the government set the maximum price that companies could charge for oil and gas. When the government lifted that cap, some politicians screamed "unfair"—prices would soon go much higher because oil companies would be able to "gouge" consumers.

Again, surprise: Prices *dropped.* Market competition held costs down better than government controls had.

Do you remember that before the '80s, it was forbidden for you to attach any "foreign" (i.e., non-AT&T) device to a telephone line? Answering machines were not allowed. They might "disrupt phone service," said the government. Of course they didn't, but we now know that only because the government let go. Today's answering machines and myriad phone choices exist not just because of technological breakthroughs—they exist because government finally stopped saying no.

Before government lifted its heavy hand, long-distance phone calls cost several dollars a minute. Companies like MCI and Sprint were not permitted to offer lower rates. Today long-distance rates are 70 percent lower—and service is better because of competition.

It's not only government that is reluctant to embrace the free market. Established businesses fear it, too. Until the '80s, the American Medical Association and state licensing boards said medical advertising would be "undignified' and "unethical." It would "mislead patients." They forbade doctors from advertising a "sale" or publicly offering to treat people for less.

In 1980, the Federal Trade Commission (yes, government does some good things) declared the advertising ban "anticompetitive." Almost immediately prices fell. When advertising was illegal, contact lenses cost $400. Ophthalmologists told me they *must* cost that much to be safely fitted. Now that there's competition, lenses are safely fitted for $50. Even though eyeglass makers have an added expense—advertising—lenses still cost less.

Businesses even resist free-market innovation that would *help* them. In 1981, the movie industry sued VCR makers, and got a court to decree VCRs "an illegal instrument of copyright infringement." Hollywood was certain that people recording programs off their TVs would destroy the movie business. The studios also tried to outlaw the renting of videotapes. Who would go to the theater if you could tape a movie off TV or rent one? Lucky for the studios, a higher court ruled against them. Now the studios make much more money from home video than from the box office.

Today it's the music business that's suing. The Recording Industry Association filed multimillion-dollar lawsuits against teenagers who download music off the Internet. The recording companies hope that terrifying a few young people will deter others from copying music. I doubt it. The industry would do better to accept the changing technology, and compete by offering downloading sites with better service, embracing the constant changes of free markets instead of fighting them.

The idea that relaxing the rules actually benefits consumers is so counterintuitive that I didn't get it even as I was watching it work. My regular sources like *Time, Newsweek,* the *New York Times,* and the other liberal media weren't writing about it. I tried the conservative media, like the *National Review* and talk radio, but didn't find it discussed there, either.

Then I discovered Los Angeles–based *Reason* magazine. It was a revelation. Here were writers who analyzed the benefits of free markets that I witnessed as a reporter. They call themselves libertarians and their slogan is "Free Minds and Free Markets." I wasn't exactly sure what that meant, but what they wrote sure made sense. It made sense to Hugh Downs, too.

Often on *20/20,* the show anchors comment on what they just watched. This part of my job always makes me nervous. Will Barbara be supportive or skeptical? Might Hugh ask a question for which I'm prepared? When my segment on "Relaxing the Rules" aired, I was relieved when Downs commented, "I hadn't known about the good things that deregulation may have brought."

Few of us had thought about it. Our belief in order and planning is threatened by the apparent chaos of unregulated markets. But the fact is that while free markets are often frightening, they create a spontaneous order that *makes most things better.*

THE CONCEIT OF THE ANOINTED

Still we don't believe it. We keep passing rules. Every week, another thousand regulations—the feds pass some, local governments pass more.

Maybe it's because they spend too much time listening to experts. There are lots of experts, smart people with specialized knowledge who are convinced that through what the Communists called "central planning," they can run our lives better than we would.

Author Thomas Sowell calls it the "Conceit of the Anointed." *You* are not to be trusted. *We* know better. There are now 150 government agencies with more than 5 million employees who spend most of every day searching for ways to protect us, make something more "fair," or just help their friends. Every year they churn out thousands of pages of new rules. But again and again, the experts' schemes go awry. They don't see the unintended consequences. The Conceit of the Anointed is so powerful that they insist on maintaining control even when they fail, and fail again.

Consider what the federal government has done to America's forests. In 2002, forest fires burned 7 million acres, destroyed 800 homes, and killed 23 firefighters. Reporters called the fires "natural disasters" or "tragic accidents," but it would be more accurate to call them "government-enabled" fires because government mismanagement let many of them happen.

Private forests weren't as likely to burn, because companies like Weyerhaeuser, International Paper, and Boise Cascade, eager to profit from their forests, manage them properly. They thin their forests, clear away flammable brush, and build firebreaks.

The government heeded preservationists' calls to leave forests untouched. If you're the interior secretary, why bother offending environmentalists by clearing forests of dense underbrush? It's not *your* money at risk. Relax, go with the flow, plot your next step up the political ladder. Problems will become your successor's problems.

So they created forests that were unnaturally dense, and we got *big* fires.

If private-sector carelessness had allowed millions of acres to burn, the CEO of the company would be public enemy number one, his wretched face plastered all over *Time* and *Newsweek*. His company would sink into bankruptcy, lawsuits, and disgrace.

But when government policy burns our national forests, there is only a sigh from the public and the press. In fact, even as the forests burned, the government argued that it should control *more* land.

TOO MANY RULES

We're conditioned to think of "public" facilities as better than "private." Public facilities are good for everybody, while privately owned things are good for only a few. But think again.

What image does "public toilet" bring to mind? Something filthy, smelly, and maybe even dangerous. That's a good description of what you find in many public parks. Yet in 400 European cities, if nature calls, you can just step over to a little kiosk, put in a coin worth about a quarter, and access a bathroom that is clean and safe. They are clean and safe because private companies run them—just as accessible as a "private" supermarket. Because someone wants to make a profit off them, however, they are better maintained than public toilets. If the quarter fee doesn't pay the full cost of the facilities; the companies make money selling advertising on the kiosks.

In the '80s, New York City bureaucrats invited the companies to bring these toilets to America. Companies were eager to comply, but they ran into American rules. First, city lawyers said, "European toilets are illegal. They have urinals; that discriminates against women." So the companies agreed to build only all-stall toilets. Then they were told that 13 separate city agencies (the Arts Commission, the Parks Commission, etc.) must grant approval. After more than a year of negotiations, many of the agencies rejected the toilets. But since people were peeing in the street, they relented, and agreed to a four-month tryout.

A French company, JC DeCaux, installed toilets at three different sites. They were nicer than public rest rooms I've seen. They actually cleaned themselves—after you left the stall, the door closed, the floor was cleaned by jets of water that shot across it, and the seat withdrew into the wall, where it was steam-cleaned and disinfected.

People I interviewed coming out of them *loved* them. Finally, New Yorkers would have a place to "go." And the kiosks wouldn't cost New York City a penny—DeCaux would recover its investment by selling advertising.

But the Anointed said the European toilets were unacceptable. They did not comply with America's new disabilities law. They had to be wheelchair-accessible. But DeCaux's CEO, Jean François DeCaux, had experimented with big, wheelchair-accessible bathrooms in London. "It was a complete disaster," he told us. "They were misused for sex and drugs, and the homeless were spending the night. . . . All the special fixtures were destroyed all the time." He asked officials to accept the European design, but NYC's bureaucrats wouldn't budge.

One deputy mayor declared the toilet experiment a huge success and said more would be installed. But after the tryout other officials decreed they must be removed. We watched as streets beneath the kiosks were torn up, the pipes to the sewer disconnected, the stalls hauled away on trucks, and the sidewalk repaved. New Yorkers went back to peeing in alleyways. The deputy mayor said the permanent toilets would soon be back. That was 10 years ago. As I write this, the city has once again announced that it's going to bring us public toilets. I'll believe it when I see it.

The Americans with Disabilities Act was just one of many hurdles to getting public toilets in NYC. The Transportation Department had a 100-page contract that must be signed. The Arts Commission must approve the toilet's "aesthetic merits," and so on.

The endless maze of rules blocks progress everywhere. I play beach volleyball near one of New York's most elegant public schools—"a gleaming 10-story palace," the *New York Times* called it. But when I visited, the school's new swimming pool was empty. Students were not allowed to use it because its depth warnings were written as "ft." instead of "feet." The pool remained unused for almost a year, until its brand new mosaic tiles were chipped away and replaced.

I'm amazed *anything* gets built. The Anointed now have so many rules that innovators need enormous courage, money, and political connections to build. The permit process often takes longer than the construction. Contractors used to call resistance to construction NIMBY—Not in My Back Yard. Now the acronym is BANANA—Build Absolutely Nothing Anywhere Near Anybody.

OSHA

The Anointed at the Occupational Safety and Health Administration (OSHA) are so confident of their wisdom, they've decided to tell every industry how its workers must work.

OSHA decreed that landscapers must not use ordinary $5 gasoline cans for their lawn mowers or chain saws. They must switch to OSHA-approved ones. The OSHA-approved ones have so many safety features, they cost $200 each.

When a man was trapped in a trench in Idaho, some construction workers quickly jumped in and rescued him. OSHA then fined the construction company $7,000—because the rescuers didn't wear approved hard hats and didn't properly secure the trench walls.

OSHA fined one company because it failed to warn employees not to ingest the toner in its copiers. The toner is black powder stored deep in the copier. People have to be told not to eat it?

OSHA regulators spend millions of dollars micromanaging workplaces. They sent a letter to beverage companies giving detailed instructions on how workers should unload trucks. The delivery companies had unloaded soft drinks for years and thought they knew how to do it, but no, OSHA had specific instructions: First, double the number of people on your delivery teams. Then "employee number one can unload the truck for an hour and employee number two can roll the hand truck. The torso should not be bent forward further than six to 10 degrees from vertical," and so on.

Privately, companies sneer at the pointless regulation, but they meekly obey it. If they complain publicly, OSHA's inspectors might retaliate. John Knott, who owns a wire-mesh factory in Massachusetts, is one of the few who'd talk to us, and sure enough, afterward he was fined. A railing is 2 inches too low. Tear it out, replace it—doesn't matter what it costs. OSHA said one of his machines was dangerous. The inspector said a worker might stick his arm in the machine when the blade inside was spinning. Knott explained that when the cover was open, the blade wouldn't turn. Didn't matter. OSHA fined him $4,000.

"They send inspectors around who invent complaints," Knott told us. "They're extortionists."

A few companies have the courage to fight back. When OSHA demanded that Dayton Tire redesign or eliminate all jobs that involved lifting things, Dayton took OSHA to court. Amazingly, at the trial, the government's experts could not agree on what was safe to lift. One said 25 pounds, another said 10 pounds, and a third said 4. One said that some workers, to be safe, shouldn't lift *any* weight. So OSHA lost the case. Still, winning cost Dayton a fortune.

Since even their own experts couldn't agree on what was safe to lift, you'd think OSHA would hesitate before trying to impose similar rules on every workplace in America. You'd be wrong. There is no end to the Conceit of the Anointed.

In 2000, claiming it would prevent injuries to workers who lift things and do repetitive tasks, OSHA decided it would set "ergonomic" standards. Lifting and repetitive work can cause painful injuries, but it's not clear that OSHA knows how to prevent them. Ergonomics is a new and uncertain science. But that didn't matter to OSHA director Charles Jeffrees, who said, "We are compelled to act. Employees are getting hurt." He wouldn't talk to me, so I interviewed Cindy Roth, an OSHA consultant who helped the government write its ergonomics proposal. Roth ran Ergonomic Technologies, which makes money telling companies how to become ergonomically correct.

The proposal said an "effective ergonomic intervention" may require "physicians, occupational health nurses, nurse practitioners, physician assistants, occupational therapists, physical therapists, industrial hygienists, ergonomists, safety engineers, and a workplace safety and health team." The rules went on for 300 pages. A company trying to deal with all that could go bankrupt just paying lawyers.

Then OSHA announced that even if you work at *home,* OSHA's ergonomics rules apply. That got my attention. Would they come into my house?

I asked Roth for an ergonomic evaluation of my home office. My "office" is just a desk with a computer, but the "certified ergonomist" whom Roth brought along found endless problems with it. First, my computer mouse was at the wrong level.

Ergonomist: You get a lot of stress on your shoulder.... So you need to get a [$300] keyboard tray that accommodates the mouse.

And my keyboard was dangerous.

Ergonomist: It induces what we call "ulnar deviation."

He told me I shouldn't sit up straight.

Ergonomist: That leads to stress on the spine.

And I should block the sunlight that comes into the room, because it will cause . . .

Ergonomist: Eye-ache and headache, maybe even neck stress.
John Stossel: And my chair?
Ergonomist: It is not suitable.

I pulled out an expensive "ergonomic" chair I'd just bought. Not good enough, said both experts.

John Stossel: A chair like this? They told me it was ergonomic.

Cindy Roth: You're going to tend to slide. You're not going to even be aware of it. These are the ways cumulative traumas develop within the body.

Across the room, my son was playing video games.

Cindy Roth: He's compressing his thigh with his forearms. He also has his head tilted this way. His neck postures are compromised. This can cause cumulative trauma disorders.

The Anointed always find problems. Fortunately, this time they had overreached to the point that the public noticed, and complained. The *Washington Post* ran a front-page story on OSHA's in-the-home plans; people screamed, and the regulators backed down. President Clinton's labor secretary, Alexis Herman, said, "Obviously, the government has no desire, or the resources, to inspect every home in this country. But we certainly need to begin to talk about it."

They're still going to discuss it, even after you told them you don't want such intrusive meddling? You bet.

That they backed down at all was unusual. It happened *only* because you caught them. Usually you're too busy to notice, and the freedom-killing rules just expand. If these busybodies have power over our lives, there is no end to what they'll mandate. They will take *all* our money and *all* our time.

THE NANNY STATE

I thought I was the only reporter in the mainstream media bothered by this regulatory overreach until I read a column by Michael Kelly, editor of the *New Republic*. He wrote:

It has been called the nanny state, but that is far too kind a term. It is too cold, too cruel, too implacable, too illiberal to be a nanny. It is the Nurse Ratched [the dictatorial ward matron in *One Flew Over the Cuckoo's Nest*] state. Government has created a brutal system of mandated behaviorism, in which the state uses its immense powers to force targeted citizens and entities to "voluntarily" accept a violation of their rights. . . . The efforts to sustain affirmative action rest on these coercive methods. So, too, do the efforts to enforce the decree that private workplaces be free of discriminatory, harassing or even rude behavior. The intrusions resulting from the Americans with Disabilities Act have mutated beyond sanity. . . . Nursie knows best.

I couldn't believe what I was reading. I wasn't alone. Here was someone from a *liberal* publication who saw what I saw. Now that he was writing about it—more eloquently than I had—others would pick it up. Even the *New York Times* would start writing about the suffocating burden of millions of little rules.

Nope.

Kelly later lost his job as *New Republic* editor—his boss, publisher Marty Peretz, said Kelly was "so far to the right, he was in breakdown lane." (Michael Kelly died covering the war in Iraq. His contribution will be missed.)

I interviewed Kelly for a story on the Nanny State that I hoped to put on *20/20*. In the story, I detailed some of the regulators' steadily accelerating assaults on smokers: They began by taxing cigarettes, then they banned smoking on airplanes, then in federal buildings. When smokers congregated outside, President Clinton proposed ordering them to stay 100 feet away from every building. California and New York then banned smoking in every restaurant and bar. Nurse Ratched always wants more.

I don't smoke, so I like a smoke-free environment, but when both owners and customers are okay with it, can't it be their choice? Can't the smokers have some bars? No.

Nanny launched a similar assault in the name of auto safety. Government first *asked* us to buckle our seat belts. It was our choice. Not anymore.

Then came air bags. First they were optional; now they are mandatory. The bags do save lives, although they are not nearly as effective as seat belts. Unfortunately, they are a small explosive device. If you are short or a child, the bag is more likely to kill you than save you. Since the mid-1990s, airbags have caused more than 200 deaths.

I interviewed Violet Cosgrove, an elderly lady who was scared to drive the new car she'd just bought. She was less than 5 feet tall, and once she learned about the air bag danger, she felt like she was sitting behind a bomb. Since the air bag was an added risk to her, could she least buy a car without an air bag? No, it was forbidden. Could she have a mechanic disconnect the air bag? No, forbidden. Could she order an on/off switch? No. Not unless she filled out complicated paperwork and begged the government for permission. Violet did file the paperwork, but she never heard back. Only when she got her congressman to intervene was she able to make this minor change to her car.

Wouldn't it at least be reasonable to allow people to have an on/off switch? Not according to Ricardo Martinez, head of the National Highway Traffic Safety Administration under President Clinton.

Ricardo Martinez: It takes a village to take care of our kids.

John Stossel: What about freedom? In a free society, can't somebody buy a car without an air bag if they want to?

Ricardo Martinez: We are a free society. On the other side of the coin, when you make rules, when you make laws, when you make decisions as a country, it's not the government *versus* the people. The government *is* the people.

That's the Conceit of the Anointed. Martinez and his fellow "experts" *are* "the people." Michael Kelly asked: "Why should the government have anything to do with that decision of yours? It is your decision. They are always protecting somebody's life, and they're always protecting somebody's life at the cost of somebody else's liberties."

Because the air bags the government required sometimes kill children, the Clinton administration moved to make it a *crime* for any parent to allow a child under 13 to ride in the front seat of the car. If I had a car pool and couldn't put all the kids in the back, I'd be breaking the law. Such a rule would probably make most parents criminals. At least the Bush administration has not pursued that proposal. But just wait. The regulators always want more.

Said Kelly, "We are increasingly prisoners of a hospital-like state. Every day you read that something has happened that is another Ratched-like intrusion into your life.... There's a million things you can do to save more lives. We can outlaw Big Macs if you want."

Maybe that's next. Lawyers have already sued McDonald's for "causing" obesity. For my "Nanny State" story, I interviewed Dr. Kelly Brownell of Yale University, who wants the government to tax you if you eat fast food. "With our nation becoming fatter almost by the day, it's a crisis," he says. *US News and World Report* called his plan "a silver bullet," one of "16 smart ideas to fix the world."

Where does this end? Will exercise police come into our homes, make us run laps, do push-ups? What happened to freedom? Patrick Henry didn't say, "Give me absolute safety or give me death."

The Anointed never stop. New Jersey and Oregon won't allow self-service gas stations. The politicians say if you pump your own gas, you might blow yourself up. The rest of us in the 48 other states manage to fill our tanks without blowing ourselves up, but New Jersey and Oregon say it isn't safe. "What if one life was lost?" say the politicians. "Would you want that on your conscience?"

The regulators believe zero risk is possible, and given the chance, they will bankrupt trying to achieve it. The cost and the delays don't worry them: They're doing this for your own good.

They'll even protect you from Halloween. In parts of Ohio, you need a special permit to go trick-or-treating. Just wait in line at city hall. It's for your safety.

I loved my "Nanny State" story, but my boss, executive producer Victor Neufeld, was unenthusiastic—he wouldn't put it on *20/20*. "I'm not bothered by those safety regulations," he said, "and I don't think most people are—they make us safer." Only after I complained relentlessly did he allow it to air—a year and a half later.

I got letters from some people who liked it, but maybe Neufeld was right. Most Americans don't seem upset about the Nanny State. I hear few complaints about regulation. Watching the news, I mostly hear people asking for *more* rules. But as Michael Kelly said:

> Every time the government tries to make life better for you, it uses force. It makes criminals out of people who are not criminals. Some poor mope who would like a large-size toilet in his house has to go out and smuggle one. The guy who smokes a cigarette down the hall from you at his desk alone in his office with the door closed is a criminal. Some mother who wants to talk to her 12-year-old in the front seat is a criminal also. All these people are criminals now. That's us. Why do they have the right to make all of us criminals because we smoke, or want to have our kids sit next to us in the car?

Because they are the Anointed, and they know best.

CHAPTER FIVE

Scaring Ourselves to Death

Fear always springs from ignorance.

—Ralph Waldo Emerson

Midway in my *20/20* career, a producer came into my office with another "scare" story. He was spitting with righteous indignation. "BIC lighters are exploding in people's pockets!" he said. "Spontaneously catching fire—they've killed four Americans over the past four years!"

He got the story from a trial lawyer. Trial lawyers are "investigative" reporters' best friends. They bring us scare stories in neatly wrapped packages, so all we have to do is take their research, and we look like big-time investigators.

But now I had a new way to think about things.

I understand why he brought me the story. BIC lighters setting people on fire was a horrible and shocking thing. Victims were saying things like "You bring it in your house, and that might be the end of your life" and "It's like a bomb." But the fact that the allegations against BIC would be a dramatic story did not mean it was the right story for a consumer reporter to put on a national newsmagazine show. Consumer reporting should focus on big risks, not unlikely ones. We rarely did.

For most of my career, I was part of the problem. I reported on statistically insignificant threats—poisonous lawn chemicals ("Danger in the Grass"), exploding coffeemakers ("Brewing Disaster"). Crusading lawyers and environmental activists got me to do stories frightening people about secondhand smoke and suggesting that Hartz Mountain flea collars were killing kittens and puppies. These stories make me cringe today, but at the time, I took the "safety" lawyers and environmentalists at their word. They were the good guys out to serve the public. They described themselves as "public interest" advocates, and I wanted to believe them because the activists had long hair and wore blue jeans—just like me. By contrast, business was run by men in suits who would do just about anything to get rich.

It took me too long to realize that the activists have selfish agendas, too. They want to be famous, or feel morally superior. And scaring people helps them raise money.

Eventually I started to wonder if our eager coverage of the activists' accusations did more harm than good. Weren't we distorting the public's understanding of what's *really* risky? Risk takers built America. But today many of us seem almost paralyzed by fear.

WHAT'S A REPORTER TO DO?

When disaster strikes, it's our job to tell you about it. If a plane crashes, that's big news—if it doesn't, it's nice, but not news. Nothing gets our adrenaline going like danger, and thousands of hardworking reporters risk their lives to keep you informed.

But we don't give you the complete picture.

Here, I must admit, my beloved free market works against calm and thoughtful journalism. It gives us an incentive to scare you. More of you will watch *20/20* if I say, "Tonight: Your water is poisoned!" than if I say it probably isn't. Bad news is what makes news. No one is out by the back fence gossiping about who's *faithful* to his spouse. It's reporters' duty to cover the bad news, but our excitement about it, and our rush to be "on top of the news," lead us to overemphasize some risks. TV news-magazines such as *20/20* and *Dateline NBC* have done stories on the danger of sharks, your mattress, washing your hands too much, not washing your hands enough, coffeepots, breakfast, fruit, vegetables, sandwiches, your shoes, your dry cleaning, dolls, cribs, crowds, day care, elevators, escalators (stairs are more dangerous, but don't make for sexy TV), libraries, school buses, playgrounds, nail salons, shopping carts, and rubber duckies.

Instead of putting risks in proportion, we hype *interesting* ones. Tom Brokaw, Katie Couric, and countless others called 2001 the "summer of the shark." Some beachgoers were so frightened, they wouldn't go in the water. They were in far greater danger of drowning, or dying in a car accident driving to the beach, but that wasn't very interesting. In truth, there wasn't a remarkable surge in shark attacks in 2001. There were about as many in 1995 and 2000, but 1995 was the year of the O. J. Simpson trial, and 2000 was an election year. The summer of 2001 was a little dull, so reporters focused on sharks.

We go nuts when a plane crashes. We in television shriek, "We're here *live*—we don't know much, but we'll keep talking, *live*," and go on about the crash for hours. The real miracle is that thousands of planes *don't* crash. Huge metal tubes filled with people actually lift themselves off the ground, slice through the sky propelled by an explosive fuel, and then glide to a stop a few feet from other huge tubes. Then they do it again. Day and night. But that's not news. It's the danger that's news. After big crashes, my bosses used to try to get me to do alarmist stories highlight-ing the ten "most dangerous" airports, or "most dangerous" airlines, or how to escape from under water after a plane crashes. (I saw that one on *Dateline NBC.*) I refused to do those stories about minuscule risks. I refused because I think reporting like that is "statistical murder."

Safety is about trade-offs. If America spends millions trying to make rubber duckies a tiny bit safer, that money is unavailable when it's time to fight bigger threats. If we scare you about minimal risks, we lead you into taking bigger risks. After we scare people with our hysterical plane crash coverage, more *drive* to Grandma's house. That raises death rates, because driving is more dangerous than flying.

WHAT'S REALLY RISKY, ANYWAY?

By 1985, I was getting so sick of our indiscriminate hyping of risks that I decided to try to rank them. My assistant and I spent six months asking scientists and government officials for data on what kills people. We came up with a "death list," which I posted on my wall. The following chart is an updated version.

TABLE I: WHAT KILLS PEOPLE

Cause of Death	Number of Deaths
Heart disease	710,760
Cancer	553,091
Stroke	167,661
Accidents	97,902

Motor vehicles 43,354

Falls 13,221

Crossing the street .6,047

Fires and burns 3,418

Choking on small objects 2,828

Electrocution 874

Bikes 800

Choking on food 640

Air crashes 570

Drowning in swimming pools 530

Bathtub drowning 320

Lightning 64

Contact with hot tap water 51

Cribs 27

Suffocation from plastic bags 25

Baseball 6

Drowning in toilets 4

BIC lighters . . . . .1?

Sources: Office of Statistics and Programming, National Center for Injury Prevention and Control. *CDC Data Source:* National Center for Health Statistics (NCHS) Vital Statistics System, National Safety Council, and Consumer Product Safety Commission.

I found the accident data fascinating. Turns out hot tap water, stairs, bunk beds, and drowning in bathtubs kill more people than most risks we hysterically warn people about.

Now that I had my "death list," I could say to that producer with the BIC lighter story, "I'll do that if you do plastic bags first; they kill twenty-five times as many people. Or let's do toilets; they kill four people *every year*. It's a big country. If we scare people about every ant, they won't pay attention when the elephants come." The producer stormed out of my office, calling me insensitive, and got someone else to do the BIC lighter story.

Then I went to my bosses and said, "I want to do an hour-long special that puts risks into perspective." They said it was a good idea and they'd get back to me. They didn't.

Then free-market competition helped me out. I got another job offer. To keep me, ABC agreed to give me three one-hour specials a year. I insisted that the first be about risk assessment. I wanted the title to be "Scaring Ourselves to Death," but ABC changed it to "Are We Scaring Ourselves to Death?"

Alan Wurzel, ABC's (now NBC's) research director, worried that such a show would get poor ratings. "Why do a show on risk assessment?" he asked. "You should do something on diet, or breast implants—something we know people will watch." I insisted, and he gave in.

ABC assigned a 12-person staff. I told the producers that at the end of the show, I wanted to say what I say in this book—that regulation itself can make life less safe by stifling innovation. Two of the three producers angrily objected, saying, "No respectable journalist would say that. We must point out that some regulations are great." (As if reporters hadn't constantly been saying that on TV for years.) They refused to go forward with my vision, and I refused to cooperate with theirs. The senior producer assigned to the program smugly told me, "You just can't say that on network TV."

I couldn't believe it. I'd fought to do this show for three years. I had threatened to leave for another job. I'd made it part of my contract negotiations. And now three producers were going to eviscerate it. After bitter arguments, we went to Paul Friedman, then executive vice president of the News Division. I was ready to quit if he took their side, but to my relief, he said, "I don't agree with you, but it's a valid intellectual argument that deserves to be made."

"Scaring" went forward. The two producers quit.

To my bosses' surprise, the show was a success—17 million Americans watched. We got 3,000 letters, many saying, "What a breath of fresh air!"

Scientists wrote in to say, "Thank God, somebody's finally saying these things. I can't believe I saw that on network television." And this marked the beginning of the second phase of my career. I was no longer the heroic consumer reporter. Now I was a traitor to journalism.

ARE WE SCARING OURSELVES TO DEATH?

What was in the show? I tried to put risk in perspective. What *should* we fear? If we scare you about blood-drinking cults and flesh-eating bacteria, how can you focus on real risks? We can't fear everything, can we?

People already have an innate fear of most things new or different. Our hysterical reporting makes it worse, creating an irrational demand for a zero-risk life.

When I speak to a large audience, I often try the following thought experiment:

Assume you are a safety regulator, and I am a businessman with a new fuel I want to sell. My new fuel will be no cheaper than oil, but it will at least give us another choice, and reduce our dependence on OPEC. The problem with it is that, unlike oil, which is just flammable, my new fuel is so flammable, it's explosive. It's also invisible, odorless, and deadly poisonous—and I want to pump it into your house.

You're the regulator. Will you approve this new fuel?

Laughter and "Of course not!" are the responses I usually get. We then debate what level of risk would be acceptable for such a new product. Should it be allowed if it kills 10 Americans a year? Five? Some audience members will approve the fuel if it would kill only two people, but most are adamantly opposed to any risk.

Then I ask one of the more passionate naysayers what kind of stove he has. Half the time he'll say gas. The audience is silent for a moment—then some people laugh.

The fuel I'm talking about isn't new. It's natural gas. We already use it—half the country has gas stoves. Natural gas is highly explosive, invisible, poisonous, and odorless. Yet we accept natural gas, even though it kills not two but 400 Americans a year, because it was introduced before we got crazy about risk. We accept coal, even though mining it is nasty and filthy and kills dozens of people every year. By contrast, we're terrified of nuclear energy. Chernobyl, the worst nuclear power disaster ever, killed only 30 people. Some say the radiation may eventually kill others, but even if that's true, natural gas kills more people every year. Nuclear power is probably *safer* than other fuels, but because it's new and mysterious, it terrifies.

Would cars be approved today? Pretend you are the regulator again. I want to introduce a one-ton machine that'll go 60 miles per hour, inches from pedestrians. (And I'll let 16-year-olds drive them!) No chance it would be approved. Airplanes? We're going to put 300 people in a tube and have it fly over a city? No way.

How can innovators keep improving our lives, and how will America compete in a world economy, when we are so hostile to new ideas? It is true that today we're exposed to far more dangerous-sounding chemicals and technologies than ever before—invisible threats like pesticides, pollutants, bioengineering, electromagnetic fields, and radiation. But that's not shortening our lives. Today *we live longer than ever.*

At the turn of the last century, half the population never reached my age (56). What's lengthened life spans 30 years is the very technology we now fear so much.

How could I put this in perspective? I decided to interview Ralph Nader. Nader's world is filled with horrible things to worry about. In our interview, he talked about "chicken contaminated with pesticides, herbicides, fungicides—sometimes contaminated with rat feces." "We shouldn't eat hot dogs," he said. "Hot dogs have a very low nutritional value. They have a high fat content." Even carpets are dangerous. We'd be better off with bare floors. "Rugs are dirt collectors, and dirt collectors mean indoor air pollution." And then there's coffee: "Caffeine is not very good for you," he told me. "On the other hand, if you take decaffeinated coffee, sometimes the process to decaffeinate it has exposed the coffee to a chemical that isn't good for you."

John Stossel: You make it sound as if you should cringe when you get up in the morning. You make life sound terrifying.
Ralph Nader: Well, life is preparedness.

It was a strange interview. As a young reporter, I admired Nader and his criticism of the auto industry. He got America to think about safety, pursuing it with single-minded passion. But now he reminds me of a train that has gone off track but won't stop. Nader has no interest in ranking risks. No juicy hot dog is worth eating.

That's not the life most of us want to lead. Worrying about *everything* won't make us live significantly longer (although it would *seem* longer).

Around the same time I was coming to a new understanding of risk, my own town, New York City, fell under the spell of the alarmists. Parents panicked when they heard asbestos was the fireproofing in the walls of many school buildings. The city closed the schools and spent $100 million ripping asbestos out of walls. This was insane. Asbestos in the walls posed no risk to children, but ripping it out spread asbestos in the air—a greater risk. Closing the schools was worse: It meant the kids played on the street, a *vastly* greater risk. But there was no reasoning with school officials or frightened parents. They were caught up in America's irrational fear of anything chemical.

Only recently, after the attack on the World Trade Center, did the Environmental Protection Agency issue a more sensible assessment of asbestos risks. After the towers fell, the agency issued a report indicating that, although 40 floors' worth of asbestos hovered in the air, the risk of disease from asbestos exposure was "very low." After decades of scaring people about exposure to even minimal amounts of asbestos, the EPA admitted the only real risk came from "long-term" exposure at high levels.

How did we get to be so fearful of chemicals?

It started in the '70s, when scientists suggested our environment might be killing us. These new, invisible threats were especially frightening—it was terrifying to think that something in our air and drinking water was slowly, silently causing cancer, miscarriages, birth defects. Toxic waste sites like Love Canal were the beginning. Once officials started looking, they seemed to find toxic chemicals everywhere.

So scientists began seeking ways to determine which chemicals caused cancers and other problems. Animal tests using proportions of chemicals that are normally consumed in real life wouldn't work because they'd need a million rats or guinea pigs to get significant results (not every animal gets cancer from the carcinogen, and a third of the animals get cancer just from living). The scientists got around that by feeding the animals huge doses of the carcinogens, then waiting up to two years to see if the animals got cancer, and the tests often cost more than $1 million.

Then California biochemist Dr. Bruce Ames came up with a brilliant solution. "Instead of testing animals," he said, "test bacteria to see if the chemicals damage DNA. You can study a billion bacteria on just one petri dish. Bacteria reproduce every 20 minutes."

The Ames test proved fabulously successful. It was hailed as a major scientific breakthrough, and became the standard test to see if chemicals cause mutations. Its first use in the '70s showed there were mutagens in hair dyes and in fireproof material in children's pajamas. Ames helped get the chemicals banned.

But then, Ames told me, "People started using our test and finding mutagens everywhere, in cups of coffee, in plants we eat, in broiled hamburgers. Most mutagens turn out to be carcinogens. I started getting a more realistic view of the world."

Ames and his colleague Lois Gold concluded that the popular assumption that man-made chemicals are more likely to be carcinogenic than natural substances is wrong. Ames told us that in "high-dose animal cancer tests, half of all chemicals ever tested, whether natural or man-made, are carcinogens. Exposure to man-made chemicals that are carcinogens is minuscule compared to the exposure to natural carcinogens in our diet. Thousands of new chemicals have been introduced over the past forty years. If they were giving people cancer, then there should be an epidemic of cancer in this country, but there isn't."

At the time, reports about the "cancer epidemic" were common. Everyone "knew" cancers were increasing. But what reporters "knew" was wrong.

It was true that lung and skin cancer were increasing. But other forms of cancer, says the American Cancer Society, have stayed pretty level, and some, like uterine and stomach and liver cancer, have declined markedly. The Society says 90 percent of the lung cancer is due to smoking, and the skin cancer is due to too much sunbathing.

More cancers are recorded now because we have better early detection, and because more people are living long enough to get cancer. Also, more of us are willing to talk about cancer. But there's no epidemic. This was not a secret. It was common knowledge to epidemiologists and cancer specialists at the National Cancer Institute, the Mayo Clinic, and elsewhere. But that wasn't on the reporter's radar. Many still don't believe it. Activists are still raising funds by wailing about the "cancer epidemic."

"Superfund sites" like Love Canal, New York, became the cancer epidemic's poster child and America's most expensive cleanup projects. Love Canal is still routinely portrayed as the worst-case scenario, a toxic nightmare in which dumped chemicals poisoned a neighborhood. But while there is nasty stuff in the dirt around Love Canal, and authorities spent a fortune to evacuate the town and bulldoze dozens of homes, they have not found evidence of higher cancer rates in people who lived there. Ever hear that reported? Didn't think so.

Chemicals that aren't killing people isn't as good a story as Poison at Love Canal or, say, *Erin Brockovich*, the fable of the woman who convinced a town that its power company was making them sick.

Erin Brockovich is one of the biggest-grossing films of all times "based on a true story." Julia Roberts is terrific as the feisty investigator bringing justice to the town. The movie brought the real Erin Brockovich lots of great publicity because the mainstream media naively treated her accusations as fact.

The genuine "true story" was different. It was never established that the power company made anyone sick. The power company looked guilty because it did what companies usually do—escaped the lawyers by settling, paying some $300 million. Brockovich herself got $2 million. That part of the movie is true.

The rest? Brockovich claimed the chemical hexavalent chromium caused uterine cancer, Hodgkin's disease, spinal deterioration, and more. Some activists suggested it made dogs attack people. Scientists roll their eyes when people claim so many different diseases caused by one chemical.

Hexavalent chromium is a carcinogen if inhaled at high levels, but the EPA says no data suggest drinking chromium causes cancer. The California Cancer Registry analyzed cancer rates in the area and found no elevation in the level of cancer, and a study of 50,000 people who'd worked *at the suspect power plants* found the workers were *healthier* than average. See that in the movie? No.

I did a "Give Me a Break" segment on that, after which the real Erin Brockovich demanded that I be fired, and held a news conference with the head of her law firm, Ed Masry, to insist that I apologize to them and the whole town.

Erin Brockovich: I used to believe John Stossel was a reporter who did consumer advocate work. After I saw this piece I am convinced he is nothing more than a corporate shill. . . . I want Mr. Stossel and his family to come out here. I want you to start drinking Chromium-6-laced water! . . . I'm not going to let that movie be made a mockery of by John Stossel.

Ed Masry: Give me a break? Stossel should be saying "Give me a brain." . . . We didn't scare anybody. Idiots like Stossel are the scary people.

Since the Pacific Gas and Electric Company case, Brockovich and Masry have gone on to sue Avon, IBM, General Electric, Coronet Industries, and the Beverly Hills School District, claiming that toxic fumes caused hundreds of cases of Hodgkin disease and thyroid cancer since the 1970s. They've successfully frightened a lot of people, but that doesn't mean anyone was actually at risk.

PROTECTING OURSELVES FROM OUR "PROTECTORS"

In America, chemical pollution is actually decreasing, although you'd never know this watching alarmist TV programs and movies like *Erin Brockovich*. Since 1976, we've made great strides: sulfur dioxides are down 67 percent, nitrogen dioxide 42 percent, carbon monoxide 73 percent, lead 97 percent. More cars are on the road, driving more miles, but smog is down by one-third.

The water is cleaner, too. When I started work in Manhattan in 1973, every flush of a toilet went straight into the East and Hudson Rivers—with no sewage treatment. To illustrate that, I flushed some food dye at CBS's headquarters and then a cameraman in a helicopter filmed the bright green color that soon appeared in the Hudson River. I did this to point out that there were 8 million people in New York City flushing away, and it all went straight into the rivers. Amazingly, nature's remarkable ability to recover on its own meant the rivers cleaned themselves enough that my friend Diana Nyad could still safely swim around Manhattan. Today, thanks to sewage treatment, the Hudson's clean enough that I swim in it.

I admit it was government that made this happen. Free markets created the affluence to pay for it, but I'm not one of those who believe markets would solve all our problems. Protecting the environment is a proper role of *limited* government.

Yet today's zealous pursuit of an ever more pristine environment brings diminishing returns—at huge expense. The expense is more than money—it's loss of freedom, and subjugation to a new, permanent class of environmental busybodies. Of course we want protection from pollution, but how much protection do we need?

When I did "Scaring," we videotaped Aspen, Colorado, because part of Aspen had been declared a Superfund site after tests found lead in the soil. Aspen was once home to silver mines, and when miners pulled silver out of ore, they left lead.

Lead is a nasty poison. If kids eat enough of it, they suffer brain damage. But lead *in soil* isn't necessarily harmful. Nevertheless, the EPA warned the citizens of Aspen that they were in danger and scheduled an ambitious cleanup. They'd remove 150 houses, dig up tons of dirt, load it onto dump trucks, and carry the dirt off.

At first, frightened people in Aspen were eager for the cleanup to begin. But then some started talking to scientists, who were bewildered by the EPA's plan. Some said the cleanup would be more dangerous than leaving the lead in the soil, because digging it up would put lead dust in the air. Thousands of truck runs carried risks, too. Wouldn't it make more sense just to cover the lead with fresh dirt? Or tell the kids not to eat the dirt? Or to eat less of it? No, said EPA toxicologist Chris Weis. He was certain leaving the dirt where it was would be "a serious problem for children." But people started to ask, how dangerous could the lead be? For decades, kids had used the toxic waste site as their playground. Now they were adults, and healthy. A committee of doctors searched through hospital records and found no cases of lead poisoning.

One of them, Dr. Robert Hunter, told me, "Nobody's sick around here from lead toxicity. If you want to go over to the hospital, I'll show you sick people. It's because they fell skiing. If you're really worried about health hazards, we should stop skiing." Lucky for skiers that the EPA doesn't have jurisdiction over *them*.

Did the lack of evidence of lead poisoning persuade the bureaucrats to reconsider demolishing homes and spending millions of your dollars? No.

They had to *save the children.*

The EPA said blood lead levels above 10 micrograms per deciliter are risky, and the officials were sure that Aspen residents were in worse shape than that. "We have to get those levels down below 10!"

In a less sophisticated and politically connected community, the EPA would simply have demolished that part of town. But after six years of arguing, Aspen residents finally persuaded officials to test their blood. EPA officials were "certain" that 99 percent of the children would show lead levels over 10. When the test results came in, the kids' levels averaged 3, among the lowest recorded anywhere in America.

Did those remarkable results get the EPA to back off? Heck no. They still planned to dig up the neighborhood because the lead in the soil was a "potential" hazard. Only after three more years of protests and testing did the EPA finally take Aspen off the Superfund list. The bureaucrats still send inspectors around to do tests, and anyone who dares dig a hole to plant a tree or expand a basement is supposed to file paperwork with the government.

When they're spending your money to fulfill their vision of the chemical-free life, the bureaucrats rarely back off.

MAKING CHOICES

What should we really worry about?

While researching "Scaring," I learned my "death list" was not the best way to put risks in perspective, because it didn't take the victims' ages into account. Risks that kill kids are a bigger social problem than risks that kill people my age, so risk specialists rank threats by comparing how many days they take off the average life.

The following chart compares threats often covered by the media. I didn't include terrorism, because it's so unpredictable. University of Pittsburgh physics professor Bernard Cohen and researchers at the Harvard School of Risk Analysis helped me prepare the chart.

CHART 1: DAYS OFF YOUR LIFE

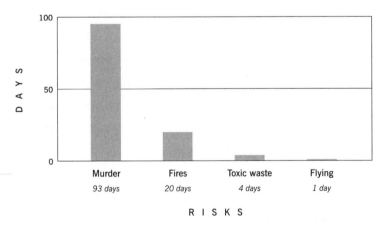

This helps explain why murder tends to lead the news. There are about 16,000 murders in America every year, resulting in about 93 days off the average life. House fires cause 4,500 deaths a year—20 days off the average life. A $10 smoke detector makes a lot of sense. It certainly makes much more sense than spending hundreds of millions of your tax dollars to purify Superfund sites so children can safely eat x teaspoons of dirt.

"Toxic waste" refers to Superfund sites like Love Canal and Times Beach, Missouri. Again, there is no proof that these sites have killed anyone, but I took the most extreme estimate I could find from an environmental group. They said "maybe a thousand Americans get cancer from these sites every year." Assuming that's true, and assuming all of them die, that would still be less than four days off the average life.

While plane crashes are big news, over the past few decades (excluding September 11), America has had fewer than 200 deaths a year from commercial airline crashes. That's less than one day off the average life.

If these were all the risks Americans faced, you might argue that the media aren't doing that bad a job. But let's expand the chart.

CHART 2: DAYS OFF YOUR LIFE

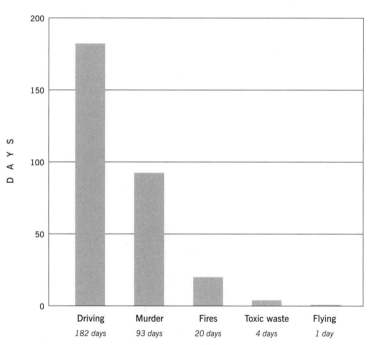

Driving takes half a year off the average life. It's 180 times worse than flying. Every month, car accidents kill 3,000 people. But car accidents aren't new and dramatic. They don't get the breathless coverage that terrorism, crime, plane crashes, and toxic-waste sites get.

The comparison gets more absurd when you add smoking to the list—6.6 years off the average man's life and 3.9 years off the average woman's. Yet smokers worry about getting brain cancer from a cell phone?

CHART 3: DAYS OFF YOUR LIFE

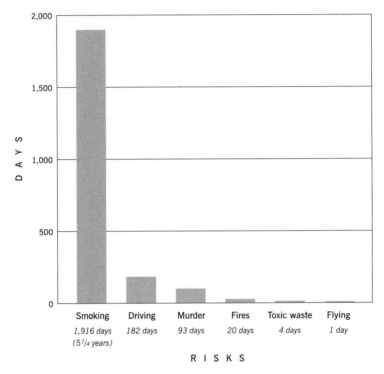

	Smoking	Driving	Murder	Fires	Toxic waste	Flying
	1,916 days (5 1/4 years)	182 days	93 days	20 days	4 days	1 day

RISKS

Want to live longer? Don't smoke, and don't drive recklessly. Exercise more, eat less fat, and practice safe sex. Boring. But much more likely to extend your life than cringing over the endless warnings about exploding cigarette lighters, pesticide residues, and toxic waste.

PANDERING FOR MONEY

I was naïve enough—or arrogant enough—to think that "Are We Scaring Ourselves to Death?" would change everybody's mind. At last, people would truly understand risk. Reporters would stop hyping tiny risks, and viewers would focus on genuine dangers.

How foolish of me. ABC actually ran an alarmist promotion *during* the broadcast of "Are We Scaring Ourselves to Death?" I was watching at home, wondering if my special might persuade my colleagues to calm down, when between commercials, I heard the scary music and an announcer breathlessly talking about pharmacists who make "deadly" mistakes.

He was promoting a report on what can happen when druggists mix drugs. Reporter John Hockenberry intoned, "Your odds of getting something bad or ineffective or contaminated are shocking!" Shocking? Ordinary five-gallon buckets kill many more people. Of course, if Hockenberry had said that, you might not have watched.

The media hysteria not only fools the public, it fools government. Regulators throw money at publicized risks—billions on Superfund and asbestos removal—instead of the riskiest risks.

Consider government-funded medical research. You would think the bureaucrats would spend tax dollars on research that would save the most lives or relieve the most suffering. But they don't. The lion's share goes to the activists who make the most noise.

In the '80s, when the National Institutes of Health were slow to spend money on AIDS research, activists in Washington, D.C., heckled President Reagan, stopped traffic, marched on Congress, and accused politicians of discriminating against gays. It worked. AIDS now gets more research money per patient than any other disease.

The success of the AIDS lobby became a model for the breast cancer lobby. Women marched on the Capitol, accusing politicians who resisted increasing funding of being "antiwoman."

Who wants to be "antiwoman?" Funding for breast cancer research joined AIDS near the top of the list of per-patient expenditures. But breast cancer and AIDS aren't the leading killers. Among diseases, breast cancer is ninth, AIDS 18th. Yet in 2001, AIDS research got $4,439 per patient from NIH, breast cancer $290, Parkinson's $175. Diabetes, which killed more people than AIDS and breast cancer combined, got $41. Heart disease, the number one killer, got just $58 per patient.

If you want your disease researched, better hope that it's politically correct, or that a celebrity gets it. After Christopher Reeve made a trip to the White House, President Clinton promised another $10 million for spinal research. Then Mary Tyler Moore went to Congress to ask for money for Parkinson's. Senator Arlen Specter fawned over her, and after she testified, he taught me a lesson in political venality. First, he said spending more money to research the actors' diseases was "fair."

John Stossel: Is that how it should work?
Senator Arlen Specter: It—how should it work? Yes, I think that's a fair— a fair way.
John Stossel: So whoever panders most to you gets the most money?
Senator Arlen Specter: Whoever panders the most . . .

The pandering question got his attention. Apparently, Senator Specter assumed I was doing what reporters routinely do: ask why this or that celebrity's disease didn't get more money. At first, he bragged that he and his committee told the National Institutes of Health what to do.

Senator Arlen Specter: The subcommittee took the lead in establishing a separate unit for women, and the National Institutes of Health followed that. We are having a special hearing on prostate cancer because the chairman of the full committee has had prostate cancer and we're having a hearing on it.

John Stossel: Because the chairman has prostate cancer you have a hearing?

When he realized I was suggesting scientists should make these decisions—not activists and Arlen Specter—he changed course without batting an eye.

Senator Arlen Specter: The decision as to how much money is spent is made by the National Institutes of Health. It is not made by the Senate or the House or the Congress.

He didn't even seem embarrassed at suddenly reversing himself.

In 1997, when President Clinton was heckled by AIDS activists at the Human Rights Campaign dinner, he smiled and said, "I would have been disappointed if you hadn't been here tonight." Then he bragged, "Since I became president, we're spending 10 times as much per fatality on people with AIDS as people with breast cancer or prostate cancer."

The audience cheered and Clinton beamed.

Am I missing something? Why is it a good thing to spend 10 times more on AIDS than on breast cancer or prostate cancer? Or, for that matter, 25 times more than on Parkinson's, which kills more people?

It's fortunate that America is so rich it can lead the world in medical research, even if politicians misdirect some of the money. But misdirecting money does kill people too. This brings me to the last and most important bar on the "Days Off Your Life" chart.

WEALTHIER IS HEALTHIER

Safety and environmental regulation takes a toll on wealth production. Some jobs are created for regulators and lawyers, but overall, regulation is a brake on an economy. If it takes five years for the factory to get permission to open, fewer factories are built, and fewer people have work. If use of a chemical is restricted, some products cost more, so consumers have less to spend on other things.

While chemicals and BIC lighters may pose slight risks, by far the bigger risk is being poor. Look at the next chart.

Studies show that if you are poor (below the poverty line in the United States, in the lowest quintile of income elsewhere), your life is *seven to 10 years shorter.* It's partly because poor people smoke and drink more, but it's mostly because poor people can't afford things that keep others alive. They drive older cars with older tires. They stay in the old house rather than move to one with a modern sprinkler system.

Wealthier is healthier. Floods in Bangladesh kill thousands of people. Floods in America are just as severe, but they rarely kill anyone, because we have wealth: We have radios to tell us about the floods, and cars in which to drive away.

When government spends vast amounts on the small risks on the right side of the chart—delaying the factory or the oil well, or closing the school to take all the asbestos out of the walls, or closing a town to take all the lead out of a Superfund site—it makes more people poorer. That shortens lives. The regulation headline should read, "New OSHA Rule to Save Six, Kill 10."

You won't see that headline. Reporters don't think that way.

CHART 4: DAYS OFF YOUR LIFE

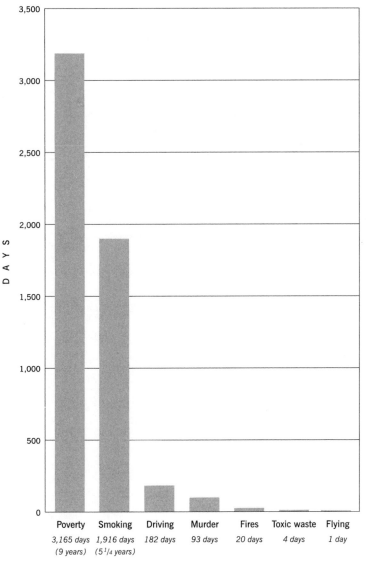

Poverty	**Smoking**	**Driving**	**Murder**	**Fires**	**Toxic waste**	**Flying**
3,165 days	*1,916 days*	*182 days*	*93 days*	*20 days*	*4 days*	*1 day*
(9 years)	*(5 ¹/₄ years)*					

R I S K S

CHAPTER SIX

Junk Science and Junk Reporting

*Everyone is entitled to
his own opinion but not
his own facts.*

—Daniel Patrick Moynihan

Sometimes I'm embarrassed by the work we do. We're supposed to double-check and get it right. We often don't.

Remember the news coverage about how schools had become much more violent? Newspaper reports said a survey found today's teachers' worries were (1) drug abuse, (2) alcohol abuse, (3) pregnancy, (4) suicide, (5) rape, (6) robbery. But in the '40s, teachers worried about (1) talking, (2) chewing gum, (3) making noise, (4) running in the halls. It was a powerful illustration of social deterioration, and reporters loved the list. It appeared everywhere—newspapers, magazines, the *Congressional Quarterly,* Ann Landers's column.

Then Yale School of Management professor Barry O'Neill finally checked the survey out. He pored through hundreds of references to it without finding the original study. Instead, he found "the *International Herald Tribune* picking it up from the *Congressional Quarterly*. They just took it from the *Wall Street Journal*." O'Neill finally traced the story back to Texas oilman T. Cullen Davis, who said *he made it up*. "When he talked to me, he said, 'I *know* what the problems in the '40s were, because I was in school then, and I know what they are now because I read the papers. I didn't make these from a scientific survey.' He had no idea that professors and government officials were all using the list that he'd sat in his house and assembled."

Journalists joke that some stories are "too good to check." This was one of those.

SCIENTIST WORSHIP

When covering what scientists say, reporters are particularly prone to getting the story wrong. Most of us have little training in science, little understanding of how it works, and too much faith in any one given scientist. When I started reporting, I thought scientists were dispassionate observers, so what they published must be objective truth. I considered the top scientific journals ironclad arbiters of fact. After all, most studies submitted to the journals are rejected, so every study that's accepted has to pass the withering scrutiny of peer review.

Then my brother Tom, who had become a research scientist and worked for some of the journals, pointed out that much of what is published turns out, a few years later, to be irrelevant or wrong. Science is not as precise as I thought it was.

Scientific *consensus* is important. When the majority of respected scientists working within their field of specialty conclude that smoking can cause heart disease or that the earth revolves around the sun, I'll believe it and report it. But now I realize that individual scientists reach dubious conclusions almost as often as the rest of us do. But when scientists reach them, we reporters are less likely to question the conclusion. Have you cut down on salt because it's bad for you? Pumped up on vitamin C to ward off colds? Forced the kids to eat spinach because it's uniquely healthy? Then you're a victim of junk science—peddled by a gullible press.

When I was a kid, my mother thought spinach was the healthiest food in the world because it contained so much iron. Getting enough iron was a big deal then because we didn't have "iron-fortified" bread. Turns out that spinach is an okay source of iron, but no better than pizza, pistachio nuts, cooked lentils, or dried peaches. The spinach-iron myth grew out of a simple mathematical miscalculation: A researcher accidentally moved a decimal point one space, so he thought spinach had 10 times more iron than it did. The press reported it, and I had to eat spinach.

Moving the decimal point was an honest mistake—but it's seldom that simple. If it happened today I'd suspect a spinach lobby was behind it. Businesses often twist science to make money. Lawyers do it to win cases. Political activists distort science to fit their agenda, bureaucrats to protect their turf. Reporters keep falling for it.

Scientists sometimes go along with it because they like being famous.

CRACK BABIES

In the late '80s and early '90s, the media used a few small studies of babies born of cocaine-addicted mothers to convince America that thousands of children were permanently damaged. Dr. Ira Chasnoff, of the National Association for Families and Addiction Research and Education, after studying only 23 babies, reported that mothers were delivering babies that "could not respond to them emotionally." He told *People* magazine that the infants "couldn't respond to a human voice." This led to a frenzy of stories on "crack babies." Many people still believe "crack babies" are handicapped for life.

It isn't true. It turns out there is no proof that crack babies do worse than anyone else. In fact, they do better, on average, than children born of alcoholic mothers. Nevertheless, *Rolling Stone* told us these children were "like no others." They were "oblivious to affection" and "automatons," and "the damage doesn't go away." Education magazines warned that soon these children would reach the schools, which would be unable to control them. *School Board Journal* warned teachers, "These children will leave your resources depleted, your compassion tested. This is something new and bad."

It was terrifying news—thousands of children likely to grow up wild and dangerous.

It wasn't until several years later that the myth started to unravel. Emory University psychologist Claire Coles had her graduate students spend hours observing "crack babies" and normal babies. Her students did not see what Chasnoff had seen. In fact, they were unable to tell which children had been exposed to cocaine.

I asked Coles what went wrong with the first study.

Claire Coles: They couldn't really tell whether they were looking at the effects of cocaine or the effects of alcohol or the effects of poverty, and everybody ignored that. They just said, "This is cocaine."

John Stossel: How could that happen?

Claire Coles: Well, they wanted to get published.

Right. It is easier to get your work published, and, more important, funded, if you find something dramatic.

Claire Coles: If you go to an agency and say, "I don't think there's a big problem here, I'd like you to give me $1 million," the probability for getting the money is very low.

It's also easier to get funded if what you conclude feeds someone's political agenda. The idea of crack babies was perfect. It met the needs of liberals and conservatives. Conservatives wanted to demonize cocaine users. Liberals wanted more money for social programs.

When Dr. Coles dared to suggest that crack babies were not permanently damaged, she was attacked by politicians, called incompetent, accused of making data up or advocating drug abuse. Dr. Chasnoff, who had helped start the scare, had no such problems.

When I confronted him, Chasnoff denied that he was pushing any agenda.

Dr. Ira Chasnoff: Neither I nor any of my colleagues were ever pushing junk science. Is everything we thought then—do we know that every bit of that is correct now? Well, obviously, the answer is no. But that's the process of science.

He said *People* and *Rolling Stone* exaggerated the implications of his research—took him "out of context." I believe it. But did he call them to correct their misleading reports? No.

VITAMIN C

When Linus Pauling said megadoses of vitamin C could ward off colds, the press reported his claim enthusiastically, and the public believed. After all, he was a Nobel Prize winner. No matter that Pauling's Nobel was in chemistry, not biology; no matter that dozens of follow-up studies found no evidence that vitamin C prevents colds. The pills still fly out of stores.

As my brother explains it, "You reporters have trouble ascertaining whether arrogance, bias, or money has colored a scientist's opinion. You gravitate to scientists considered the 'elite.' But the irony is that elitism fosters arrogance and does not immunize against error. Pauling, for example, was spectacularly right about the fundamental principles of chemistry, but he was wrong about the structure of DNA, as well as about vitamin C."

Scientific communication is very stilted, as if to convey impartiality. Scientists are happy to have nonscientists view them as uniquely unbiased, and reporters fall into the trap of believing them. But supposedly "dispassionate" scientists are as passionate about their ideas as any entrepreneur. They have all sorts of reasons to lose perspective, to get carried away with hope and excitement. If they discover something, they may be famous. If they don't, they may have wasted years in some windowless laboratory.

Several years ago, two physicists in Utah, Stanley Pons and Martin Fleischmann, announced they'd solved the mystery of cold fusion. They'd found a way to create energy from a cup of water. It was a stunning announcement. If they were right, we'd never have to buy oil from OPEC again.

Pons and Fleischmann were so confident, they skipped peer review and just held a press conference. Then they went to Congress to ask for millions. The only reason they didn't get it was because scientists all over the world had furiously begun trying to duplicate their results. It was soon clear that they couldn't. Nevertheless, Pons and Fleischmann still managed to convince some Japanese companies to set them up in a laboratory in the south of France. It's now 14 years later, and sadly, they still haven't created cold fusion.

EMPIRE BUILDING

Empire building is another corrupter of science. The U.S. government now has an antisalt bureaucracy that churns out thousands of pamphlets and runs public service announcements that warn Americans to cut back on salt.

We should eat "no more than 2,400 milligrams a day," says Dr. Jeffrey Cutler, the official who runs the government's antisalt campaign. "It should probably be lower, but that's a reasonable interim goal."

Do you follow your government's recommendations? I feel sorry for you if you do. Two thousand four hundred milligrams a day makes for a miserable diet. Three dill pickles put you over the limit.

Cutler decided that Americans should eat less salt because high blood pressure can lead to heart disease, and eating less salt can lower blood pressure. It's a plausible theory, but it *doesn't* prove that less salt leads to less heart disease. Too many other things may be going on.

Experts on blood pressure told us there isn't enough scientific research to justify the government's antisalt campaign, and there definitely isn't enough to justify Cutler's 2,400-milligram limit.

"I can't imagine how they came up with that number. I mean, there isn't a single bit of evidence that suggests 2,400 milligrams is better than 2,100 or 3,700," says Dr. Michael Alderman, who headed the American Society of Hypertension, America's biggest organization of specialists in high blood pressure. He and others told us *some* people should cut back on salt, but for most people, it's pointless. One study even found that those who ate the least salt were *more* likely to have heart attacks.

"It's not clear to me that there's any evidence that a lower-sodium diet is going to lead to a longer or better life," Alderman says. "Eating less salt does lots of things to the body, not all of them good."

I confronted Dr. Cutler at his office at the government's huge National Heart, Lung, and Blood Institute (the institute's recent budget was $2,569,794,000).

John Stossel: In the *Journal of the American Medical Association,* [it says] reducing salt in diet has little effect on blood pressure.

Dr. Jeffrey Cutler: My study has not concluded that.

John Stossel: We just called up ten leading cardiologists, major hospitals. Nine out of ten said they don't think this is a reasonable program. I mean, nine out of ten.

Dr. Jeffrey Cutler: I don't know what kind of sample you . . .

John Stossel: People at Stanford, Johns Hopkins. It suggests you're just trying to build a bureaucracy.

Dr. Jeffrey Cutler: I don't accept that.

I can't read Cutler's mind, so I don't know that he pushed his antisalt campaign because he wanted to build himself a little empire. But consider the choices of the bureaucrat: If he finds that Americans "eat more than twenty times the salt your body needs," he may be on *Good Morning*

America, and his supervisors may assign more people to work for him. He's important.

If he finds no threat, he is just another bureaucrat.

THE "FACTS" VS. THE TRUTH

One good thing about science is that in the long run the truth usually comes out. The media may be gullible, but other scientists are skeptical. They keep testing—questioning—so gradually we keep moving closer to the truth.

When I began reporting, I assumed America's courts would help this process along. But now I realize lawyers are more concerned with *winning* than with truth. If the lawyers have money on the line, truth may not matter much at all. Since reporters pay so much attention to court decisions, a lawyer who can sell junk science to a few judges and juries can get reporters to sell that junk science to the world.

That's what happened with silicone breast implants. Lawyers used the media to terrify the nation.

In the 1990s, lawyers told women that Dow Corning, an evil chemical company that made silicone, was responsible for their "being poisoned by their own bodies"! Silicone from their breast implants was probably leaking into their breasts and would soon give them cancer and autoimmune diseases. One lawyer got on a TV news show and told women they had "time bombs" in their breasts.

The women's fear and anger were palpable. At least one was so desperate to remove her implants, she took a razor to her own breasts. At an anti-implant demonstration, an ABC cameraman captured the fury of the women when a skeptical reporter dared ask, "Where's the evidence that the implants cause these diseases?"

Demonstrators: *We* are the evidence! We are the evidence! We are the evidence!

Woman with Breast Implants: It's in throughout my blood. And it's eating at my muscle tissues.

Demonstrators: *We* are the evidence!

At the time, about a million American women had implants. While some women had complaints (sometimes scar tissue made their breasts as hard as baseballs), most were satisfied with the surgery.

Then doctors reported that about 1 percent of women who have breast implants—10,000 American women—had connective-tissue disease. To reporters, that was evidence that implants caused the disease. But 10,000 illnesses didn't prove anything. It turns out that the same percentage of women *without implants* got the disease.

That fact wasn't publicized. Instead, lawyers ran ads on TV like: "Your breast implants may be making you sick! Call us, Kind Lawyers Who Protect Women, 1–800 . . ."

Women called; the lawyers brought them into court. With the help of "expert" witnesses who said implants caused disease, they convinced juries that Dow Corning had recklessly poisoned women. Two of the most influential experts on breast implants were Drs. Nir Kossovsky of Los Angeles and David Smalley of Memphis. Both had tests that they said detected whether a woman's immune system was affected by silicone. But then surgeon Leroy Young at the Scripps Research Institute tested the "expert's'" tests. Young sent Dr. Smalley blood from women who *didn't* have breast implants—and they all tested positive. The tests were bunk.

But juries didn't know that.

One jury awarded $4 million; another, $7 million. Then came a $25 million verdict. Facing thousands of lawsuits, Dow Corning declared bankruptcy.

But where was the science? Studies by the Mayo Clinic, Harvard, Brigham and Women's Hospital, and others concluded that women with implants were no sicker than those without. It didn't matter. The *"doesn't cause connective-tissue-disease stories"* got much less media attention. People *still* think implants cause disease.

And the lack of scientific evidence didn't stop the lawyers. Even after America's top scientists concluded that implants did not cause disease, the lawyers kept suing, and winning. After all, they didn't have to convince a majority of scientists—they just had to convince a jury.

SCIENTIFICALLY CLUELESS

Reporters are easy to convince, too. Most of us are so clueless about science, we assume unusual numbers of cancer cases near a chemical plant means the chemicals caused the cancer, but *association is not causation.* There is no more reason to blame the chemicals than to blame diet soda for making people fat because you see lots of fat people drinking it. The cluster of cancers may have been caused by a hundred other factors, or it may be "statistical noise."

The "Texas Sharpshooter Fallacy" is a good analogy. A drunken Texan shoots a hundred bullets into the side of a barn. Then he walks up to the barn, draws a bulls-eye around the biggest cluster of bullet holes, and claims he was aiming for that. Clusters of cancer may be just as random, but if a power line or chemical plant is nearby, lawyers and reporters get excited.

"Dose makes the poison" is another basic principle that somehow eludes reporters. Remember the cranberry panic? In 1959, the government said a weed killer used on cranberry crops gave rats thyroid cancer. San Francisco and Chicago banned cranberry sales. Supermarkets pulled products containing cranberries off their shelves. Then scientists pointed out that the rats had been given huge doses of the chemical, concentrations equivalent to humans eating 15,000 pounds of berries every day. At doses that high, lots of things are harmful. Water is essential to life, but 6 feet of it drowns people. The scientists' cautions made little difference. Only after President Kennedy publicly drank cranberry juice did the panic subside.

Even if the rats got cancer from smaller doses, it still wouldn't prove that the cranberries were a threat to people, because *chemicals that harm animals don't necessarily harm humans.* Saccharine was once banned because it caused cancer in rats. But it turned out that saccharine interacts with rat urine in ways that do not apply to humans. People are different from rats. Now we consume vast amounts of saccharine, without harm.

Saccharine probably *saves* lives by reducing obesity; it certainly makes life more pleasant.

I fell for the animal-test myth when I did a scare story on the chemical dioxin. I was told tiny amounts of it kill guinea pigs. I didn't realize that this doesn't prove tiny amounts are harmful to us.

In 1977, an explosion in a factory near Seveso, Italy, released a cloud of dioxin that blew over much of the city. In the following weeks, residents complained of headaches and diarrhea, and many developed a painful skin rash. By then, the people in Seveso learned they had been exposed to dioxin—at 10,000 times the safe level. The army strung barbed wire across town. Environmentalists predicted big increases in cancers and lung disease. They told pregnant women their children would be born with birth defects, and demanded that Seveso be sealed off permanently.

But instead, the Italian government just gathered the most contaminated material, including carcasses of animals that had been killed in the explosion, covered it all with plastic and dirt, and planted trees and grass on top of it. That was it. Then they waited. The death and disease didn't come. Twenty years after the explosion, I walked in the public park that now sits on top of the dioxin contamination. People ate fruit from trees that grow in the soil. We drank water from the drinking fountain. People in Seveso are as healthy as people in the rest of Italy.

Why didn't they get sick? Because dioxin that kills animals doesn't necessarily hurt us. You'd think Americans would have known this, because for years, workers in American chemical plants had been exposed to vast amounts of dioxin—practically bathed in it. Yet they were as healthy as the rest of us.

But that didn't matter when dioxin was found in America. The scientifically illiterate media, hysterical about most chemicals, led American authorities to overreact.

In Times Beach, Missouri, a man had sprayed some dioxin on some dirt roads, hoping to hold down the dust. It wasn't a lot of dioxin; the people in Italy had been exposed to a thousand times more 10 years before. But the EPA *destroyed the whole town anyway.*

I contributed to the hysteria. Based on data I'd been given on tests on rats and guinea pigs, I reported that "dioxin is incredibly deadly." I knew nothing about the Seveso experience, and nothing about the healthy American chemical plant workers who'd spent years exposed to dioxin. The activist scientists who fed reporters the deadly-dioxin scenario were not about to tell us that there was no proof dioxin hurts *people.*

Local residents were convinced dioxin was making them ill, and I rushed to put them on TV.

First Times Beach Resident: We have medical problems that my children didn't have before we moved in!

Second Times Beach Resident: My son's had pneumonia twice in the last two
    and a half months, and today we had to take him back to the
    doctor because he had a strep throat again!
First Times Beach Resident: We can't take much more!

It was powerful television. But as I walked though Times Beach with other reporters—all of us wearing normal clothing—next to EPA officials who looked like astronauts in white biohazard suits, I started to wonder if we were leading people astray. The government evacuated Times Beach, then bulldozed the homes and buried much of the town. It cost millions of tax dollars and terrified people who lived there. The terror and dislocation surely hurt people more than dioxin buried in soil ever could have. Years later, the official who urged that the town be bulldozed said, well, maybe he had made "a mistake."

When I returned several years later, the entire area was surrounded by a high fence patrolled by armed guards. It looked like a fortress.

Something was off. In Italy, life is basically back to normal. In America, less dioxin, buried in soil, created a hugely expensive fortified wasteland.

Was the EPA at all embarrassed about this? Not a bit, said William Farland, the EPA's director of risk assessment.

John Stossel: So Italy's being careless?
William Farland: No, I wouldn't say Italy's being careless.
John Stossel: Well, either they're being careless, or we're being stupid.
William Farland: No, I don't think it has to be one way or the other. There
    continues to be the possibility for human exposure if that
    material remains in the soil.

A *possibility*. That was enough for government to destroy the town. Of course, in Times Beach there were all those people who said the dioxin had made them sick. But if the people in Italy weren't sick, why were people in Times Beach so sick?

Because when chemical scares erupt, people attribute normal aches and pains of life to the chemicals being vilified on TV, said Dr. Karen Webb, chief medical officer at St. Louis University, when I interviewed her years later for a special we called "Junk Science." Webb studied the residents of Times Beach and found they were no sicker than other Americans.

"They might *get* sick," I suggested.

Dr. Karen Webb: *Anybody* might get sick. We are all going to get sick. Life's a terminal event. One in five pregnancies ends in a miscarriage. One-third of all people get cancer sometime during their life. It *happens*, and it's *not* related to dioxin.

John Stossel: So why are we spending tens of millions of dollars to wall off a town and burn the dirt?

Dr. Karen Webb: Beats me. And I tell you something—as a taxpayer, I'm rather outraged. We need to stop spending money on something that hasn't ever even been shown to cause a death.

She should also be outraged at reporters like me who, when scientists told us Times Beach and Love Canal were chemical death traps, didn't question whether those most eager to talk to us had agendas of their own. Some hated corporations; some wanted to be famous; some thought publicity might get them more grant money. I should have seen that they weren't the dispassionate observers I thought they were.

BIAS

We are quicker to spot bias when business funds research. Corporate money sets off alarms. Several years ago, a study found oat bran lowers cholesterol. People rushed out to buy oat bran muffins, even though the fat in muffins surely outweighed any oat bran benefit to anyone's heart. People started selling oat bran beer and oat bran toothpaste, but once reporters realized that the research was funded by the Quaker Oats Company, they noticed you had to eat vast quantities of oat bran to see any effect, the exciting oat bran news faded away. But we in the media are less vigilant when it comes to detecting researchers' political agendas—especially when the researchers' and reporters' politics are in sync. Consider this astounding statistic propounded by feminists: Did you know 150,000 women a year die of anorexia? The *Washington Post* and other media simply accepted the number, but think about it—150,000 is absurd. Triple the number killed in cars? Triple the number of Americans killed during the entire Vietnam War? The real anorexia death toll is somewhere between 50 and 1,750. The 150,000 number was touted in books by feminist heroes Gloria Steinem and Naomi Wolf. (Wolf corrected the number in later editions.) Who in the media wanted to second-guess them?

Another widely reported piece of feminist dogma held that "domestic violence causes more birth defects than all medical causes combined." The news reports said the research came from the March of Dimes. But Clark University philosophy professor Christina Hoff Sommers, author of *Who Stole Feminism?*, was more skeptical than the supposedly skeptical reporters. She called the March of Dimes, which told her there was never any such study—it was a rumor that wouldn't go away. Again, reporters believed the feminist myth, even though the numbers made little sense.

Christina Hoff Sommers: What they were saying is that the battery of women was responsible for more birth defects than alcohol, crack, genetic disorders, spina bifida—all these things combined. . . . When it comes to feminist victim statistics, common sense has gone out the window.

John Stossel: Why would feminist groups want to distort numbers?

Christina Hoff Sommers: Many of them believe they're involved in a gender war, and in any war, the first casualty is truth.

Maybe that's why the *New York Times* called the Super Bowl the "Abuse Bowl." The *Times* claimed that on Super Bowl Sunday "more women than usual will be battered . . . in their homes by the men in their lives. It's an inevitable part of the post-game show." It is a game "for men conditioned by the sports culture to act out their rage on someone smaller."

The extreme-left group Fairness and Accuracy in Reporting (FAIR) helped organize a news conference where activists declared Super Bowl Sunday "the biggest day of the year for violence against women." *Good Morning America* interviewed a psychiatrist about it. The *Boston Globe* wrote about violence hot lines flooded with calls on Super Bowl Sunday. CBS and the Associated Press labeled it "the day of dread."

Then Ken Ringle of the *Washington Post* bothered to check the record. In a story titled "Debunking the 'Day of Dread,' " he wrote, "None of the activists appears to have any evidence that a link actually exists between football and wife-beating." It was another politically correct myth. My favorite part of Ringle's story was what he learned about the 40 percent climb in hot line calls reported in the *Globe* article. The reporter, Lynda Gorov, admitted she never saw the study but had been told about it by FAIR. "FAIR's [Linda] Mitchell said the authority was Walker [the psychiatrist interviewed on *Good Morning America*]. Walker's office referred callers to another psychiatrist, who said, 'I haven't been any more successful than you in tracking down any of this.' "

I fell for one piece of dubious research. A well-publicized report from the American Association of University Women (AAUW) said teenage girls were losing self-esteem. "Sixty percent of elementary school girls and sixty-seven percent of elementary school boys say they're pleased with themselves. By high school, girls' self-esteem has fallen by half, and only twenty-nine percent say they're happy with themselves."

That depressing survey persuaded me to do a *20/20* report on the advantages of all-girl schools. The expert from Harvard said girls are pushed into what she called "the silence ghetto," where they are "isolated from the rest of the class because they're never called on."

My goodness—it's so sad. My daughter was just entering a coed school—was I condemning her to a "silence ghetto"?

Sommers examined the AAUW report more carefully than I had, and noticed that the poll didn't really say what the AAUW said it did. The researchers focused on just one part of the poll: More boys than girls said it was "always true" that "I am happy the way I am." But that doesn't prove girls have self-esteem problems. Maybe the boys were just bragging. Maybe the girls were just more mature about answering "always" questions. In fact, *most* of the teen girls said it was "sort of true" or "sometimes true" that they were happy the way they were. But the AAUW ignored those answers, proclaimed a crisis anyway, and sold it to us in the media.

Had I examined the report more carefully, I would have noticed that there were plenty of examples where girls did *better* than boys. Girls and boys said teachers liked being around girls more, and both girls and boys thought girls were smarter. In its quest to portray girls as "victims" needing government money for "gender-equity" programs, the association ignored those answers.

I didn't catch it. I joined the pack of reporters chanting about girls' low self-esteem. That hurts people, says Sommers, because when reporters hype "research" like that, the public demands action, and politicians pander. "Do you realize there are public schools out there that don't have money for pencils, that don't have money for textbooks, and we're going to spend precious federal funds for basically busybodies?" she said. "We're going to have gender-bias experts and gender-bias facilitators offering workshops . . . addressing a crisis that doesn't exist."

Liberal activist groups are adept at using the media to help their cause by feeding us "studies." A group called the Food Research and Action Center wants the government to spend more on food programs. Sure enough, their study found that astonishing numbers of children were "hungry": "One in four American children under age 12 is hungry or at risk of hunger in America."

The report got lots of press. Some reporters spun the report so it sounded worse than it was. Dan Rather somehow changed kids who were "sometimes hungry" into "children in danger of starving."

Starving? The Food Research and Action Center never counted calories. They didn't even ask people what they ate. Instead, they asked: "Do you ever cut the size of meals?" "Do you ever eat less than you feel you should?" Naturally, some people said yes to those questions. It didn't mean America is "hungry," let alone "starving." In fact, in America, one of the poor's biggest problems is *obesity*. Look around—Americans aren't starving.

Reporters don't deliberately choose to tell half-truths. But we tend to seize the first plausible-sounding explanation that seems to cut through the confusion of life. Then, once we've formed a belief, we're not inclined to consider contrary evidence. If it's called "scientific" research, we're particularly gullible.

We like to think we're superior to the people who, centuries ago, burned "witches" for no better reason than a neighbor's belief that his crop failure or impotence was caused by that woman's action. But reporters are still prone to the same mental errors that caused these killings: seeing patterns where there are none, finding causes where there is only coincidence, ignoring our sources' political agendas, and turning scanty evidence into panic.

CHAPTER SEVEN

Government

*The natural progress of
things is for liberty to yield
and government to gain.*

— Thomas Jefferson

A|fter September 11, the president and Congress quickly agreed what must be done about airport security: federalize it. The vote in the Senate was 100–0. Democrats and Republicans alike said it was obvious that government had to take charge. September 11 proved airport screening was too important a job to be left to (sneer) private companies.

The opposite is true. Important jobs are almost always done better by private companies.

It is true that until September 11 profit-seeking companies paid low wages to airport screeners, many of whom seemed half asleep. But the private companies were doing everything government ordered them to do. The small knives the hijackers used were legal under FAA rules. So were the open cockpit doors. The FAA *never asked* for tighter security.

Now it has. The politicians feel pressured to do something. But why assume *government* workers are what we need to make us safe? Do you think security would have been better on September 11 if government screeners had been on the job? If you think government employees do things better, visit your local Department of Motor Vehicles.

Government rarely does *anything* better. Even with taxpayer subsidies and special breaks on parking tickets, the U.S. Postal Office can't figure out how to deliver mail and packages as well as private companies like UPS and FedEx.

On September 11, it was *government* that failed. Law enforcement agencies didn't detect the plot. The FBI had reports that said young men on the terrorist watch list were going from flight school to flight school, trying to find an instructor who would teach them how to fly a commercial jet. But the FBI never acted on it. The INS let the hijackers in. Three of them had expired visas. Months after the attack, the government issued visas to two dead hijackers.

The solution to such government incompetence is to give the government more power?

Congress could have done what Amsterdam, Belfast, Brussels, Copenhagen, Frankfurt, Hamburg, London, Paris, and Rome did: set tough standards and let private companies compete to meet them. Many of those cities switched to private companies because they realized government-run security wasn't working very well. Private-sector competition keeps the screeners alert because the airport can fire them. No one can fire the government; that's a reason government agencies gradually deteriorate. There's no competition.

So why, when we urgently want better screening, would we turn to an institution that has such a dismal record for getting things done? Because when crises happen, it's automatic: Our first reaction is "Bring the government in!"

Senate majority leader Tom Daschle coined a rhyme: "You can't professionalize if you don't federalize."

What nonsense. In a "Give Me a Break" I did on this, I pointed out that NASDAQ counts billions of stock trades every day and gets it right, that Visa processes a billion transactions a day and gets the bills mostly right. *But government can't even count the votes in Florida.* So why do we think government would screen passengers well?

Everybody I work with laughed. They said, "That was a great piece." Then they said, "But of course we've got to have the government do it."

Why don't they get it? MSNBC's Jerry Nachman wrote a *New York Times* op-ed wondering why so many reporters are enthusiastic about new government programs. "Three-quarters of the stories we cover could be labeled under an omnibus umbrella: The government doesn't work. . . . So why would journalists, the same ones who uncover these stories and win all the big awards for doing so, believe that a bigger government, collecting more tax money and accumulating yet more power, would be more effective . . . than it isn't now?" It bewilders Nachman; beats me, too.

Today airport screening is handled by the U.S. Transportation Security Administration. Security is tighter now because we spend billions more on it. The TSA hired thousands of extra screeners and doubled or tripled their pay. Bob Poole, director of transportation studies at the Reason Foundation, in Los Angeles, says, "The TSA's approach is a typical example of governmental overkill. Afraid of being called on the carpet by members of Congress upset over long lines and delays at airports, they hired more than three times as many screeners as the private contractors used."

When you throw lots of money at a problem, things usually get better. But competing *private* companies would have done it better and cheaper. Watching the mob of government workers at some airport security checkpoints lately suggests TSA stands for "thousands standing around."

FREE MARKETS ARE BETTER

The editor of this book challenged me on this, saying, "How can you draw such distinctions between government and private enterprise? Democracy is a sort of free market. We choose representatives and get exactly what we ask for. Isn't that just as good?" No, because under private enterprise, we get to vote more often, and for more things. Free-market competition demands competitors adjust *constantly* (millions of changes a day, if not per second) if they are to keep pleasing (winning the votes of) customers.

Democracy is a kind of market, but a horribly slow and clumsy one. We elect only once every several years, and we don't choose representatives under conditions of open competition. The political class has so rigged the system that 98 percent of congressional incumbents are reelected. Now that incumbents have also enacted contribution limits, it's even harder to raise enough money to mount a challenge.

More important, politics is a package deal; government responds to collective choice, usually the wishes of a majority. You get all of Gore's promises, or all of Bush's promises. But you can choose between *20/20* and a dozen other newsmagazines on TV. There are many different restaurants, with many different combinations of cuisine, quality, and price. Imagine that you bought food like you vote for president. You get two choices, donkey meat and elephant meat (every now and then, another choice is available in certain states, where the food's producers solicited enough signatures on a petition to get into the grocery store). Every four years, everybody gets together and votes for donkey or elephant meat. No matter how you vote, you have to eat what the majority picks.

When I go to the grocery store in a reasonably free market, I can pick elephant and you can pick donkey or we can make entirely different choices. We don't have to make our decision together, and we are not bound by each other's decisions. The constant competition among millions of us making millions of different choices forces entrepreneurs to give us better choices.

This is why government can never do *anything* as well as the private sector. Government means one-size-fits-all rules that are hard to customize or change. If government does something clever, its rigidities eventually make it lose ground. Failing may take a while; in the Soviet Union it took 70 years. But government services will eventually decay. Whether it's public schools, public toilets, the post office, or the TSA doesn't matter; government cannot do it as well.

In 2000, the city of Austin, Texas, began marketing bottled water to the public for "promotional purposes." The water is merely city tap water, poured into tanker trucks and then bottled. Austin sells a case of 24 bottles for $6.00. Unfortunately, each case costs the city $8.90, so Austin loses $2.90 per case sold. Only a government monopoly, with no competition and no incentive to try harder, can sell tap water for more than the price of gasoline, and still manage to lose money.

By contrast, the market performs miracles with such regularity that we take them for granted. The average supermarket now offers us 30,000 different products; I complain if they don't have mint-chocolate-chip DoveBars. A few years ago I went to Italy, where a complete stranger, who didn't even speak my language, gave me a car. All I had to do was give him a plastic card and sign a piece of paper. I stuck that same card into a slot in a wall, and a bank I'd never done business with promptly gave me $600 in cash. A month later the bill came and was accurate to the penny. The private sector performs miracles like this every day.

The Soviet Union, where huge wheat harvests repeatedly could not find their way to retail stores, is a good example of how it's almost impossible to get people what they need in the absence of a free market.

Even in so called "mixed economies," like those so praised in Europe, the bloated government sector destroys innovation.

When personal computers were invented, politicians in France were clever enough to decide that France should embrace them. In 1983, France created the Minitel Computer Network. The government gave every home a free computer! It served as an electronic phone book and also let people do banking at home. You'd think that this early head start would have given the French a huge lead in the computer age, but that's not what happened. Entrepreneurs in Silicon Valley and Seattle (is it just coincidence that these are the metropolitan areas farthest from Washington, D.C.?) left France in the dust. Today, Minitel is a dinosaur. In 1997, even Prime Minister Lionel Jospin said that Minitel was causing France to lag dangerously behind other countries in embracing the Internet and entering the information age.

The government officials in charge couldn't keep up with the hundreds of millions of spontaneous experiments flying about in the United States, where private entrepreneurs, not government, called the shots. As economist F. A. Hayek put it, "Order generated without design can far outstrip plans men consciously contrive." The French government's response was to offer Minitel in six colors. Pathetic. No one wants it.

Yet politicians continue to offer all kinds of sweet-sounding plans that promise to make our lives better. Why do we think these ambitious plans will succeed, when they can't even fulfill their most basic duties? The Bureau of Indian Affairs, for instance, cannot find the money it was supposed to keep safe for Indians. More than $2 billion is unaccounted for. Yet as activist Russell Means told us, "No one is even reprimanded. No one's indicted. No one's demoted. No one is fired. No one is even named."

At the Pentagon, the accounting discrepancies total *$2 trillion.* "They may have it. They just don't know where it is," David Walker, head of the General Accounting Office, told me. How can they *not find* that much money? Walker says the Pentagon has bought things with it, but doesn't know what. "They don't know that they have it," he says. "They may buy it again."

No private company could get away with keeping its books that way. The investors would be all over it. It would go bankrupt. The managers might go to jail. When I said that to Walker, he answered, "We're not a private company."

There you have it. Government doesn't have to follow the same rules. When they lose money, they just demand we give them more. And we do.

What they don't lose, they often waste. In a national park in Pennsylvania, we videotaped a beautiful building with a gabled slate roof, lots of cobblestone masonry, a porch, and windows. It cost taxpayers $330,000. It's an outhouse. And no, I don't mean a bathroom; it has no running water. It's just an outhouse.

I doubt officials would spend *their own* money on such an elegant outhouse, but when it's a government project, different standards prevail. The Parks Department assigned more than a dozen park service engineers and architects to the project and gave them two years and $100,000 just to design the outhouse. To oversee construction, the department spent $80,000 to have a supervisor from Denver live in Pennsylvania for a year. The outhouse had to meet all government construction rules, which meant hiring minority-owned firms, conforming to size requirements mandated by the Americans with Disabilities Act, paying union-approved construction wages, and filling out all the paperwork that goes with those regulations. Parks Department officials decided the outhouse had to have windows, a porch, and a slate roof. Local slate wasn't good enough, so special slate was trucked in from Vermont. The outhouse had to be "landscaped," not with ordinary flowers—that wouldn't do—but with flower seed that cost $750 a pound. The paint had to be epoxy that cost $78 a gallon, not the $25-a-gallon stuff you'd probably buy. This is how a government outhouse gets to cost $330,000.

Park officials claimed that "at that location, any facility" would cost "over $100,000." If you work for the government monopoly long enough, you believe such things. We checked with local real estate agents and found a real house—a huge one, 15 rooms—beautifully restored and detailed, just a few minutes away. It was for sale for less than the outhouse cost.

Our skeptical questions about the outhouse didn't change Parks Department policy. Officials didn't even seem embarrassed about what they'd done. After my story ran, the Parks Department went on to build an outhouse in Montana that cost a *million* dollars. (It's a four-holer.)

"WE'LL CUT THE WASTE"

The politicians always promise they will cut the fat, streamline the process. But they almost never do.

Around 1900, America had 6 million farms, and the Agriculture department employed 3,000 people. Today there are 2 million farms, but the Department employs 100,000 people. At this rate, soon there will more bureaucrats than farmers.

Last year, the Agriculture Department paid subsidies of almost $200 million to make sure some sheep and goat ranchers made a profit. Why? Because in 1954, nine years after World War II, congressmen argued it was crucial to "national security" that America have enough wool to make soldiers' uniforms. Today most military uniforms *aren't even made of wool,* but no matter, the Agriculture Department still gives the farmers handouts.

Government also wastes money making sure rich and politically connected people get to fly places cheaply. We videotaped passengers boarding a Colgan Air flight to Hot Springs, Virginia. Hot Springs is hardly a busy travel hub. Why did Colgan fly to there when it's not a profitable route? Because the Transportation Department deemed the route "essential air service" and subsidized it. What was "essential" in Hot Springs? Most of Colgan's passengers went to the Homestead, an elegant resort. As I write this, Hot Springs is no longer on the essential air service list, but there are still 126 other subsidized routes. Some congressmen thought it was a good idea.

Government spends even more when it has a very popular cause, like mass transit. In Los Angeles the brilliant city planners spent two decades digging up huge parts of town to create a subway—a beautiful one, with gleaming elevators, escalators, shiny new high-tech train cars, and lots of open space. The cost is phenomenal: $50,000 per foot of track.

Unfortunately, the subway carries half as many passengers as expected, because it doesn't go where most people want to go. The planners built a tunnel that runs in a straight line. But people commute every which way, in a thousand different directions.

The result? There is no "mass" in Los Angeles's mass transit. A Reason Foundation study found that today's new rail lines are so underused, each ride costs taxpayers $9 dollars.

Subsidizing buses would have been much cheaper. Even paying for people's taxi rides might have been cheaper. But buses and taxis aren't sexy enough for politicians with grand visions.

COMPETITION

Of course, no politician considered calling in the private sector to help. I assume it never crossed their minds, because most people assume things like mass transit are services only government can deliver. I assumed only the government could dig subway tunnels, yet years after I came to New York, I was surprised to learn that private companies built New York's first subway lines and ran them until the 1940s. The city only took over after it had bankrupted the private lines by refusing to allow them to raise the "five-cent fare."

People assume only government can provide "public goods" like clean drinking water. But that's not true, either. In Jersey City, New Jersey, the city water department let the pipes rust. The water tasted foul and sometimes failed safety tests. City workers told the mayor there wasn't much they could do. In fact, they said, water prices would have to be raised . . . just to maintain the lousy service they had.

So the mayor, Bret Schundler, did something unusual. He put the water contract out for bid, inviting competition from private companies and from city workers. A for-profit company turned in the lowest bid. Critics said its low price and desire for profit would lead it to deliver even worse service. That didn't happen. Within months, the private company fixed the pipes government workers said couldn't be fixed. Jersey City's water now, for the first time in years, meets the highest cleanliness standard. And the private company saved taxpayers $35 million.

Why could the company do so much better than the city waterworks? Because its skills are honed by competition. The private company's survival depends on performance, and the mayor told us he made it clear to them that if they screw up, "They're fired. They're toast. I don't care. If they blow it, we're going to give the contract to somebody else." That threat focuses the mind. That's the difference between private and "public" enterprise.

Of course, critics of privatization said the private company would make life hell for the workers. That didn't happen either. The private company hired some of the men who used to work for the city, and when I asked them about it, they said that while they were working harder now, they liked it. They had better tools, and dealt with less bureaucracy. Hard work was okay, they said, because they were accomplishing more, and as one man in a hard hat put it, "that feels good."

When Pinellas County, Florida, put its ambulance service up for bid, critics there, too, warned that private enterprise would soon abuse the ambulance drivers. But private employers know that if they want to retain their best employees, they have to treat them right. It turned out that the workers liked working for the private ambulance service better. "We work harder," nurse Debbie Vass told us, but "the system is way cool. You have state-of-the-art, brand-new equipment. That is so different from the way things were. Before, it was a struggle just to have a pillow on your stretcher." The improvements after privatization astonished the county's politicians. Not only were taxes lowered because the county was now paying less for ambulances, but the workers were happier and ambulance service was better.

At the new private ambulance headquarters, paramedics—not just dispatchers—now answer the phone. They can give you medical advice while you wait for the ambulance. The ambulances arrive sooner because a new satellite tracking system tells the dispatcher which ambulance is closest. Better service—for less money. "Our taxes were lowered eight years in a row," said Chuck Kearns, Pinellas County EMS director. "Competition has proven to get us higher quality, faster ambulances, and lower costs. The people in our ambulance service are excellent. But then again, they have no choice. If they're not excellent, they're history." There it is again: that competition that brings out people's best efforts.

GOVERNMENT STAGNATION

By contrast, government can't get its act together, even when thousands of lives are at stake. The Federal Aviation Administration still uses antiquated vacuum tubes in its radar system. Vacuum tubes are so primitive, manufacturers took them out of our TV sets dozens of years ago. But FAA officials can't quite manage modernizing. It's not that they haven't tried. They've spent billions trying. It's just that government monopolies don't modernize well.

They don't have that problem in Canada, because in 1996, Canada privatized air traffic control. It sounds frightening. In America, Congress decreed that air traffic control is "inherently a government job." Critics said it would be insane to trust passengers' lives to a (sneer) private profit-seeking company, which would cut corners to make more money. But in Canada, the private company didn't. Its managers knew the company's profitability depended on its safety record. Today, Canada's privatized air traffic control does the job well—for one third less.

American air traffic controllers still keep track of planes on little pieces of paper. They'd slide them around, the way a bartender slides beer down the bar. In Canada, computers have replaced paper and pencil.

Controllers who used to work for the government were skeptical at first, but four years after privatization, they told us they were thrilled at the changes the private company had brought.

Andy Vasarins: We went through a divorce. We left the government behind. We left the number of management layers behind.

Bill Snelgrove: If the government was still here, we'd be falling behind the eight ball every day. Delays, delays, delays. We would gridlock this airport.

How many other things would work better if government would let go?

We take it for granted that building highways is a job for government, but when competition is allowed, private enterprise works better there, too. We never think of government as the cause of traffic jams, but it is! Traffic jams are the automotive equivalent of the human lines at the DMV or the post office. In fact, when competition is allowed, traffic patterns miraculously improve. A company rented the empty space in the middle of the 91 Freeway in California, and used it as a toll road—a better one. It has no tollbooths; computers scan the cars as they drive by (you don't even have to slow down) and bill people electronically. Since traffic jams lower profits, the private company did innovative things to keep traffic moving. It has cameras trained on the road, so if a car breaks down, they see it, and someone quickly comes to help. If you run out of gas, they give you a free gallon. Tolls change according to how many people are using the road ("congestion pricing"). A ride that costs $4.75 at rush hour might cost 50 cents at midnight.

It worked. The private toll road got people there faster. But once the operators started making a profit, local government bought them out.

GOVERNMENT ALWAYS GROWS

I shouldn't be surprised that government took over the 91 Freeway, because government always grows. Sadly, Thomas Jefferson's quote at the beginning of this chapter was prescient. It doesn't matter that government fails and fails again; the politicians always want to do more. President Clinton received thunderous applause from Democrats and Republicans when he told Congress, "The era of big government is over." But since then government's only gotten bigger. As of this writing, 488,327 new pages have been added to the *Federal Register* since Clinton's speech. Every year, there is another spiderweb of rules for you to obey, and more taxes to pay. Government *always* gets bigger—under every administration—both parties. Republicans *talk* about shrinking government, but they've never done it.

How big should government be? It's not a question we normally ask. We should. America grew fastest when our government was small. From 1776 to 1915, government expenditures were less than 3 percent of gross national product. Is that the right amount? Or is 5 percent better? Ten percent? Even the Bible has a warning about that. The people of Israel demanded a king, but God warned against it: "This will be the manner of the king who shall reign over you: he will take your sons, and appoint them to him, for his chariots. . . . He will take your daughters to be perfumers, and to be cooks, and to be bakers. He will take your fields, and your vineyards, and your olive groves, even the best of them, and give them to his servants. "He will take the tenth of your seed, and of your vineyards, and give to his officers" (1 Samuel 8:11–15).

A tenth? What kind of puny threat is that? Today, the sad truth is that government (federal, state, local) is about *40 percent* of the economy. This is not what the founding fathers had in mind.

Today government runs trains, subways, schools, parks, public housing, welfare, Medicare, Medicaid, Social Security, a war on drugs. It subsidizes students, farmers, ranchers, Indians, researchers, volunteers, small businessmen, rich businessmen, and artists. It polices the world and, at home, polices our speech, jobs, schools, sports, and bedrooms. Maybe if it weren't doing all those things—badly—it would do a better job doing what it *should* do: like protect us from terrorists.

The founders said government should have *limited* duties. They laid it out in Article 1, Section 8, of the Constitution: Government should keep the peace, coin money, establish a post office, postal roads, and the courts, and secure time-limited copyrights and patents. For 150 years, that's about all it did. The focus was on guaranteeing individual liberty.

In the 1930s, Franklin Roosevelt changed that. His New Deal decreed it was government's job to get people jobs, retirement benefits, and health care. Every administration since has expanded the New Deal's programs, and started new ones.

Economist Walter Williams says, "If you want to take all liberty away from all Americans, you have to know how to cook a frog." When a frog is killed by water heated slowly, he doesn't notice the rise in temperature. If it happened suddenly, he'd jump out. It's an apt metafor. I mind the loss of freedom most, but since freedom is hard to measure let's track the growth of government.

CHART 5: FEDERAL SPENDING 1789–2003

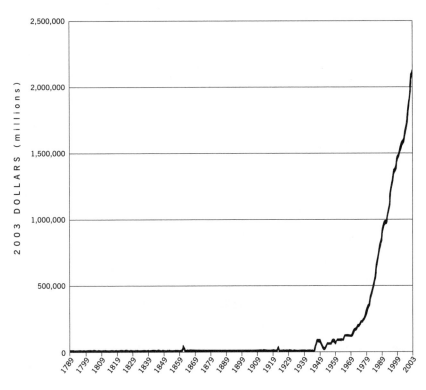

When America began, government cost every citizen $20 (in today's money) per year. Taxes rose during wars, but for most of the life of America, spending never exceeded a few hundred dollars per person. During World War II, government got much bigger. It was supposed to shrink again after the war but never did. Instead, it just kept growing.

Now the federal government costs every man, woman, and child an average of $10,000 per year.

You probably don't know you pay that much, because the government is sneaky about how it taxes you. Paying withholding taxes each pay period dulls the pain of the income tax, and a hundred other taxes are hidden. For my special "John Stossel Goes to Washington," we followed St. Louis construction worker Bill Thurston and totaled the little-known taxes he paid as the day went by. It started with the tax on the electricity that powered the alarm clock that woke him. Bill paid two taxes on his toothpaste. He paid a sewer fee so the water could drain, and a tax on the water. Daring to drive to work cost him more: He pays personal property tax and sales tax on his truck. And when he buys gas there's a county gas tax, a state gas tax, and a federal gas tax.

At work, Bill's boss needs two employees just to calculate how much to withhold from paychecks. They make sure every employee pays local income tax, state income tax, federal income tax, FICA, and Medicare.

Because Bill's wife works as a nurse, the Thurstons pay a marriage tax of $1,000 a year. Then there's grocery tax, property tax, utility tax, FCC tax, a county tax on cable TV, five taxes on the phone (line tax, local tax, municipal tax, county tax, state tax), and finally, a sin tax on the beer they drink.

Add it up. Collectively Americans now pay more in taxes than we do for food, clothing, and shelter combined. Yet government keeps getting bigger. I fear nothing will stop Jefferson's "natural progress of things." Why does government keep growing? It's not just that politicians want more power. Representative democracy has a built-in bias toward increased spending.

Political scientist James L. Payne examined the record of 14 congressional appropriations hearings and found that of 1,060 witnesses who testified, only seven spoke against spending money, while more than 1,000 testified in favor. Even a politician who believed in limited government would have a tough time resisting a constant onslaught of needy people saying, "*This* program is crucial."

The testimony is lopsided because of the "concentrated benefits—diffuse costs" problem: Benefits of government programs go to a few, but the costs are spread among many. If sheep and goat ranchers get $200 million in handouts, it costs each of us less than a buck. What are you going to do about that? Go to Washington and protest? I doubt it. For a buck, you probably won't even write your congressman, let alone take him out to dinner or give him a $2,000 campaign contribution. Yet the sheep ranchers have an incentive to spend $199 million lobbying if it gets them $200 million back.

Economists call that "rent seeking." A 1987 advertisement in the *Durango (Colorado) Herald* spelled it out perfectly, telling readers why they should support a big federal water project: "Because someone else is paying the tab! We get the water. We get the reservoir. They get the bill."

That was remarkably honest, but this doesn't help America. It just makes government bigger. In the end, we all lose.

LIMITED GOVERNMENT

Don't get me wrong. I'm not saying we don't need government. I'm no anarchist. The worst places in the world are the places that have no security, almost no rules. We need rule of law. But do we need so *much*?

The founders' vision of *limited* government is one of the greatest philosophical achievements of humanity because it protects people while leaving them free to pursue their own interests. That freedom is what makes so many other good and creative things possible.

CHAPTER EIGHT

Welfare for the Rich

*Law grinds the poor, and
rich men rule the law.*

—Oliver Goldsmith

The Welfare Reform Act put a five-year time limit on welfare payments. Both Republicans and Democrats seem to agree this was a good thing. Reform moved millions of poor people away from dependency.

So when do we take rich people off the dole?

President Ronald Reagan talked about "welfare queens," but America's biggest welfare queens are rich people.

All over America, the rich have their hands out. Their lobbyists fawn over politicians, giving them little bits of money—campaign contributions, plane trips, dinners, golf outings—in exchange for huge bits of *your* money. Millionaires who own your favorite sports teams get subsidies, as do millionaire farmers, corporations, and all kinds of well-connected people. I got some of your money, too.

I'M A WELFARE QUEEN

In 1980, I built a beach house. A wonderful one. Four bedrooms—every room with a view of the Atlantic Ocean.

It was an absurd place to build. It was on *the edge of the ocean*. All that stood between my house and ruin was a hundred feet of sand. My father told me, "Don't do it, it's too risky. No one should build so close to an ocean."

But I built anyway.

Why? As my eager-for-the-business architect said, "Why not? If the ocean destroys your house, the government will pay for a new one."

What? Why would the government do that? Why would it encourage people to build in such risky places? That would be insane.

But the architect was right. If the ocean took my house, Uncle Sam would pay to replace it, under the National Flood Insurance Program. Since private insurers weren't dumb enough to sell cheap insurance to people who built on the edges of oceans or rivers, Congress decided that the government should step in and do it. It meant if the ocean ate what I built, I could rebuild and rebuild again and again—there was no limit to the number of claims on the same property in the same location—up to a maximum of $250,000 per house per flood, you taxpayers will pay for it.

Thanks.

I did have to pay insurance premiums, but they were dirt cheap—mine never exceeded a few hundred dollars a year.

LUCKY SO FAR

Why does Uncle Sam offer me cheap insurance? "It saves federal dollars," replied James Lee Witt, head of the Federal Emergency

Management Agency (FEMA), when I did a *20/20* report on this boondoggle. "If this insurance wasn't here," he said, "then people would be building in those areas anyway. Then it would cost the American taxpayers *more* [in relief funds] if a disaster hit."

That's government logic: *Since we always mindlessly use taxpayer money to bail out every idiot who takes an expensive risk, let's get some money up front by selling them insurance first.*

Of course the insurance has encouraged *more* people to build on the edges of rivers and oceans. The National Flood Insurance Program is currently the biggest property insurance writer in the United States, putting taxpayers on the hook for over $640 billion in property. Subsidized insurance goes to movie stars in Malibu, to rich people in Kennebunkport (where the Bush family has its vacation compound), to rich people in Hyannis (where the Kennedy family has its), and to all sorts of people like me who ought to be paying our own way.

When we did the story on this, producer David Sloan was shooting B roll (pictures) on the elegant Outer Banks of North Carolina, and a man who saw our camera invited Sloan to videotape inside a luxurious beach mansion he was renting. Sloan accepted, and was surprised to see, taped to the refrigerator, a picture of presidential hopeful (then majority whip) Richard Gephardt. "Why is his picture here?" Sloan asked. "He's an owner of the house," answered the renter.

Aha, an interesting surprise twist to our story: A Missouri congressman owns expensive beachfront property insured by taxpayers. We called Representative Gephardt's office and asked to interview him about flood insurance. I was excited. He and I had something in common: We were both welfare queens. I thought he might say something like, "Yes, it's disgraceful—we shouldn't get special protection because we are rich enough to build on beaches. I'm trying to end this boondoggle." But when I interviewed him, he just smiled blandly, and kept saying Congress would "look into the program."

Why subsidize affluent people like Gephardt and me? Why not let us sink or swim on our own? If my house erodes away, it should be my tough luck. FEMA director Witt at least attempted an answer: "The American people are pretty compassionate toward their neighbors."

Government flood insurance is so "compassionate," the program didn't even raise my premiums when, just four years after I built my house, a two-day Northeaster swept away my first floor. I could still use the place, since the kitchen and bedrooms were on upper floors, though some guests were unnerved when a wave sloshed through the bottom of the house. After the water receded, government bought me a new first floor. Now the view was really spectacular—you saw water everywhere.

I asked Witt why taxpayers should have to pay for my new first floor. "Should we just walk away and say, 'We're not going to help you'?" he responded.

Yes! Government should walk away and let us beach-land owners take our own risks with our own money. Then I'd think more carefully about where I'd build. Federal flood insurance payments are like buying drunken drivers new cars after they wreck theirs.

I never invited you taxpayers to my home—you shouldn't have to pay for my ocean view. Actually, I don't have such a great view anymore. On New Year's Day, 1995, I got a call from a friend. "Happy New Year," he said. "Your house is gone." He'd seen it on the local news. (Or rather, he saw the houses next to mine, and nothing but sand next to them.) The ocean had knocked down my government-approved flood-resistant pilings and eaten my house.

It was an upsetting loss for me, but financially I made out just fine. You paid for the house—and its contents. I'm not proud that I took your money, but if the government is foolish enough to offer me a special deal, I'd be foolish not to take it. I take a big home-mortgage deduction, too; that's another form of welfare for the rich.

I could have rebuilt the beach house and possibly ripped you taxpayers off again, but I'd had enough; I sold the land. Someone now has built an even bigger house on my old property. Bet we soon will have to pay for that.

SO ELIMINATE THE STUPID GIVEAWAY

National Flood Insurance is a disgrace that should be repealed, but neither Democrats nor Republicans have expressed any interest in doing so. Once such welfare programs are established, they almost never go away. We welfare queens come to feel entitled to your money, and we'll fight hard to keep it.

I interviewed beachfront homeowners in New Jersey, asking why they should be entitled to "welfare." They got angry:

First Homeowner: We create a lot of employment here—look at the dishwashers and the chefs and the waitresses and the waiters.

John Stossel: This is welfare for you rich people.

First Homeowner: I am not rich.

John Stossel: People who are making $25,000 have to—pay taxes . . . to protect you.

Second Homeowner: They've bailed out the S&L's and they help the farming people.

John Stossel: So since there's welfare for all these other rich people, you should get some too?

Third Homeowner: Sound management is what it is. It's got nothing to do with welfare.

Sound management? It's never welfare if it goes to you.

In any case, their homes were on the line. They had money and connections. No one's going to take *their* entitlement away.

FEEDING AT THE FEDERAL TROUGH

Today's biggest welfare queens are probably farmers. This is odd because farmers were once the most self-sufficient of Americans.

When I make speeches about free markets at Farm Bureau conferences, farmers applaud enthusiastically. But now most of them get subsidies: $200 billion in direct handouts this decade, plus another $200 billion in artificial price supports (which force everyone to pay more for food).

Farm supports are as destructive as the old welfare payments to poor people were. Just as addictive, too: Subsidies are supposed to help farmers recover from low prices caused by overproduction; but the subsidies lead farmers to plant more crops, which brings more overproduction, which lowers prices, making farmers even more dependent on subsidies.

The subsidies wreck the lives of farmers in poor countries because they can't compete with subsidized American farmers (or with even more subsidized European farmers). Hypocritical politicians blather constantly about helping the poor, and demand more of your tax money for foreign aid. But simultaneously they pass farm subsidies, which rig the system so all over the world, poor farmers stay poor.

Why shovel all this money to American farmers?

Because we like farms. Farms are romantic. No one wants to lose the family farm. Of course, most handouts don't go to family farms. They end up going to big farm corporations because the big, established companies are most skilled at using the system. Fortune 500 firms like Westvaco, Chevron, John Hancock Life Insurance, Du Pont, and Caterpillar get hundreds of thousands of dollars in subsidies.

Another reason farmers get this ridiculous handout is that farmers are good at panhandling. Every state has a politically aggressive farm lobby, and every politician wants to stay on its good side. Watching the 2000 election's Iowa caucuses was nauseating. At Vice President Gore's rallies, they played country music, while Gore regaled crowds with farm stories. "Every summer," said Gore, who grew up in a fancy Washington, D.C., hotel, "we went back down to the farm. I was in the 4-H club."

Even so-called shrink-the-government Republicans will make government bigger for farmers. The candidate the press called the most "conservative," Alan Keyes, said farm supports are absolutely necessary: "It's a question of America's moral decency."

Oh, please. Most American farmers do just fine—better than most other Americans. Subsidies go to corn growers who earn more than $200,000 a year, even to "farmers" like my ABC colleague Sam Donaldson, who got thousands of dollars in wool and mohair payments because he and his wife raised sheep and goats on their New Mexico ranch. Donaldson calls the payments "a horrible mess" (he's sold the livestock, and no longer collects subsidies), but like me compares them to the home-mortgage deduction, saying, "As long as the law is on the books, it's appropriate to take advantage of it." Rich people take extra advantage: David Rockefeller got $352,187; Ted Turner, $176,077; and basketball star Scottie Pippen, $131,575.

Farmers argue, "We need subsidies—because the food supply is too important to be left to the uncertainties of free-market competition." But the opposite is true. Farmers who grow beans, pears, and apples receive *no* government subsidies, and thrive. Free markets are what are best at producing ample supplies of *everything*. Food is no exception.

Notice any shortages of unsubsidized green beans, pears, and apples? Me, neither.

Besides, America is the fattest country in the world. Trust me. We don't have a food-supply problem.

Yes, some farmers have a tough time. Some will go broke and lose their farms. That's sad. But it's also sad when people at Woolworth or TWA lose their jobs. Allowing businesses to fail is a key ingredient of the creative destruction that allows capitalism to work. Those who fail move on to jobs where their skills are put to better use. It makes life better for the majority.

THE BIGGEST PIGGY?

When public interest groups compile lists of corporate welfare recipients, a company named Archer Daniels Midland is usually at the top of the list. You may never have heard of ADM, because it's name rarely appears on consumer products, but it's huge. Its products are in most processed foods.

ADM collects welfare because of two cleverly designed special deals. The first is the government's mandated minimum price for sugar. Because of the price supports, if the Coca-Cola Company or Pepsi wants to buy sugar for its soda, it has to pay 22 cents a pound—more than twice the world price. So Coke (and most everyone else) buys corn sweetener instead. Guess who makes corn sweetener? ADM, of course. Now guess who finances the groups that lobby to keep sugar prices high?

ADM's second federal feeding trough is the tax break on ethanol. Ethanol's a fuel additive made from corn, kind of like Hamburger Helper for gasoline, except that it's more expensive, so no one would buy it if government didn't give companies that use ethanol a special 52-cent-a-gallon tax break. That costs the treasury half a billion dollars a year. ADM produces half the ethanol made in America.

Why does ADM get these special deals? Bribery. Okay, it's not bribery—that would be illegal. ADM just makes "contributions." Through his business and his family, former ADM chairman Dwayne Andreas gave millions in campaign funds to both Mondale and Reagan, Dukakis and Bush, Dole and Clinton. President's Nixon's secretary, Rosemary Woods, says Andreas himself brought $100,000 in *cash* to the White House. He even paid the tuition for Vice President Hubert Humphrey's son. Republicans, Democrats, it doesn't matter. ADM just gives.

It also flies people around on its corporate jets. When we contacted Andreas to ask for an interview, he arranged to fly us to ADM's Decatur, Illinois, headquarters in one of ADM's jets. I've seen private jets before, but ADM's was a step above. A flight attendant served us excellent food on gold-plated china. The camera crew and I loved it. Bet the politicians like it, too.

A limo took us to Dwayne Andreas's office. Once the cameras were rolling, I brought out the questions about "corporate welfare." I foolishly thought I could get him to admit he was a rich guy milking the system. I thought he'd at least act embarrassed about it. Fuggeddaboutit. He was unfazed.

John Stossel: *Mother Jones* [magazine] pictured you as a pig. You're a pig feeding at the welfare trough.
Dwayne Andreas: Why should I care?
John Stossel: It doesn't bother you?
Dwayne Andreas: Not a bit.

I still wonder why he granted the interview. I asked him about his bribes—I mean, contributions. For example, Andreas gave the Democrats a check for $100,000. A few days later, President Clinton ordered 10 percent of the country to use ethanol.

John Stossel: And the purpose of this money wasn't to influence the president?

Dwayne Andreas: Certainly not.

John Stossel: So why give him the money?

Dwayne Andreas: Because somebody asked for it.

Because they asked for it? Give me a break.

PANHANDLERS

In a special we called "Freeloaders," economist Walter Williams said: "A panhandler is far more moral than corporate welfare queens. . . . The panhandler doesn't enlist anyone to *force* you to give him money. He's coming up to you and saying, 'Will you help me out?' The farmers, when they want subsidies, they're not asking for a voluntary transaction. They go to a congressman and say, 'Could you *take* his money and give it to us?' That's immoral."

There's always justification. The politicians need your money for national security, research, job protection, or to "protect the food supply." After spending time on the golf course with lobbyists, politicians will find a way to justify almost anything. They justify giving subsidies to prosperous companies that sell goods overseas by saying that the resulting exports will be "good for America." They will be. But does Sunkist need taxpayer help to sell oranges? McDonald's to sell McNuggets to the Third World? Gallo to sell cranapple juice? Let them do their own marketing. My employer, Disney (which owns ABC), got tax money to create better fireworks at Disney World. Really.

Self-professed free-trade advocate George W. Bush gave the steel industry billions of dollars by raising tariffs on steel. This helps the steel industry but takes jobs from people who work in industries that have to buy steel. In addition, since the tariff means everything made of steel costs more, every American who buys anything with steel in it is hurt; the tariff adds $100 to the price of your car. The tariffs are just a way of favoring politically connected voters at everyone else's expense.

The shipping industry also gets billions in handouts. Without them, American shipbuilders say, they can't compete with low-cost ship-builders overseas. American politicians should say, "They're more efficient overseas? Fine! We'll save money and buy their cheaper ships." Shipping goods would cost less, and American taxpayers would be richer. But we don't do that—because the shipping industry has friends like former Senate majority leader Trent Lott. He makes sure Congress keeps your money close to home—*his* home.

Without moving the tripod, our camera could pan from Lott's Mississippi home to the shipyard that got half a billion dollars of your money to build a ship the Defense Department never even requested. Senator Lott didn't even seem ashamed of that. "Pork is in the eye of the beholder," he joked. "Where I'm from . . . [pork] is federal programs that go north of Memphis."

SPORTS TYCOON FREELOADERS

Real estate tycoon Jerry Reinsdorf bought the Chicago White Sox for $20 million and, when I interviewed him, said the team was worth more than $100 million. George Steinbrenner's New York Yankees are worth more. You'd think these people would pay their own way. But they don't. You pay for their sports palaces.

The sports tycoons sell the idea of the stadium as "public interest." Their politician friends tell voters that a stadium will "bring jobs," be "good for the city," "pay for itself." That's bunk. Study after study finds stadiums cost cities far more than they return.

The mayor of Cleveland bragged that his new $170 million baseball stadium would create lots of jobs. "Assume it did create a thousand jobs," economist Mark Rosentraub, author of *Major League Losers,* told me for "Freeloaders." "It's in excess of $170,000 for every job. You could have done better just saying to the people who would have been hired, here's $50,000—start a business."

Supporters of stadium subsidies say, "It's important to a city to have a professional team—great for civic pride." Said Rosentraub, "Then, be honest and say, 'Look—we're going to spend $700 million so you feel better about yourself. If you think it's worth it, then do it.' " When George Steinbrenner said he'd pull the Yankees out of New York City unless he got a new stadium, Mayor Rudy Giuliani rushed in to try to give him what he wanted. (Giuliani, a big Yankee fan, loved presiding over victory parades.)

If George Steinbrenner wants a stadium, why doesn't he build one with his own money? He wouldn't talk to us about it. In fact, most wealthy owners we called would not talk about subsidies. But Jerry Reinsdorf did. Maybe he thought I was going to ask him about the greatness of the White Sox. He told me the government "had to" fund his stadium.

John Stossel: You could have raised the money privately.

Jerry Reinsdorf: No, I couldn't have. Because you have to pay it back.

John Stossel: You couldn't have paid it back? You couldn't have made enough money here?

Jerry Reinsdorf: No. I could not have made a—I didn't realize that this was going to be a debate, or I probably wouldn't have agreed to the interview. But, but, but—but anyway, if you want it to be a debate, we can continue doing it that way.

John Stossel: Let's have a debate. You're a freeloader. You're taking money from poor taxpayers to make you, a rich guy, richer.

Jerry Reinsdorf: The people that own sports franchises don't do it to get richer. They could get richer someplace else.

John Stossel: That's fine. Then do it with your money. Don't take the public's money.

Jerry Reinsdorf: You mean, if somebody walks up to you and hands you money, you shouldn't take it? The fact is—I was offered this stadium by elected officials.

Bingo.

Reinsdorf got his stadium after Illinois governor James Thompson leaned on some legislators. A few years later, the park was built, and the governor threw out the first ball. Governor Thompson and Reinsdorf are friends from law school. Cozy.

Taxpayers basically built a palace for baseball fans, and the ones who made out the best are rich baseball fans. The new stadium has a six-level dining room with an expansive view of the playing field. For $700 extra per season, fans can order roast beef in an exclusive club.

It's Robin Hood in reverse. Politicians take money from taxpayers and give it to people like Reinsdorf (and George W. Bush, who, along with his fellow owners of the Texas Rangers, got taxpayers to build the team a stadium). The politicians help rich folks get richer at taxpayer expense.

I confronted Governor Thompson about it.

John Stossel: Aren't you just taking tax money and giving it to your rich friend?

James Thompson: Oh, yeah, but it was—it was your tax money, it wasn't
our tax money. I mean, the whole baseball field is built on
the hotel/motel tax. Chicagoans don't pay hotel-motel tax.
Guys from New York like you pay hotel-motel taxes. What
a great deal.

How smug and clueless. Even if the money came from tourists, it
wasn't free money. Higher taxes deter some tourists from going to
Chicago. In addition, every penny taken in taxes is a penny that might
have been spent somewhere else—maybe in bowling alleys or shoe
stores. That's the part of the transaction the press and the politicians
don't see. It's like Frederic Bastiat's story of the broken window:

In a small town, a teenager breaks a shop window. Everyone calls him
a vandal at first, but then someone points out that a window installer
now has to be paid to replace the window. The window installer then will
have enough money to buy a new suit. A tailor will then be able to buy a
new desk. And so on. All that money circulating shows that the whole
town will benefit from the economic activity generated by the boy's vandalism (or from building a stadium).

It's nonsense, of course. The circulating money is seen; *what is not
seen* is what would have been done with the money if the window were
still whole. The shopkeeper might have expanded his business, or
bought a new suit or a new desk. The town is no better off because of a
broken window.

In such simple form, the fallacy is obvious. But the same fallacy is
found in newspapers every day. It's found every time politicians propose
subsidizing a new stadium. In their right hand, they hold out the promise that increased business activity will replace the tax money spent. But
they don't show the left hand—the jobs created by the money that people would have spent if it hadn't been taxed away.

When the government bailed out Chrysler with $1.5 billion in loan guarantees, the media said the bailout was a big success because Chrysler stayed in business. What they didn't report—what they could not report—was what was not seen: the homes not built, the businesses not expanded, with the money others could not borrow because government took it and gave it to Chrysler.

Every scheme to create jobs through government spending means people who work and pay taxes have less money to spend on projects *they* would choose. But we in the media miss that. I can interview the people who got jobs or benefits from the government project, but I can't find the people who didn't get a job because money was diverted.

It's why they're still talking about building Steinbrenner a new stadium.

ISN'T YOUR HOME YOUR CASTLE?

Occasionally, politicians are so eager to help their rich friends that they'll take your home to do it.

The legal doctrine of "eminent domain" (which means "superior ownership") allows government officials to take possession of your property if they decide they need it for the greater good. Traditionally this meant building highways, bridges, and parks, and eminent domain was used only in unusual situations.

But today government officials use eminent domain to help private companies—Kmart, Home Depot, baseball teams, shopping malls. Hurst, Texas, condemned 127 homes that stood in the way of a developer's plan to expand a mall. Toledo, Ohio, got a $28.8 million HUD loan to forcibly relocate the owners of 83 perfectly nice homes that were condemned to make way for a Jeep factory. A county in Kansas condemned property belonging to 150 families to make way for NASCAR's

Kansas International Speedway. What? You thought your deed meant you could stay on your property? No. The majority of voters elected me, and now I'm kicking you out to help some big businesses.

Occasionally people are able to thwart the government-business collusion. We visited a neighborhood in New Rochelle, New York, that politicians decided to flatten to make room for an IKEA furniture outlet. The mayor boasted that a spanking-new store would replace a "blighted" neighborhood. Blighted? This was someone's private property, a perfectly nice group of homes and businesses. I told the mayor it looked better than the neighborhood around his office. But he was having none of it. He said the homes had to go.

Now, I like IKEA stores. They sell good stuff at great prices. They are good things to have around. But let them build them on their own damn property.

Why should homeowners be *forced* out? Why do the politicians get to decide? The people who lived in the neighborhood couldn't believe what was happening to them.

Dominick Gataletto, Homeowner: Is it right to tear people from their homes? Is that right? I've been here 67 years, and you don't just wipe that away simply because a furniture store wants to come in. This is America.

First Woman: I've never felt so powerless in my whole life. What's wrong with my American dream? Why is IKEA's American dream better than my American dream?

Second Woman: Where is the freedom? What freedom do we have when we have businesses that will just come in and say, "Oh, you have to move"?

Actually, the business can't force anyone to move. Only government gets to use force; IKEA was just the favored business that day.

Courtesy of the author

When I criticized business every week, I won an armful of Emmys. Now that I criticize government, I no longer win Emmys, but I do get interesting notes from viewers. . . .

MS

From:
Sent: Friday, January 23, 1998 2:31 AM
To: stossel@abc.com
Subject: YOU SUCK

GET OFF THE AIR. GET OFF THE AIR. GET OFF THE AIR. THE ONLY THING MORE ANNOYING THAN THE INCREDIBLE STUPIDITY OF WHAT YOU PUT ON THE AIR IS THE WHINING, NASAL SOUND OF YOUR VOICE. YOU MAKE THE SPICE GIRLS LOOK LIKE BRAIN SURGEONS. YOU ARE THE ABSOLUTE WORST. YOU ARE AN IDIOT. DO THE WORLD A FAVOR AND COMMIT SUICIDE. YOU SUCK. YOU BLOW. YOU STINK. IF MEN ARE FROM MARS AND WOMEN FROM VENUS, WHAT PLANET DO YOU COME FROM? GET OFF
THE AIR. GET OFF THE AIR. GET OFF THE AIR.

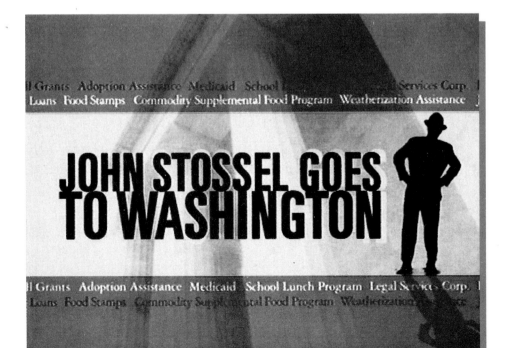

Here's how a free market works: ABC had long talked about giving me one-hour specials but didn't act on it until I got a job offer from another network. Here are three of my favorites: We filmed "Greed" at the Vanderbilt mansion in Asheville, North Carolina. In "John Stossel Goes to Washington," we showed that government doesn't follow the same rules you do—it just keeps spending and misplacing your money. "Freeloaders" focused on the biggest welfare queens: rich people.

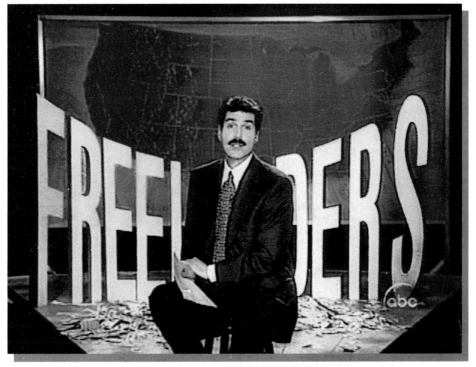

All photographs courtesy of ABC News/ABC Photo Archives

FIRES
PESTICIDES
AIR POLLUTION
MURDER
DRIVI
SMO
POV

ABC decided my first special, "Are We Scaring Ourselves to Death?" was too controversial to run without reaction, and perhaps rebuttal, from a studio audience. They invited regulators, union officials, and others who were skeptical of

my argument that poverty shortens lives more than plane crashes, pesticides, exploding BIC lighters, and other threats hyped by the media.

Okay, I admit it—I'm a freeloader, too. A northeaster swept away the first floor of my beach house, but cheap insurance from the federal government meant that you taxpayers paid for my repairs. I could have been noble and turned the money down, but when government wantonly hands out dollar bills, it's hard to say no. Congress should end this subsidy.

I told Donald Trump he was a bully when he tried to force Vera Coking *(below)* out of her home so he could expand his casino in Atlantic City. Trump's response? "Nobody talks to me that way." Coking kept her home, but only after a four-year legal struggle. Usually, when businesses collude with government to take people's private property, they succeed.

When I first appeared on camera on KGW in Portland, I was terrible. As my news reading improved, my stuttering got worse. I did live TV when I had to—in the photo below I'm comparing products on John Davidson's syndicated show—but I hated it, because I was afraid I'd humiliate myself by stuttering.

Courtesy of the author

Courtesy of the author

John Stossel just got word. He's pregnant!

Here's what happened.

Emmy award-winning Consumer Editor John Stossel heard about certain doctors who were telling women they were pregnant. And offering to perform abortions. The only problem—some of the women <u>weren't</u> pregnant!

So he sent a female researcher for a pregnancy test, but with one catch. The lab specimen she brought with her was supplied by Stossel.

To find out what happened after Stossel received the most surprising news of his life, watch his two part "On Your Side" report, tonight and tomorrow.

6&11pm Channel 2 News
Nobody does it better.

After I got better known as a consumer reporter, I had to disguise myself to go undercover. A CBS makeup artist gave me this beard for an exposé of crooked diamond dealers.

To expose deceitful abortion doctors, I sent female researchers to six clinics with my urine for testing. Two of the clinics told them they were pregnant, which made for good advertising copy.

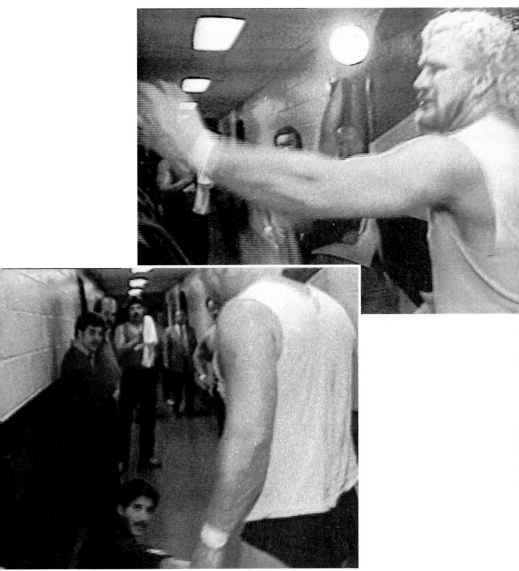

All photographs courtesy of ABC News/ABC Photo Archives

I've confronted lots of people on air, but the only time I ever got hit was when 280-pound wrestler Dave Schultz, a.k.a. Dr. D, didn't like me calling professional wrestling "fake." Once I was on the ground, he asked, "Is that fake?"

What's wrong with these pictures? EPA scientists in biohazard suits condemned the entire town of Times Beach, Missouri, while reporters like me followed them in street clothes. Scenes like this made me start to wonder whether chemicals such as dioxin were as dangerous to us as government agencies and the media make them out to be.

When I was a young, desperate-to-please reporter in Portland, Oregon, I eagerly rode elephants, stuck my arm in the mouths of circus lions, and did whatever else someone suggested might make good TV.

This lovely structure was built by the Parks Department in Pennsylvania. Building it took the government two years and cost $330,000. It's an outhouse—no running water, just an outhouse—and a prime example of how your tax money can go literally into the toilet.

Courtesy of *Pocono Record*

Thanks to the Fifth Amendment, government can't just *take* your property. It has to give you "just compensation." Trouble is, the government, not you, gets to decide what's "just." Officials pay only what they say your home is worth. It's often much less than what *you* think its worth.

The New Rochelle politicians insisted an IKEA store would be "urban renewal" that would be "good for the community." That conceit infuriated Dana Berliner, a lawyer for Washington, D.C.'s Institute for Justice. Says Berliner: "It's always what the 'community' wants. The 'community' wants to be more upscale. It figures it can get there by sacrificing some of its members, forcing them to move when they don't want to, forcing them to accept less money than they would sell for and forcing them into court if they aren't happy. It was to prevent just such abuses, the tyranny of majority over minority, that the founders wrote our Constitution."

The Institute for Justice is a public-interest law firm that defends individuals politicians trample. In New Rochelle, Berliner didn't have to take the case to court. Making noise was enough. After our cameras (and others) showed the public what the politicians were trying to do, IKEA backed down.

But Donald Trump didn't back down. In the early '90s, the billionaire already owned Trump Plaza, Trump Tower, Trump Parc, Trump International Hotel, Trump Palace, Trump World's Fair, and Trump Taj Mahal. But he wanted more. He wanted to expand one of his casinos in Atlantic City.

Vera Coking was in the way. The elderly widow had lived in a house in Atlantic City for more than 30 years, and she didn't want to move. Trump offered Coking $1 million if she'd sell. She said no.

This annoyed Trump. He told reporters her house was ugly, and it would be better if it were torn down to make room for a parking lot for limousines waiting outside his casino.

I wouldn't think that was "public use," but before you could say "corporate welfare," New Jersey's Casino Reinvestment Development Authority filed a lawsuit in 1994 to "acquire" Coking's property. They told Coking that she must vacate her home within 90 days or the sheriff would forcibly remove her.

Suddenly the $1 million offer was off the table. The Authority said Coking's house was worth only $251,000—one-fifth what Trump paid for a smaller lot nearby.

It looked to me as if the government was robbing Vera Coking to pay off Donald Trump. The government officials wouldn't talk to me about it, but Trump did.

John Stossel: In the old days, big developers came in with thugs with clubs. Now you use lawyers. You go to court and you force people out.

Donald Trump: Excuse me. Other people maybe use thugs today. I don't. I've done this very nicely. If I wanted to use thugs, we wouldn't have any problems. It would have been all taken care of many years ago. I don't do business that way. We have been so nice to this woman.

Trump said Coking turned down his offer because "her lawyer wants to get rich, and everybody wants to get rich off me."

John Stossel: So don't pay it. Let them stay. Basic to freedom is that if you own something, it's yours. The government doesn't just come and take it away.

Donald Trump: Do you want to live in a city where you can't build roads or highways or have access to hospitals? Condemnation is a necessary evil.

John Stossel: But we're not talking about a hospital. This is a building a rich guy finds ugly.

Donald Trump: You're talking about at the tip of this city, lies a little group of terrible, terrible tenements—just terrible stuff, tenement housing.

John Stossel: So what!

Donald Trump: So what? . . . Atlantic City does a lot less business, and senior citizens get a lot less money and a lot less taxes and a lot less this and that.

Sadly, claims that people will be deprived of "this and that" can now be used by politicians to condemn your house.

It didn't seem right to Vera Coking.

"This is America. My husband fought in the war and worked to make sure I would have a roof over my head, and they want to take it from me?"

Usually the Donald Trumps of the world and their partners in government get what they want. But Vera Coking was lucky enough to get media attention, and to have the Institute for Justice take her case to court. In 1998, a judge finally ruled against Trump and the government, finding that taking the property would benefit Trump, not the public. Vera Coking got to keep her home. She still lives there, surrounded by Trump's hotel.

One little victory for the people.

JUSTICE

The rich and their political cronies will always try to manipulate government to benefit themselves. It's good we have a free press to keep an eye on them and groups like the Institute for Justice that sue when politicians ignore what the Constitution says about government's *limited* powers.

I was skeptical when I first learned about the institute's plans to protect individuals' rights by suing. I said to institute directors Chip Mellor and John Kramer: "You're going to preserve liberty by filing *more lawsuits*? Give me a break. Lawsuits do more harm than good."

In this case, I was wrong. The institute's suits have broken up business-government cartels that prevented people from buying cheap caskets and taxi rides, or choosing which school their children attend. They saved people from having their homes bulldozed. The institute's work shows that some lawsuits are necessary. Some.

CHAPTER NINE

The Trouble with Lawyers

*Laws do not persuade
just because they threaten.*
— *S e n e c a*

I'm known as a lawyer hater. Once my 11-year-old asked me, "Daddy, how can you hate lawyers? All your, like, friends are lawyers!" He had a point; I don't hate all lawyers. We *need* lawyers.

We need them to preserve the rule of law. We need them to defend us if others cheat us, steal from us, trample on our rights. However, we also need nuclear missiles—to keep other nations from trampling our rights. But we consider missiles a necessary evil. We try not to use them, because they harm innocent people.

We should treat lawsuits the same way. Lawsuits are necessary, but *evil*. They may not be as violent as missiles, but they cause enormous harm. Just one lawsuit can wreck your life. Even if you win, the lawsuit can take all your time, and all your money. That's why even the *threat* of litigation *terrifies*. One of the legal system's heroes, Judge Learned Hand, compared litigation to "sickness and death."

Tort lawyers, the ones who sue businesses that make products that hurt people, claim to help "the little guy," but based on what I've seen in my reporting, for every person they help, they hurt five. For every dollar of good they achieve, they take five. That's because lawsuits hurt innocent people, too.

To film "The Trouble with Lawyers," we went to a suburb of San Francisco. When people saw me and our camera, they seemed terrified. They hid—slammed doors, pulled shades down. A few brave souls who eventually came out to talk said they were afraid to attend community meetings or let the kids play outdoors. They lived in fear, they said, because of one woman: Patricia McColm. "It's like an atomic bomb right in the middle of our neighborhood," said one of her neighbors.

Patricia McColm is not a bomb, of course—she just sues people a lot. She sued a department store, saying she slipped on dust and hurt her ankle; a supermarket, claiming her foot had been run over by a cart; the local Bank of America because her foot was hit by a door. She filed a claim against the city of San Francisco, saying she slipped in a puddle at city hall, spraining her ankle and tearing her nylons.

"She tells you if you do things, you will be *sorry*," said Adrienne Taliafar. High school student David Greenbaum said he could no longer shoot baskets in his own driveway because McColm sued his family, saying the noise of the bouncing ball caused her physical and emotional distress. His parents fought the suit, but they ran up against the ugly truth of our legal system: Even when you're in the right, you still lose. After eight years and $35,000 in legal bills, they and their insurance company gave up. They took their hoop down and paid McColm a $5,000 settlement.

She's won many settlements. Does that mean some of her suits are valid? Arbitrators did find for her in a few instances and McColm says that every one of her suits is justified. But her neighbors scoff at that. "Absolutely not," said one. Stephen Theoharis, the attorney hired to defend her neighbors, said, "She *extorts* people because she knows that she's imposing costs of defense. She has absolutely nothing to lose," he said. "A company has to consider legal fees." Bank of America did fight her in court, and after a trial, it won, but it had to pay its own lawyers $27,000. The American legal system is unique in that its rules favor attackers. A lawyer who sues can win millions, but she can't lose much; maybe some time, some expense money—but even if her case is a bad one, and it goes against her, she just walks away. She doesn't have to pay for the damage her lawsuit did to you; she doesn't even have to say she's sorry. She can move on to sue the next guy. No wonder Patricia McColm's neighbors hide.

I wanted to interview McColm, but she said it didn't fit her schedule. When we were taping, she watched us from an upstairs window. A few months later, she sued *me*—for "slanderous comments." (A judge eventually dismissed her suit.)

At the courthouse, the clerks knew her well. They demanded that ABC not show *their* faces for fear she'd sue them. It's one of the sad, unintended consequences of lawsuits: fearful silence. People told us, "No, I can't talk to you about McColm. It's too dangerous."

Lawsuits kill the open debate that's helped make America free.

Patricia McColm isn't even a lawyer. She went to law school but failed the bar exam. She files suits *pro se,* arguing her own cases.

Imagine how much damage *real* lawyers can do.

THE INVISIBLE FIST

As a believer in free markets, I should like lawsuits, since they promise a free-market solution. Unlike clumsy, one-size-fits-all government regulation, a lawsuit is an individual remedy. Walter Olsen, of overlawyered.com, calls trial lawyers the "invisible fist," a supplement to the free market's "invisible hand."

This should be a good thing: The threat of lawsuits should act as a deterrent, force people to toe the line, make products and services safer and better. But something has gone horribly wrong. Our unique legal system makes litigation too inviting. As a result, we have armies of lawyers who attack our goodwill toward one another, our access to critical information, and our freedom to make informed choices. They deter innovation because anything new and risky exposes the inventor to dangerous legal liability. It's safer not to try.

When I started doing consumer reporting, lawyers were my best source. Their mission, they explained, was to protect consumers and get victims compensation. I thought, "Hey, they're just like us consumer reporters—they want to punish bullies and rip-off artists. They can do it better than I can because they have power. My television reports just alert the public; lawyers can make the bad guys *pay*."

This partnership between reporters and trial lawyers is not a good thing, but it's hard for us reporters to resist, because trial lawyers are a perfect source. They do most of the work for us. We don't need to make phone calls to search for victims; the lawyers identify the most telegenic of them, the people whose stories make you cry, and they'll bring them right to our office.

Then they identify the "bad guy" for us. We don't need to do much original investigating, since the lawyers use their subpoena power to force companies to turn over just about every record they've ever produced. The lawyers usually find some dirt (bet they'd find dirt on *you* if they got all your papers) and hand it to us. We double-check it—but we're following the lawyers' script.

I felt so self-righteous doing those stories. The lawyers and I were the good guys fighting the bullies.

Now I realize that it's the *lawyers* who are the bullies, and I was just part of their hustle. My reports on, say, "the dangers of asbestos" got them more clients, softened up juries, and encouraged business defendants to settle to avoid looking bad on TV. ("That jerk Stossel is at our headquarters door with a network camera!" Who wants publicity like *that*?)

The lawyers got richer. But was the public safer? No. The lawyers claim they make us safer, but now I understand that the opposite is true. Lawsuits make America less safe.

SAFETY LAWSUITS MAKE LIFE MORE DANGEROUS

How can this be? Clearly, lawsuits have a deterrent effect that *seems* to make life safer. But tort lawyers attack the very people we need most in order to be safe: innovators, companies that make safety devices, hospitals, drugmakers, paramedics, those who stand on the front line between life and death. The lawsuits *threaten* the people who make us safer.

In the 1980s, trial lawyers made millions claiming vaccines caused autism and neurological disorders in children. It's impossible to know whether these problems were caused by the vaccines. Some kids get terribly sick after vaccinations, but in any group of millions of kids, some will get sick. And the FDA had approved the vaccines. But that didn't matter. A persuasive personal injury lawyer only has to convince one jury that a drug company cruelly sold a vaccine that wasn't as safe as it might have been. Then other lawyers sue. Drugmakers and other producers of good things settle to avoid destruction by a thousand invisible fists. Even if companies are in the right, they often pay up to avoid the defense costs these legal missiles would force upon them. Then the lawyers brag that they saved x lives because y company did z. Sounds good. But it misses the bigger picture.

Before the vaccine suits were filed, 25 companies researched and manufactured vaccines. In an era of AIDS, anthrax, SARS, and who knows what bioweapon might come next, vaccine research is crucial. But many drug companies have given it up. After the lawsuit, some said, "Who needs this liability? We don't make much profit off vaccines. Let's stick to our pimple-cream or shampoo business." Today only five companies make vaccines. Are we safer with five vaccine makers instead of 25? No way.

Lawyers brag that they made football helmets safer, and they did make them thicker. But does that mean the kids are safer? Not necessarily. Some schools can't afford $100 per extrathick helmet, so they give up football programs. The kids play on the street. That's less safe, but there's no one to sue.

Maryland's Peter Angelos, who made enough money from asbestos litigation to buy the Baltimore Orioles, told me, "If it wasn't for the American lawyer, your basic civil rights today would be gone." Tort lawyers constantly portray themselves as defenders of the "little guy," as warriors who protect us from the big bad businesses that want to violate your civil rights.

But these Kings of Torts are not your basic civil rights lawyers. They are avaricious parasites. "It is true that our liberties are tied up with our legal system," says Yale law professor John Langbein, but "the fallacy is the claim that our liberties require us to permit hucksters like the tort barons to abuse our legal system." The tort lawyers' law firms have become monstrous bulldozers that crush entrepreneurs and kill jobs.

THE ASBESTOS MONSTER

No one disputes that asbestos can kill. During World War II, workers who built warships breathed in huge amounts of it; films of the shipyards show people working in what looks like snowstorms. Many shipyard workers who inhaled the asbestos "snow" got lung diseases and a deadly cancer called mesothelioma.

Those sick people deserve compensation, and bosses who knew of the risk but allowed workers to be exposed anyway deserve to be punished. That's what the tort system is supposed to do.

But that's not what's happening. Today, most people and companies that were instrumental in exposing people to asbestos are dead or bankrupt. The number of mesothelioma deaths is declining.

But the lawsuits continue to grow, like cancer. After asbestos maker Johns Manville filed for bankruptcy, the lawyers moved on, sniffing after the money. They sued glassmaker Pittsburgh Corning, insulation maker Owens Corning, Armstrong World Industries, WR Grace, USG Corporation, Federal-Mogul Corporation, and Kaiser Aluminum of Houston. Those companies all filed for bankruptcy. Harvard Law professor Christopher Edley Jr. says there "is no asbestos industry anymore."

That didn't matter to the lawyers. The lawsuit bulldozer moved on; now it's attacking Sears, Roebuck; Chiquita Brands; Ford; GM; Chrysler; and 6,000 other companies. Most have only the most distant connection to asbestos. Nevertheless, when the lawyers threaten to bring a thousand "victims" into court (many are healthy—"but they might *get* sick"), the companies will almost certainly do what others did: buy the lawyers off—I mean, settle—rather than risk ruin by fighting the suits.

You may not care about the 6,000 companies now being squashed, but you should, because you pay the bill. The money to buy the Baltimore Orioles, or cover some lawyer's $25 million Gulfsteam jet, comes out of your pocket in the form of higher car prices or insurance premiums. The horrors of September 11 cost insurance companies $43 billion. Asbestos litigation will cost about $200 billion. *You* helped buy Peter Angelos his baseball team. Did he thank you?

The lawyers' "public service" costs you every time you buy something. Lawsuits add $500 to the price of a car and $3,000 to every pacemaker. Even haircuts cost more because hairdressers now buy lawsuit insurance in case someone has a bad hair day.

But an even greater cost is the loss of all the good things *we don't get to have in the first place.* Genentech says fear of suits led it to halt its research into an AIDS vaccine. Other entrepreneurs give up on promising ideas because innovation—any change—risks opening the door to the lawyers.

Several years ago, ABC News reported on how a hip replacement changed Carol Kornblum's life. "I'm with my grandchildren," she said. "I can play basketball with them. It's like a new life." But when she wanted to replace her other hip, she found the maker of the plastic used in the hip joint had taken it off the market, not because it's unsafe—it isn't— but because he thought he might be sued.

Such losses are everywhere. For years, an Arizona couple cooked free Thanksgiving dinners for the poor. Then they gave it up because they feared someone would sue, claiming food poisoning. Girl Scout camps have eliminated horseback riding. Olympic gymnast Tim Daggett told me gymnastic programs have been crippled by fear of lawsuits. "The YMCAs, the Park and Recreations, the Boys and Girls Clubs, the high school programs, they are vanishing," he said. The Boy Scouts say fewer people are willing to volunteer to be leaders. Some parents are afraid to coach Little League.

Lawsuits have killed honest job references. Now employers often say *nothing* about bad or dangerous workers. When an airline fires a pilot for flying drunk, they don't tell the other airlines that he's a drunkard. It's safer to say nothing.

INFORMATION POLLUTION

Lawsuits also disrupt the information flow that helps us protect ourselves. We ought to read labels. We should read the labels warning that microwave popcorn or McDonald's coffee can burn us, or that some antibiotics won't work if you take them with milk. But who reads labels anymore? I rarely do, because legalese has smothered their usefulness. The label on a candle says, "A burning candle is fire . . . do not eat the candle." Thanks for the tip. A sleeping pill prescription warns, "Drug may cause drowsiness." A stepladder now comes with *41* instructions:

DO NOT OVERREACH.

KEEP STEPS DRY AND CLEAN.

WEAR SLIP-RESISTANT SHOES.

And so on. Is this useful? No. It's verbal pollution. People respond to it by ignoring labels we *should* read.

Again, lawsuits designed to make life better make it worse. Some people are helped, but more are harmed.

JOBS

Then there's the loss of jobs. So far, the asbestos bulldozer has demolished about 60,000 of them. I interviewed Glenn Bailey, president of the Keene Corporation. We talked in his nearly empty office in New York City; it felt like a morgue. Bailey never made asbestos, but he bought a company that once did. Now, he says, "We've been sued to death." One more vibrant business, and its employees, were gone.

How sad for America. The producers suffer while the parasites who feed off them thrive.

I asked Peter Angelos why he deserved to make millions while others suffered. He didn't bat an eye.

"That's the system," he said. "That's the American system. The purpose of bringing litigation was not for me to get rich. It was for the purpose of compensating the victims of these companies. If some people have lost their jobs because of that, certainly, we did not intend that result, but nonetheless, we can't be held responsible for that."

Like many plaintiff's lawyers, he talks proudly about how he makes America safer. (It's *always* about "safety," not the huge fees.) They brag that they protect us from evil big business—asbestos and tobacco companies or the makers of the Dalkon Shield (an IUD). But *lawyers* didn't discover that the Dalkon Shield or asbestos or cigarettes can shorten lives; *scientists* discovered that, and then the lawyers, like vultures, rushed in to feed off the carcass. The big tobacco suits were filed after the bad news about tobacco was already out. The vast majority of asbestos and Dalkon shield lawsuits were filed *after* the products were already taken off the market.

COMPENSATION

The lawyers claim that even if they fail to punish the bad guys, their lawsuits at least get compensation to victims. But this is a lousy way to compensate injured people. Astonishingly, most of the money doesn't go to the victims—it goes to the lawyers. The plaintiff's attorneys get 30 or 40 percent; then there are the court costs; and of course the defense lawyers have to be paid. The poor victim is left with less than half the money spent on litigation and settlements. No wonder the defense bar doesn't scream about reforming this disgusting system. It's a racket for *both* sides. The lawyers fight, then shake hands on their way to the bank. What kind of victim-compensation system is that? It takes two or 10 or 20 years to get your money—and the lawyers take *most* of it?

Asbestos litigants often get less. We interviewed a group that won their suit but were furious because they had "peanuts after lawyers got through with us." "Peanuts" isn't exactly correct. Many won several thousand dollars, but their lawyers got *millions*—$300,000 per hour in one case.

This is a not a fair way to compensate victims.

YOU THOUGHT THE PEOPLE YOU *ELECTED* MAKE THE LAWS?

In addition to enriching themselves at your expense, trial lawyers now set policy for the whole country. All by themselves.

In Albuquerque, New Mexico, Stella Liebeck's family took her to McDonald's for a cup of coffee. She held it while sitting in her grandson's car. "He has a little sports car," she told me. There was no cup holder, and "everything is slanted. So I put it between my knees and steadied it with my left hand and tried to get the top off. And it just went, *pssh*."

The coffee burned her. Her lawyer, Reed Morgan, sued. He argued that McDonald's coffee, at almost 190 degrees, was too hot. A jury awarded them $2.9 million (later reduced to $640,000). I understand why the jury gave her money. Liebeck is a sweet lady who was burned severely—she had to have skin grafts. Other people had complained to McDonald's about the temperature of its coffee. The jury chose the victim over a corporation.

Lawyer Reed Morgan proudly says he performed a "public service" because his lawsuit got McDonald's and other fast-food chains to lower the temperature of their coffee.

But did we intend to have Reed Morgan set policy for the whole country? Food industry consultants say most customers prefer take-out coffee *really* hot, so it's still hot when they get to where they drink it. But after Liebeck's lawsuit, McDonald's and other fast-food restaurants lowered the temperature 30 degrees. I'd rather have my coffee hot. Reed Morgan may call what he did a "public service," but why does Morgan get to make the decision for *all* of us?

Because he's a lawyer—and lawyers can be nuclear missiles.

THE FOULEST, RANKEST SCANDAL

The lawyers say, "Don't blame it all on us; we're just doing the will of the people. We do what our clients ask us to do, and we win only when an independent jury agrees with our argument."

But that's not exactly true. These days, lawyers often choose their clients. They decide which industry will be a lucrative target (tobacco, asbestos, paint, whatever), and then they recruit "victims."

Once they have a big pool of victims, they keep suing until they win. They almost always win eventually. Antitobacco activist John Banzaff says trial lawyers lost 700 lawsuits against "Big Tobacco" before finally winning one.

Facing another 700, or perhaps 7,000, suits, the tobacco companies settled. The settlement got fawning press coverage because most reporters bought the lawyers' spin: Big Tobacco has been brought to its knees—those evil executives who lied to us will now be punished, and they will have to pay for health care for smokers to compensate taxpayers for Medicaid money spent on smokers. State attorneys general fell over one another to get in front of the cameras to tell America that, thanks to their fine work, Big Tobacco would pay "the public" a whopping $206 billion.

It sounded good, but if you look closely at this deal, it looks like what in my consumer-reporting days we called a scam.

"It is the foulest, rankest scandal I have seen in 20 years in Washington," said Michael Horowitz of the Hudson Institute for a *20/20* story ABC called "What a Deal!" Said Horowitz, "Lawyers are going to get richer. Tobacco companies are going to get richer. And who's going to pay for it? Poor old Joe, who's now going to pay 80 cents a pack more."

Tobacco companies will get *richer*? Well, yes. It turns out it isn't evil tobacco executives who are paying for this deal. The bad guys who lied about cigarette science are gone, and even if some were still around, they wouldn't have to pay, because tobacco companies just raised their prices. Since all the major cigarette producers were party to the settlement, none needed to worry about losing market share. Tobacco company stocks went *up* when the deal was announced.

It's today's smokers who must pay. Don't they owe taxpayers the money? No. "The whole idea that the healthy people are being victimized by smokers is exactly backward," says Harvard Law School economist Kip Viscusi, one of many researchers who've pointed out that smokers already cover the costs of their bad habit by paying an average of 56 cents in tax every time they buy a pack. Also, "What the state calculations don't take into account is that smokers don't live as long as nonsmokers," says Viscusi. In other words, the gruesome truth is that smokers *save* America money because they die sooner, thereby collecting less in Social Security and pension money.

The tobacco settlement is Robin Hood in reverse. It's poor people who smoke most, so the poorest people in America will pay hundreds of billions to the states (New York is spending some of the money on a golf course, North Carolina on tobacco farmers and a tobacco museum), and to a group of lawyers. Very rich lawyers. Some will make more than $100,000 per hour. I can't tell you exactly how many millions each lawyer will get, because the lawyers say that's a secret.

Who *are* these lawyers? Well, the politicians contracted the work out to private lawyers. The biggest suits were pressed by America's most famous courtroom missiles, real-life Kings of Torts Ron Motley, Dickie Scruggs, Joe Rice, and Bob Montgomery. They were already multimillionaires; now they'll be billionaires.

Some states farmed the lucrative legal work out to—surprise—the politicians' lawyer friends. Texas's attorney general, Dan Morales, told some lawyers he'd give them the case if they gave him a million-dollar contribution, according to superlawyer Joe Jamail, who turned him down. Other times the money went to—surprise—politicians' relatives. Hugh Rodham (as in Hillary Rodham Clinton) is in on the deal. Dickie Scruggs, Trent Lott's brother-in-law, is too.

Taxing poor smokers and giving billions of it to already rich lawyers doesn't seem fair, so I confronted Christine Gregoire, Washington State's attorney general, about it. Gregoire was the lead lawyer among the state officials who'd made deals with the attorneys who won the settlement. She told me, "We wouldn't have $206 billion. We wouldn't have the opportunity to save lives, but for those private lawyers partnering with the attorneys general of this country."

Without the trial lawyers, they couldn't get the money? Wait a second! We do, in America, have something called legislatures, and usually, when we want to discourage use of a product or to tax users to pay for medical care, our representatives decide that. If Americans want rules requiring colder coffee or higher cigarette prices because we think that's good for our health, we can vote for representatives who support that. That's more democratic and *cheaper* than a lawsuit, because wads of money don't go to buy lawyers new jets and yachts.

But instead of voting for a tax, the politicians did a deal with their lawyer friends.

"They made payoffs, plain and simple," says Horowitz. "Fat, obscene, unethical, intolerable payoffs to their pals."

The state attorneys general and the trial lawyers deny that the tobacco deal was about political payoffs. But nearly all the attorneys general who sued are Democrats, and nearly all the trial lawyers are Democrats, and now the Democratic Party's biggest contributors are the trial lawyers. I confronted Gregoire about that.

"You're paying them off here," I said.

"This is about saving lives—most importantly, children's lives," she said.

They are always *saving the children.*

Does a select group of lawyers really get to decide cigarette-tax and coffee-temperature rules for the whole country because their law degrees give them license to act like nuclear missiles? Well, yes.

EXTORTION

Of course the tobacco companies didn't *have* to settle, and McDonald's didn't *have* to cool its coffee. But how could they resist? How can any company resist? When you're fighting the lawyers, even if you win, you lose.

My view of the system is not shaped just by what I've learned as a reporter. I've had unfortunate firsthand experience. People who didn't like what I said about them on TV have sued me. And I brought suit myself when I got whacked by that wrestler who didn't like my saying pro wrestling is fake.

I won every case, so I should be happy with the process, but I'm not, because under America's peculiar legal system, only the lawyers *really* win.

Last time I was sued for libel, for example, a Philadelphia jury came down on my side. Vindication! But the process took years, and ABC still had to pay defense lawyers almost $1 million. How is that winning?

This is why American lawsuits resemble shakedowns. Even some lawyers admit it. Yale law professor John Langbein said in "The Trouble with Lawyers," "No matter how blameless you are, you say to yourself, 'I'm going to settle out. I'll pay tribute.' This is not far removed from what Al Capone used to do to shopkeepers on the West Side of Chicago."

I keep learning about the new ways clever lawyers are finding to make money with their Mafia-like powers. To help the disabled, Congress passed the Americans with Disabilities Act, which requires businesses to install wheelchair ramps and handicapped parking spaces. It's not clear that the disabled have been helped, but a new group of extortionists— oops, I mean "disability rights lawyers"—has certainly found a lucrative racket—I mean "public-service legal enterprise."

In 1998, California lawyers Russell Handy, Esq., and Mark Potter, Esq., sued hundreds of small stores for doing things like not posting those blue Handicapped Only signs. Their terrifying 30-page lawsuit demanded a "jury trial" because the storeowners were guilty of "discrimination against persons with physical disabilities" because of "lack of appropriate accessibility signage." The plaintiff "suffered a loss of his civil rights and his rights as a person with physical disabilities to full and equal access to public accommodations, which includes shame, humiliation, embarrassment, anger, chagrin, disappointment and worry."

Really. This is typical of the mass smears lawyers write into legal threats. It costs the lawyers nothing extra to accuse everyone of everything.

The horrified small-business men imagine their pictures in the newspaper—over a caption identifying them as the evil person who "discriminated" and "humiliated" disabled people—so they whimper to their lawyer (if they can afford one), who tells them it would cost too much to fight the lawsuit. They settle by posting the blue signs and paying thousands of dollars in "attorney's fees."

Isn't that extortion? Russell Handy told us he "loves this area of law" because, like the legislature, he's "helping the disabled."

If anyone's helping the disabled, it's Dave and Donna Batelaan. They are disabled themselves. In Florida, they have a little store where they sell and repair wheelchairs. Since their customers are disabled, they didn't have a special handicapped parking sign. Guess what? *They* were sued— by a lawyer named Tony Brady, who runs a similar shakedown—I mean public-service law practice. When I accused Brady of shaking them down, he said, "Is it a shakedown in a personal injury case where the lawyer says if you don't settle for $10,000, I'm gonna go to a jury?"

Yes, Mr. Brady, under America's legal rules, it is.

When I ask lawyers about these problems, they usually say, "America has the best legal system in the world."

I went to Houston to talk to Joe Jamail about it. In 1995, Joe Jamail took home $90 million and was at the top of *Forbes* magazine's list of richest lawyers. Visiting him was like visiting a king. Everyone deferred to him—practically bowed and scraped. No one wants to be on the bad side of a lawyer that good.

Jamail says he's good because he fights hard. Once he thought an opponent had gotten out of line. So he "hit him in the mouth and knocked him down in a corner and tried to kick his brains out." *This* is the kind of lawyer people should want? "Well," he replies, "do you want some asshole that's going to sit back and let you get killed by some guy that's just absolutely abusive and insulting?"

He's right. If you're fighting a war, you want to hire the toughest guy. You want to have bigger missiles than your opponent. But innocent people get hurt when disputes are resolved by hired guns who fight that hard. And we consumers have to pay for the battle.

The newest way for lawyers to get rich has been to combine cases into a class-action suit. This is an efficient way to get justice when lots of people were hurt by the same thing. *Brown v. Board of Education* was a class-action suit. Individually the kids couldn't afford to sue, but as a group, they could integrate the schools. In theory, class actions are a good remedy.

But the lawyers have made it a scam. Even Joe Jamail said he's so disgusted by class actions, he won't participate. What's so disgusting? Case after case like this: A General Mills supplier accidentally used an "unapproved" chemical. No one was hurt. Class-action lawyers sued on behalf of all buyers of General Mills cereal. The company settled by giving customers coupons for free boxes of cereal. The lawyers got almost $2 million. Thanks, guys!

In a class-action lawsuit against Bank of Boston, plaintiffs got a few dollars each while the lawyers took millions. It turned out that winning *cost* some class members money, because the lawyers' huge fees were deducted from clients' mortgage escrow accounts.

Such scams happen all the time, but you don't hear about them, because the deals are so complex that only lawyers understand them. McDonald's, Blockbuster, Federal Express, Ameritech, in fact most large companies have paid settlements. The companies go along because it's cheaper to pay than to fight, and they then pass the cost on to you. At the moment, you may be a plaintiff in seven to 10 class-action suits, although you probably don't even know about it because the lawyer didn't need your permission to include you in his suit.

DO EVEN THE CLIENTS WIN?

Since lawsuits raise prices and deprive us of valuable things, you'd assume that tort lawyers at least help their clients. Sometimes they do, but a surprising number of clients are unhappy, even when they win. When I started consumer reporting and met victimized consumers I couldn't help, I sometimes referred them to lawyers.

"*They'll* help," I thought. "They're in the justice *business.*" How naive. After I made a referral, the consumers often told me, "I just got ripped off again! The *lawyer* ripped me off."

It usually wasn't that the lawyers had broken laws. It's just that almost everything they do is so ruinously expensive.

As a consumer reporter, I've watched most every American industry find ways to do things better, faster, and cheaper. The computer I'm writing this book on costs less, yet is more powerful than earlier models. Cars get better. Supermarkets offer more for less. Most every business is better.

But not the law business. In law, *everything* is slow and expensive, and our choices are limited.

For $1 I can buy a newspaper, and every day it's different. But try to get a divorce or a simple will for less than $200—lawyers charge more than that for boilerplate that's nearly identical for every client.

The lawyers defend their fees and snail-like pace, saying, "We've got to make sure you get *due process.*" Glad they're so concerned. But when there's no money in a case, people have trouble even getting a lawyer, let alone getting due process. When there's money, lawyers insist on tons of due process. They'll waste time obsessing about *everything.* In the O. J. Simpson trial, they even quibbled about the jewelry the other lawyers wore. Other businesses pad bills, too, but *competition limits it.* There's less competition in law because lawyers *outlawed* competition from outside their profession—they prosecute paralegals who offer cheaper alternatives, calling it "unauthorized practice of law."

Long as the O. J. circus was, it was relatively quick because it was a criminal case. A criminal defendant has a right to demand a speedy trial.

What keeps most lawyers busy is civil cases, the ones in which they argue about money. Civil cases take *years*. The process is so painfully slow that it almost makes me feel sorry for the people who sue *me*. The guy in Philadelphia who said I slandered him, damaged his reputation, had to wait four years just to get me into court.

The essence of my story was that Irwin Rogal, a dentist, ran a dental "mill," telling people (including me, after he examined me for a *20/20* story) we had jaw problems, and then charging big bucks for dubious "treatments." In his lawsuit, he claimed he had not recommended treatment to me. Reasonable people could differ on this; he went back and forth on the recommendation during a 40-minute exam.

Sounds simple for a court to resolve. The exam was on videotape. The jury could watch the 40-minute tape and then decide. But that never happened. Instead, the dentist's lawyers and mine spent *three years* sending legal papers back and forth. My lawyers (did I mention they were paid by the hour?) demanded that the dentist produce vast amounts of paperwork detailing "all persons other than your attorneys with whom you have had written or oral communication" and "each workshop or seminar in which you have participated as a speaker, including, but not limited to your seminars for dentists, physicians, lawyers and headache sufferers," as well as the "date, the location, the attendance, the amount charged to each attendee...."

The dentist's attorneys demanded that we "state the title and author of each book that was used as a source of information, the name and date of publication of each newspaper, magazine, pamphlet ... documents ..." In case we didn't know what documents were, they spelled it out: "Any abstracts, accounts, accounting records, accounting advertisements, agreements, bids, bills, bills of lading, blanks, books, books of accounts, brochures"—that's just the A's and B's. The demands went on and on.

Years later, the trial finally came. But instead of spending one hour to watch the tape of the exam, the lawyers had *days* of testimony, and the jury never saw the full 40-minute tape. Instead, we had war. War is what a lawsuit *is*. Each side played snippets of the videotape. His side played a few minutes that made it seem as if he *hadn't* recommended treatment; my side played a few that demonstrated he *did*. This happened again and again, three-minute snippets—for days. It was ridiculous. That's what got to me most, watching my case: the extravagant waste. Even with lawyers charging hundreds of dollars an hour, the judge just let it go on and on.

I finally won, but the ordeal cost ABC a fortune. Why couldn't the judge say, "Shut up. This is a waste of time and money. We're just going to play the tape"? "Because most judges are afraid to offend," says Joe Jamail. So these lawyers are just self-indulgent, right? "No, they were being paid," says Jamail.

"We have lawyers running the system, and the problem with that is that lawyers don't have an obligation and a commitment to the truth," says Professor Langbein. "They have an obligation to *win*. So we've got a combat system rather than a truth system. All over America, every day, in our daily lives, in our personal lives, in our business affairs, we're making decisions to investigate the facts and decide what action to take . . . but none of us do it the way it's done in the law courts, and for good reason: What's done in the law courts is absurd. It's distortion and trickery."

Expensive distortion and trickery.

Court reminds me of a religious ritual. We don't get speedy justice, but we get lots of pompous ceremony. Judges wear robes. We call them "honorable," whether they are or not. Many lawyers put the silly word "esquire" after their name. It once meant "English landowner"; now it means nothing. Lawyers say the ceremony is necessary to maintain "respect for the law," but wait a second: These folks can take *all our money,* and *our freedom.* Doesn't that get them enough respect?

The pompous rituals suggest there's magic in the law, work only lawyers can do. That makes it easier to resist reform.

FIXING IT

Destructive litigation is a particularly American problem. In most countries, if you sue, and the court finds you're wrong, *you* have to pay the other guy's legal costs. It's called "loser pays." We are the *only* advanced country in which I can sue you, wreck your life, be wrong, and then just walk away. It's the reason Americans file some 90 million lawsuits a year—one every three seconds. Lawsuits are too lucrative—and risk-free—to resist. But under "loser pays," Patricia McColm, the dentist, the class-action extortionists, and other bullies might have to compensate those of us they sued. It would make it harder to bully people into settling.

Lawyers complain that "loser pays" would discourage Americans from going to court. They're right. But *that's okay*—given the harm lawsuits do, it's *worth it.* We should avoid using lawsuits, the way we avoid using our missiles.

Remember when the National Football League tried instant replay to check refs' calls? There is a lot at stake every game, so it seemed reasonable to check the tape every time there was a dispute. But fans and players hated it. It stopped the momentum of the game. So the NFL limited the number of challenges allowed, and imposed a penalty—loss of a time-out ("loser pays")—when a challenge loses.

Let's do the same thing to the legal system.

"Loser pays" is just one of many possible reforms that have been successfully blocked by the trial lawyers. Illinois congressman Henry Hyde's 1994 reform bill failed in committee, and nothing serious has happened since. The trial lawyers win in legislatures because they fight better than *anybody*. Think about it. Practice makes perfect. Trial lawyers fight people *every day*, so they've become experts at it. They may not be right, but they know how to win. They twist the truth in diabolically clever ways. Even "loser pays" they distort—they marginalize it by calling it the "English rule." But it's *not* the "English rule," it's the *rest of the world* rule.

"We have a legal system that is a flop—a laughingstock," says Professor Langbein. "We have a legal system which encourages people not to want to do business in this country."

The American legal system isn't even working for the lawyers. Even though law is now the highest-paid profession, the lawyers aren't happy. Many say they went to law school hoping to do good, but now find themselves working incredibly long hours doing tedious work that's often more about money than justice. A survey of California lawyers found most would change careers if they could. Something's very wrong when America's brightest young people are choosing a profession many won't like, where they're not building something, not making the economic pie bigger, just fighting over who gets which slice, making each slice cost more, and taking our freedom in the process.

CHAPTER TEN

The Left
Takes Notice

*Distrust all men in
whom the impulse to
punish is powerful.*
— Friedrich Nietzsche

Where I work (in network TV) and live (on the Upper West Side of Manhattan), they say "conservative" the way they say "child molester." It's the worst thing to be called. Everyone here agrees: Conservatives are repressive, uptight, fearful of new things, and above all, indifferent to the suffering of the poor.

People here talk about the "far right, extreme right, hard right, religious right, unapologetic right," but never about a "left." What you might call "the left" doesn't exist in my neighborhood. It's just enlightened thinking to favor more safety and environmental rules, tougher gun control, abortion on demand, and higher taxes to fund good-government projects.

Anyone who disagrees is seen as not just wrong, but selfish and cruel. Once at a dinner party, I found myself arguing that the welfare state perpetuated poverty; the other guests shrieked at me, and then my wife jumped in—on *their* side. I was so dismayed by that, I threw a piece of cake at her. (And it was a cake she had baked.) I was upset because I'd spent years discussing these ideas with her, and thought she'd come to see their value. But at that dinner party, I was an alien, even to my own wife.

Leftist thinking is simply the culture I swim in. More property programs? More safety regulation? Who could not want that? Everyone I know wants that. When I question other reporters about bias, I get blank stares. It's like asking fish about water. "What water?" say the fish.

The hometown newspaper for most everyone in my business is the *New York Times*. It shouldn't have much influence, because its readership is so small—about a million people a day (compared to the networks' 30 million viewers), and I assume readers who reach, say, page A16 total only a few thousand. Yet the *New York Times* matters more because other media copy it—sycophantically. When I worked at WCBS-TV, the editor clipped articles from that morning's *Times* and gave them to us as our assignments. The newscast was a video version of the *Times* (shorter and dumber because we did only the most TV-friendly stories). That's how bias in the *Times* becomes bias on TV, not to mention in *Time, Newsweek,* and the rest.

On August 19, 2000, the front page of the *New York Times* featured a picture of the North Pole; the accompanying news story said: "The North Pole is melting. The thick ice that has for ages covered the Arctic Ocean at the pole has turned to water . . . something that has presumably never before been seen by humans and is more evidence that global warming may be real and already affecting climate."

Oops . . . Ten days later the *Times* apologized, saying it "misstated the normal conditions of the sea ice there. A clear spot has probably opened at the pole before, scientists say, because about 10 percent of the Arctic Ocean is clear of ice in a typical summer."

But by then the *Washington Post, USA Today,* AP, NPR, American TV networks, Canadian TV, and papers in London had repeated the story. *NBC Nightly News* talked about "a mile-wide stretch of water where ice should be." CNN said the ice cap "is losing its ice." CNN, CBS, and Canadian TV interviewed the same "global warming expert" who was quoted by the *Times*.

THAT CONSERVATIVE ON ABC

This media climate helps explain why some people call me "that conservative on ABC."

I'm hardly what I would call conservative. I happen to think consenting adults should be able to do just about anything they want. I think prostitution should be permitted. (If quarterbacks and boxers make money with their bodies, why can't a woman make money with hers?) I believe homosexuality is perfectly natural, that the drug war should be ended, that flag burning and foul language should be tolerated, and most abortion should be legal. This is conservative? Real conservatives should be insulted.

But the mainstream media are tilted so far to the left that they call me conservative.

I guess they call me that because I believe the free market is a good thing—but what's conservative about the market? It's unplanned, unpredictable, scary, noisy. "Libertarian" is a better term for my beliefs. But it's a lousy word. People think it means "libertine," and the Libertarian Party has had flaky people like Howard Stern run for office. Maybe "classical liberal" is a better term for what I am. Liberals were originally the ones who advocated freedom and tolerance.

Not lately.

THE JADED CRUSADER

I was discussing my first special, "Are We Scaring Ourselves to Death?", on a talk radio program when a caller said, "Watch out for Howard Kurtz. He's the enforcer for the liberal interest groups." I thought it was a silly comment. Howard Kurtz writes about media for the *Washington Post*. He'd never written about me, and I saw no reason to "watch out."

But a few months after the broadcast, I received an angry phone call from a leftist group demanding that I respond to accusations about my heresy. They were going to put them in their newsletter. I declined. One hour later, a call came from Howard Kurtz.

He told me he was writing a lengthy profile of me for the *Post*, and wanted to come to New York to interview me. Now I think it's unfair to call Kurtz an "enforcer" for the liberal interest groups. The timing of the call was probably coincidence, but it was clear I was now "a problem" on the media radar screen.

Kurtz's article was titled "The Jaded Crusader."

He quoted Sidney Wolfe of the Ralph Nader–founded group Public Citizen, saying I was "a menace . . . doing a massive amount of damage." And Nader himself: "He's the most dishonest mass-media journalist I have ever encountered."

At the time, my work was watched by about 20 million people. Presumably some of you thought it was good, but Kurtz found only critics to quote.

That *Washington Post* article was the first major assault on my "leap from consumer advocate to friend of industry," as the *Post* put it.

Hello? Why am I no longer a consumer advocate when I scrutinize government? Doesn't government cheat consumers, too?

Why am I a "friend of industry" because I like free markets? Many in industry despise free-markets, and try to use cronyism and government connections to rig the system to avoid free market competition. I'm a friend of entrepreneurship, but is there something wrong with that? Entrepreneurship brings us many of the best things we have.

But this is how the press operates. In the culture where I work, it is assumed that business does evil in pursuit of profit, while government and consumer groups do the Lord's work.

Even basic free-market principles are doubted, if not mocked. One of my worst battles with ABC legal review was over a "Give Me a Break" segment on rent control. Limiting rent increases may sound good to tenants, but it hurts most renters because landlords have no incentive to renovate or to build new apartments. Also, since people would be fools to leave rent-controlled apartments, the market's natural turnover is asphyxiated. The elderly don't move out to make room for young families. Families don't move on when they outgrow their apartments. Virtually all professional economists agree that rent control causes housing shortages. Walter Williams said, "Short of aerial bombardment, the best way to destroy a city is through rent controls." My piece merely complained that under rent control, privileged New Yorkers like Carly Simon, Mia Farrow, and Alistair Cooke paid minuscule rents for huge apartments, while newcomers had to pay a fortune, or had trouble finding any housing at all.

It seemed like a straightforward piece to me, but an economically illiterate ABC lawyer kept blocking it. He argued that in New York City, ending rent control would hurt the poor. He demanded that we interview more economists and "soften" the tone of the piece. Later I learned that the lawyer lived in, you guessed it, a rent-controlled apartment.

BOYS AND GIRLS ARE DIFFERENT

My first special after "Are We Scaring Ourselves to Death?" was "Boys and Girls Are Different: Men, Women, and the Sex Difference."

Strangely, saying that boys and girls are different was controversial on network television in 1995. My boss, executive producer Victor Neufeld, said, "You are going to catch hell for this one."

All I said in the show was that gender differences are probably *not* entirely the result of sexist child-raising and sexist media propaganda, that research now suggests there are genuine differences in the way men's and women's brains operate. At conception both sexes begin life as the same clump of cells, except for the Y chromosome in males. Waves of testosterone must be added for that clump of cells if the fetus is to become male.

Brain researcher Dr. Laura Allen of UCLA told us, "Testosterone kind of rides a roller coaster until birth. We know the first rise of testosterone causes the development of the male sex organs. We don't know what the second rise of testosterone does. I suspect it causes our brains to be different. . . .

"As I began to look at the human brain more and more, I kept finding differences, and about seven or eight out of 10 structures that we actually measured turned out to be different between men and women." Other researchers told us these brain differences may explain why women are often better at reading feelings, men at reading maps.

One could still argue that these differences develop because of some very early sexist parenting, except that differences show up in newborns.

June Reinisch, former director of the Kinsey Institute, told us, "When they look at babies in the first 72 hours of life, they find that males and females are not identical in the way they behave. Males startle more than females. If you give a little puff of air on their abdomen, they [are] much more likely to startle than females," while "females rhythmically mouth, they suck on their tongues, they move their lips and so forth, more than males do." Infant girls sit up without support earlier than boys, while boys crawl away from their caretaker earlier than girls. This happens before parents have much influence.

It wasn't a sexist show. It just said men and women are not the same—that we should celebrate our differences rather than deny they exist. "Equality means that people should have equal opportunities," said June Reinisch. "It doesn't mean that everybody is the same, or that we want everybody to be the same. Difference is good."

This was controversial?

I did "Boys and Girls Are Different" because watching my own kids and their friends made me question what I'd been taught about gender. At Princeton I had absorbed the teachings of the egalitarian wing of the women's movement, and when I started work as a reporter, I believed it totally. Clearly, the horrible history of patriarchal discrimination was the only reason men and women behaved differently. Now that we were enlightened, everything would change. There would still be physical differences, but if parents and society treated boys and girls identically, other gender differences would vanish.

Then I had kids, and saw what an idiot I was.

I was obsessive about eliminating every sexist influence. I pored over my daughter's books and changed the "he's" to "she's." I prevented my friends and relatives from giving her the "sweet little girl" treatment, and tried to raise her in a totally gender-neutral way. The only video entertainment I brought was She-Ra, Princess of Power. It depicted women as leaders and superheroes.

My gender-neutral parenting didn't take. I threw balls to my daughter, and she drew faces on them. She and her girlfriends *talked* about things, smiled at me, and looked adults in the eye. My son and his friends kicked the ball, and ran around crashing into walls.

I know this proves nothing. I hadn't controlled all the social influences—and even if I could, my two kids don't make up a trend. But I kept noticing biology at work. I had some aggressively antigun friends who wouldn't allow toy guns in the house; they soon found their sons "shooting" with carrots.

So I started reading more about the science, and quickly learned that it went well beyond Dr. Allen's and the Kinsey Institute's work. There was lots of research that suggested what parents had said for years was true: Males and females are biologically hardwired to be different. The research just hadn't been publicized, because it wasn't politically correct.

My favorite experiments were the ones done at the University of Rochester and York University. Rochester students were blindfolded and then walked through a maze of tunnels that run underneath the campus. Then they were asked how to get to a particular college building. The men said things like "Go through the next doors, take a left and a right, then a left."

Women said things like "How would I know?"

Men's brains are somehow better at sensing where they are. Women, on the other hand, tend to have a better memory for detail. York University students were asked to wait two minutes in a cluttered room while an experimenter got something ready. That request was a trick. The real purpose of the test was to see what people remembered. After the students left the cluttered room, the experimenter asked what was in the room.

Women gave stunningly detailed answers, like "On the right-hand side of the desk, right here, was a briefcase with your initials at the top. Then there was a clock with an 'I am 40' button on it. In the middle there were York University envelopes. There was a thing of Clearasil and a Bazooka Joe comic. . . ." And so on. Men said things like "What was in there? I dunno . . . some stuff."

The researchers were just excited about studying why these differences exist. But some feminists said this kind of research shouldn't even be done.

I interviewed Gloria Steinem. I'd admired her for what she'd accomplished, and assumed that when I brought up the science, she'd say, "Of course there are differences, but sexism makes them worse." No. She wouldn't admit *any* differences! Sexist parenting is what makes boys different, she said dismissively. "We badly need to raise our boys more like our girls."

Feminist lawyer Gloria Allred appeared on the show to say I shouldn't even be doing the show. "We take attacks from the media on our skills and our abilities and our talents and our dreams very seriously," she said. "This is harmful and damaging to our daughters' lives, and to our mothers' lives, and I'm very angry about it."

What? Is she a leader of the thought police? My show wasn't even an "attack"—it was an attempt to understand differences. It's better to act on the basis of what is true than to maintain that it has no right to be true. And we can't know what's true unless we have free inquiry. Acknowledging gender differences doesn't mean the women's movement was wrong or should be reversed. I don't want it reversed! Who wants to go back to the days when my daughter would be discouraged from becoming a lawyer or doctor, and when men barely got involved with nurturing their children? Nevertheless, the "equality feminists" had become so dominant in academia and the media that they felt they had the right to demand that gender differences should not even be discussed. Free inquiry is often exactly what the left doesn't want.

Dr. Allen said that feminist political correctness was so stifling on many campuses that scientists had been frightened away from trying to study gender. Colleagues told her, "Don't do this kind of research."

Leftist dogma is so pervasive on campuses that the novel ranked "most influential" in their lives by the largest number of readers responding to a Library of Congress and Book of the Month Club survey is almost never even mentioned in women's studies courses, even though the book was written by a woman. The novel is *Atlas Shrugged* and it continues to sell more than 100,000 copies a year. But the left doesn't want Ayn Rand's ideas discussed.

At the time I did "Boys and Girls Are Different," cities, to get more women into fire departments to avoid accusations of sex discrimination, were "gender-norming" qualification standards. Since men have twice the upper-body strength, some fire departments just dropped the strength test. Kate O'Beirne of the Heritage Foundation put it in perspective: "If I, as an all-suffering taxpayer, have to be evacuated from a building, I used to be carried by a male firefighter. I am now dragged by my ankles, as my head hits every single stair going down three stories. I prefer being carried. I assume most taxpayers prefer being carried."

I passed that thought on to Gloria Steinem. I love her response: "It's better to drag them out because there's less smoke down there. We were probably killing people by carrying them out at that height."

It was so bizarre, I couldn't believe what I was hearing. Then she said sex differences shouldn't even be researched. "It's really the remnant of anti-American, crazy thinking to do this kind of research," O'Beirne says. "It's what's keeping us down, not what's helping us."

Don't even do the research? It's the censorship by the thought police that's truly un-American.

TAMPERING WITH NATURE— OR WITH KIDS?

I learned more about that from the reaction to another special, "Tampering with Nature," which challenged scaremongers who were preaching environmental doom and gloom.

Living with nature, I pointed out, really means running around naked, maybe killing a rabbit with a rock, then dying young, probably before age 40. That was natural life for most of human history.

Tampering with that way of life has been *good* for people. While too much tampering can be bad, building houses, and cultivating land and fertilizing it with chemicals, have allowed us to nearly double our life spans without crippling nature.

Yet on Earth Day every year, and in schoolrooms most every day, environmental activists tell kids that humankind is the enemy.

We filmed "environmental educators" telling schoolchildren in Los Angeles that President George W. Bush and his "friends in the oil business" were polluting the land and killing caribou in Alaska. They got the kids to write letters to their congressmen complaining about the President. This they called "nonpartisan" instruction.

I thought the activists were indoctrinating, not educating, children. Afterward, the kids were frightened. They feared massive floods, increased cancer, and drowning in our own garbage. They were convinced America was dying in a sea of pollution. Kids said that because of global warming "Alaska was melting" and "cities will soon be under water."

Boy: Floods will happen, and we won't be able to breathe. And if we can't breathe, we'll probably go extinct.

John Stossel: Is America getting more polluted?

Children: (In unison) Yes.

John Stossel: Is the water and air getting more polluted?

Children: (In unison) Yes.

Why not tell the kids the truth? As I said earlier, the EPA reports that over the past 30 years, the air and water have been getting cleaner. But the kids don't believe it.

John Stossel: The government says over the past 30 years it's been getting cleaner.

Children (All at once): No. They are so wrong. He's lying!

There is a reason the children fear the earth is dying: It's because the environmental movement "has been hijacked by political activists who are using environmental rhetoric to cloak agendas like class warfare and anticorporatism that in fact have almost nothing to do with ecology," said environmentalist Patrick Moore, a former director of Greenpeace who quit the organization. He quit because he came to believe that the environmental movement had become an industry addicted to raising money through unscientific scaremongering.

The biggest scare now is global warming. Here, too, the activists (and the media) tell only part of the story. It made headlines when 1,600 scientists signed a letter warning of the "devastating consequences" of global warming. But I bet you never heard that 17,000 scientists signed a petition saying there's no convincing evidence that greenhouse gases will disrupt the earth's climate. That was less exciting "news."

There's no doubt that there's been a slight warming, about one degree in the past hundred years, and it looks kind of scary if you isolate that.

CHART 6

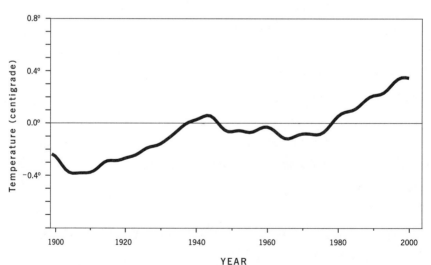

But when you get some historical perspective, you see it is not such a big deal. In fact, over the past 10,000 years, there have been big cycles of warming and cooling, and for most of those years, the earth was warmer than it is today.

CHART 7

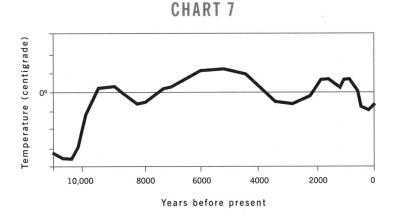

"Tampering with Nature" pointed out that it is by no means clear that human action affects temperature much, or that "fixes" like the Kyoto treaty would do any good. If the treaty were ever implemented, Kyoto's costs would certainly make life harder for millions of poor people. The "environmental educators" didn't want viewers to hear that, and so they set out to undermine my reporting.

If you watched "Tampering with Nature" you didn't get to see the *first* group of schoolchildren we interviewed. Just days after consulting with activists, the parents of some of the kids in that first group suddenly withdrew their consent. With the help of the Environmental Working Group, an organization that had been criticizing my reporting and asking ABC to fire me, they distributed a letter claiming I had manipulated their kids.

Their campaign got lots of publicity. "Stossel oughta pick on kids his own size," wrote the *New York Daily News*. "More underhanded reporting from ABC News" crowed TomPaine.com, the Web site funded by Bill Moyers and his son. "Stossel's Latest Stunt Puts Him at the Back of the Classy," was the headline in the *Chicago Tribune*. The *New York Times* reported that "several parents said they had given ABC permission to interview their children after they had been led to believe that their children would be asked straightforward questions about environmental issues." However, "Mr. Stossel asked leading questions to get them to say what he wanted."

I never asked the kids "leading questions." I asked, "Is America getting more polluted?" and "What will happen to the earth?" That was enough to bring out their litany of doom. Some of the parents who later complained were present at the taping. We heard no complaints then. They were all smiles, and many told us it was a "great experience." It was only *after* the activists got involved that some parents changed their minds about wanting their kids to be on TV. ABC chose to honor their request. We threw out that videotape and interviewed another group of kids. I asked the same questions—and got the same frightened answers.

No one needs to "lead" kids to get them to say things like "Alaska is melting." The activists' indoctrination has misled them about the state of the earth. The activists don't want objective reporting on the environment; they want to scare people. What the Environmental Working Group is afraid of is not bias—it's truth.

THE ORGANIC FOOD HOAX

Unfortunately, a year earlier, I'd given them a perfect chance to discredit me. I made a dumb mistake in a *20/20* report on organic food. Promoters make organic food sound so great. "All natural. No pesticides.

No chemicals. Pure as Nature." They've convinced people that organic food has almost magical qualities. Our cameras caught customers in "health food" markets fondling organic vegetables as if they were religious icons. No wonder organic food is the runaway hit of the food business. It costs much more, but if it's healthier, it's worth it.

But it isn't. "Unfortunately, you've been hoaxed," said Dennis Avery. "Organic food is less good for you and less good for the environment." Avery, a former research analyst for the State Department who directs the Hudson Institute's Center for Global Food Issues, pointed out that the organic food craze is founded on myths.

The biggest myths are that organic food is healthier because it's pesticide-free, and that it contains more nutrients. Neither claim is true.

Organic food is rarely "pesticide-free." Tests by Consumers Union and the U.S. Agriculture Department found pesticide residue on organic food, too. That's because much of what's called organic food isn't really organic, and even if it were, pesticides from other fields often spread to organic crops. In my report—this was my mistake—I said "our tests" found no pesticide residue on organic or conventional food. Turned out a producer misunderstood the scientists who did the testing for us. They had searched only for bacteria. They did no tests for pesticide residue.

Not that pesticide residue matters much anyway. Clearly, organic food is less likely to contain synthetic pesticide residues than regular produce is, but so what? Farmworkers and their children are exposed to much higher levels of pesticides, and they are as healthy as anyone else. Anyway, 99 percent of the pesticides we ingest are natural ones, produced by plants to fend off pests. These natural pesticides may be loved by devotees of organics, but they contain chemicals that are known to be endocrine disrupters, neurotoxins, and carcinogens. In 1999 the National Research Council concluded that "the total exposure to naturally occurring carcinogens exceeds the exposure to synthetic carcinogens."

Don't get me wrong: I'm not saying the natural pesticides are a threat.

There's no evidence that these tiny residues of pesticides—natural or synthetic—hurt anybody. A National Academy of Sciences report says the level of the chemicals is "so low that they are unlikely to pose an appreciable cancer risk."

The point was that even if organics were pesticide-free, the gain wouldn't make up for the downside of organic food: It's more likely to be infested with bacteria because it's grown in "natural" fertilizer. Natural fertilizer is the health food business's euphemism for cow manure. (The much-criticized "nonorganic" produce is grown in nitrogen fertilizers. Although organics advocates sneer at the chemicals, "chemical" nitrogen is perfectly healthy; air is 78 percent nitrogen, after all. We have a choice between foods grown in nitrogen taken from the air, and "organic" food grown in cow manure.)

Cow manure, of course, is crawling with bacteria. It's fecal matter. Before organic farmers use manure, they are supposed to heat it by composting it for 120 days at a minimum temperature of 131 degrees to kill any dangerous bacteria. But Avery says lots of organic farmers don't bother. "They're not even using thermometers," he says. "They're out there dumping stuff in piles and guessing."

There are plenty of dumb food-safety scares (food dyes, nitrites, NutraSweet, cyclamates, etc.), but bacteria are genuinely dangerous. Last time you had the flu, it might not have been flu. It might have been *E. coli* or salmonella. "Approximately 76 million [one in every four Americans] get sick each year with one of these organisms," said Dr. Lester Crawford, who ran the Food and Nutrition Center at Georgetown University. Most of the time you don't know you've been sickened by your food—you assume it's a virus.

Some people get seriously sick. The Centers for Disease Control say every year thousands of Americans die from bacteria in food.

So we decided to run tests to see if Avery was right. Does organic food contain more bacteria? *20/20* paid Dr. Michael Doyle of the University of

Georgia to run the tests. There was good news: Broccoli, parsley, and celery —organic and conventional—were generally bacteria-free. But a third of the sprouts and prebagged lettuce called spring mix had "sewage contamination." There was more bacteria on the organic than on the nonorganic produce.

This is not a huge deal. America's food supply, including organic food, is basically safe. Even if *E. coli* is present in produce, washing it well may get rid of it.

But the important point is that organics' big selling point—that the stuff is better for you—is bunk. This is good news for poor people. Many parents who can't afford to pay twice as much for organic peanut butter feel sad about depriving their kids of "the healthiest" food. If they only knew the truth: The cheaper stuff is just as good.

"They've got us worrying about exactly the wrong thing," said Avery. "If we've got no deaths from pesticides and 5,000 deaths from bacteria, it's pretty clear to me that we should be worrying now primarily about the nasty new bacteria."

When I confronted Catherine DiMateo of the Organic Trade Association about the bacteria, she had a careful answer.

Catherine Dimateo: It's as nutritious as any other product.
John Stossel: Is it more nutritious?
Catherine Dimateo: It is as nutritious as any other product on the market.

Now *there's* a sales campaign to dream about: "More expensive—not more nutritious." When the organics industry representative is on national TV, she has to admit the truth, that organics are no more nutritious. But in the health food stores, the sales staff passionately tells people organics will make them healthier, happier, stronger, and smarter. Sales keep rising.

If organics are no healthier, are they at least better for the planet?

Even that isn't true, says Avery, because organic farmers waste so much land. They're forced to use more because they lose so much of their crop to weeds and insects. "Agriculture takes a third of the earth's surface right now," he says. "If overnight all our food supply were suddenly organic, to feed today's population, we'd have plowed down half of the world's land area not under ice to get organic food."

The real environmentalists are today's *conventional* farmers, says Avery, the nonorganic ones. They have performed an environment-saving miracle by using chemical fertilizers and pesticides, and genetically engineered seeds. "Today's modern farmer produces more food on less land, and the food he produces is safer than it's ever been," says Avery. Yet "his reputation has been trashed all over the Western world by organic farmers who claim they're better, but offer no evidence."

THE TOTALITARIAN LEFT

I think that's news the public should hear. But the left does not want such ideas broadcast. Organic food faddists and environmental activists expect media cheerleading, and they usually get it. Marian Burros of the *New York Times* has done 100 columns praising organic food. No wonder some activists said, "How dare John Stossel suggest organic food is no better?"

Well, organic food *is* no better. Unfortunately, my mistake gave my detractors a chance to discredit the entire report.

After the story aired, people wrote long letters of complaint to my bosses. Some objected to my "tone." Some criticized the bacterial test we used (although it was the same one the government uses). Some said I, or my sources, were "in the pocket of big chemical companies." Buried among these attempts to intimidate was a question that went to the heart of the error in the story: Who tested the produce for pesticides?

The producer confidently provided the names of the scientists who did the tests, and said he had their research results in his office. Unfortunately, none of us double-checked that. Instead, we had long discussions about the critics' objections to the bacterial test (scientists told us the complaints were specious), and about other issues raised in the complaint letters. We somehow overlooked the question about pesticide tests.

Jim Rutenberg didn't. The *New York Times* media reporter diligently asked for the names of the scientists, got them, called them, and was told they hadn't tested produce for pesticides, only for bacteria. Rutenberg shocked us with the news.

Many anxious phone calls later, the producer, who was on his way to Africa to do a *20/20* story, reassured us by phone that the tests had been done; Rutenberg must have talked to the wrong scientists. He was certain he had pesticide test results in his office. He was immediately summoned back to search for them. Unfortunately, he never found any. Apparently he'd confused the bacterial tests with pesticide tests. Or confused tests on chicken with tests on produce. In any case, we had done no pesticide tests.

Now I had become news. It seemed my mistake was trumpeted in headlines in every newspaper read by everyone I knew. ABC called me back from a family vacation in Massachusetts to attend a meeting where we would decide what to do. I had time for one last hike on the Appalachian Trail and stopped at a Parks Department building to ask for directions. I was met by a trail guide wearing a T-shirt that proclaimed "100% Organic!" "Aren't you Stossel, that guy who lied about organic food?" he asked me. I mumbled something about how I hadn't exactly lied, and that the crux of the story was true, but he just glared and sullenly gave me directions. Fearful of where they might lead us, my family just took a shorter hike and returned to New York.

I apologized for my mistake before a nationwide audience on network television, and all transcripts of the story were withdrawn from abcnews.com. This course of action was decided on after a series of meetings that went all the way to the top of ABC News. The producer who gave us the wrong information was suspended, and I was reprimanded for not double-checking.

The apology was torturous. I stared at the camera for three long minutes and confessed what I'd done wrong. I thought that this humiliation would be the end of the story. But the nasty publicity was just beginning.

What happened after my mistake shows what the left does when it's orthodoxy is challenged. The Organic Trade Association and environmental activist groups wrote my bosses more long letters, demanding that I be fired. Correcting the record was not sufficient; reporters like me must be taken off the air. (I should be grateful they don't want me killed.) One created a Web page titled "Give Me a Fake," and got the trial lawyers' favorite public relations firm, Fenton Communications (which previously brought us the breast implant scare) to spread word of my "fakery." In a headline, a far-left group called Fairness and Accuracy in Reporting distorted my mistake into intentional deceit: "Stossel Fabricated Data." TomPaine.com bought a big ad in the *New York Times* that went on about my "journalistic fakery" and "fabricated and distorted evidence."

Give me a break. Here's the entire error: "And what about pesticides? Our tests surprisingly found no pesticide residue on the conventional samples or the organic."

That was it. Two sentences. (Though I was wrong twice; the show reran before we realized it contained a mistake.) If I had just said "tests find no significant residue," it would all have been true. What bothered the organic food extremists was not a lie, but the truth—the truth revealed in the rest of the report: Organic food costs much more, but is no better. Can't have *that* get out. No wonder the Organic Trade Association demanded ABC "withdraw all archived files containing the story."

CNN, *USA Today,* the *Wall Street Journal,* the *Washington Post,* the *Los Angeles Times,* the *Chicago Tribune,* and others wrote about my mistake. The *New York Times* ran two stories. *The Nation* ran four attacks in one week, explaining that I was a traitor, a consumer reporter who was now a "darling of corporate polluters," willing to make false allegations "to advance a speaking career on the anti-regulatory rubber-chicken circuit." (I do, for the record, speak for fat fees on the "rubber-chicken circuit." I do it because I like sharing the ideas I present in this book. I donate my speaking fees to charity.)

Why so much fuss when the important part of the story was true?

Because a TV reporter questioned the totalitarian left's gods—the "natural food" movement, environmental groups, government regulators, trial lawyers. The totalitarian left is the large and influential part of the political left that is unwilling to debate. They want those who disagree with them muzzled, fired, silenced. They are apoplectic that their worldview, long treated with reverence by the mainstream media, would be subject to skeptical reporting. No reporter may deviate from the party line: Activists, government regulation, and anything "natural" are good; capitalism and chemicals are bad. I must be fired, if only as a warning to others.

Compare the outrage over my mistake to what *didn't* happen when others in my business made bigger mistakes. Dan Rather changed "sometimes hungry" children to kids "in danger of starving." *60 Minutes,* conned by Fenton Communications and other activists peddling junk science, so frightened the public about a pesticide in apples that some mothers poured out their apple juice. Then they told people the Audi 500 would suddenly accelerate without anyone hitting the gas pedal. Both scares were unfounded, but there was no fuss in the media.

The media view the reporters who wrote those stories as just good, objective thinkers who occasionally make a mistake. I, however, had become a heretic. To the left, one contrarian on network TV is one too many.

CHAPTER ELEVEN

It's Not My Fault!

Liberty means responsibility.
That is why most men dread it.
                    —George Bernard Shaw

I *cringe* to admit I sued the World Wrestling Federation. I don't like it when people respond to every injury with a lawsuit. But wasn't I justified? I was in pain. I thought it was important to teach the WWF that it can't go around having reporters beaten up.

Also—I might as well admit it—I was really pissed. I'd been sucker punched by that goon. And after he pummeled my ears, loud noises *hurt*. When my daughter was born, her crying hurt so badly that I would put her down and cover my ears. This is not a good way to begin fatherhood.

So I wanted revenge. *I was a victim.* I sued, and won a fat settlement.

What's wrong with that? Aren't victims entitled to compensation? Well, yes. But compensating victims has an unintended consequence: It encourages us to *be* victims, to hold on to our "victimhood." When you reward something, you get more of it.

Today if you steal money, mutilate your husband, kill your parents, it may be because you're a victim. If you're Washington mayor Marion Barry, caught smoking crack, you're a victim of a racist plot. If you're caught groping the office staff, you're a victim of frotteurism, a disease that compels you to fondle breasts (a dentist in Philadelphia claimed that and sued for disability payments). Caught driving drunk? You're not really responsible. You're a victim of alcoholism.

Don't blame me, it's not my fault.

It's not that Americans are fragile, inclined to victimhood. The country was founded by tough adventurers. They didn't want handouts. They wanted government to leave them alone. This self-sufficiency *built America*. It's also a natural part of human nature. Watching kids on the playground, you see how they test themselves against new obstacles. They struggle to climb, fall, then climb again. No one tells them to do this. Overcoming obstacles makes people feel good about themselves.

In the past few decades, we've corrupted this spirit by passing well-intended laws meant to make life kinder and more "fair." They accomplish neither.

THE AMERICANS WITH DISABILITIES ACT

When legislators passed the ADA, they bragged it would "protect 43 million Americans." *Forty-three million?* The number should have raised alarms—it meant one in six of us was disabled. How is that possible? If one in six of us is disabled, what exactly does "disability" mean?

The law defines it as "an impairment that substantially limits your life activities, a record of such impairment, or being regarded as having such an impairment." Wonderfully vague. Vague laws are great for "disability rights" lawyers. The American Bar Association devoted *70 pages* of text to just trying to explain what the word "disability" means. What is an "impairment"? What's a "substantial limitation"? Is being stupid a disability? Feeling compelled to fondle women? Being fat? Who knows? When it goes to court, some judges say no, some say yes. The breast-grabbing dentist didn't win his suit, but that was cold comfort to his insurance company. It still had to pay lawyers' fees. Many businesses settle to avoid these costs.

The ADA requires employers to "accommodate" disabled employees. Maybe I can collect some money. Did my ear pain from my bout with the "wrestler" qualify me for special "accommodation"? How about my stuttering? Maybe *that's* why I don't have Peter Jennings's job. Should I sue ABC?

It's by no means clear that the law has helped the truly disabled. In fact, it's made it *harder* for some to find work.

FEWER JOBS FOR THE DISABLED

Consider the threat the ADA poses to an employer who *wants* to do the right thing. The minefield starts with the job interview. For a *20/20* piece titled "Getting In on the Act," Julie Janofsky, a labor lawyer, patiently explained to me that certain disability-related questions are forbidden. For example, if you come to my office with your arm in a sling and ask me for a job . . .

John Stossel: Can I ask, "Are you disabled in some way I should know about?"

Julie Janofsky: No. You cannot ask if I'm disabled, even if I come in with my arm in a sling.

John Stossel: It would be discriminatory just to ask?

Julie Janofsky: That's correct.

John Stossel: Can I ask you if you've been addicted to drugs?

Julie Janofsky: No. You cannot ask any questions about prior drug addiction.

John Stossel: Can I ask you if you're addicted now?

Julie Janofsky: Yes, but not to legal drugs. You can ask me if I'm addicted to marijuana and cocaine now. You can't ask me if I'm addicted to Valium now, because if I'm addicted to Valium now, I'm protected under the ADA.

How are employers supposed to understand this? I confronted Gilbert Casellas, head of the Equal Employment Opportunity Commission under President Clinton. He said the ADA is a wonderful law, and had the nerve to say it *isn't complicated*. "None of this stuff is rocket science," he said.

"That was a perfect setup line," I thought, so I asked him about Janofsky's example:

John Stossel: If you come to me applying for a job, and your arm is in a sling, can I ask you why your arm is in a sling?

Gilbert Casellas: You can ask—you know what? I'm going to ask you to stop the tape, because we're getting into—

John Stossel: You want to check—?

Gilbert Casellas: We're getting into a complicated area of what you can and cannot ask at the appropriate time.

Oh, I see; we're into a "complicated area." Knowing what job interview questions are illegal is too complicated for the head of the EEOC, but every employer is America is supposed to understand it. At his request, we stopped taping while he consulted with one of his assistants. They discussed the issue for about five minutes, and then Casellas indicated he was ready to resume. So I repeated the question:

John Stossel: You come in with your arm in a sling, I can't ask you what's wrong?

Gilbert Casellas: You can ask me whether I can do the job.

John Stossel: You say the interview rules are simple. You run the EEOC— you don't even understand them well enough. You have to stop and ask your assistant what the rule is.

Gilbert Casellas: Well, because you asked me a specific question, using a specific situation.

That's the point! Every employer is in a specific situation, and lawyers are ready to pounce if they don't do everything according to the law. And the laws are now so complex, it's impossible to obey all of them. Exxon gave Joseph Hazelwood a job after he completed alcohol rehab; he was made captain of the *Exxon Valdez.* One night Hazelwood had several drinks, then went to his cabin and let a subordinate steer. The ship then ran aground. Exxon was sued for allowing it to happen. So then Exxon decided employees who've had a drug or drinking problem may not hold safety-sensitive jobs. The result? You guessed it—employees with a history of alcohol abuse sued, demanding their *right,* under the ADA, to hold safety-sensitive jobs. Exxon *can't* win. They get sued if they do, sued if they don't.

What would the head of the EEOC say about that? Amazingly, he said, "That's an easy case." Exxon's restrictions "illegally discriminated."

So I asked if that meant Exxon should *not* have had to pay billions of dollars for the *Valdez* spill?

Casellas answered, "Well, you know, that's another issue."

Not *his* problem.

Well-intended but complicated and unpredictable laws like the ADA eventually hurt the people they were meant to help. They cause employers to avoid the disabled. One poll found that since the ADA was passed, the percentage of disabled men who were employed *dropped*. Why? Some employers told us it was because their lawyers tell them disabled people are "dangerous" because they can become legal liabilities. "Once you hire them, you can never fire them. They are lawsuit bombs," one told me. "So we just tell them the job has been filled."

This unintended consequence of the ADA shouldn't have been a surprise. If you give some workers extra power to sue, employers avoid those "lawsuit bombs."

So the disabled get fewer job offers, while the lawyers get richer.

MORE VICTIMS

Legislators envisioned the ADA helping the blind and people in wheelchairs, but it's mostly people with sore backs and lazy people who have come to use the law. When you give everybody the chance to say, "No, you can't fire me, because my back is sore," you *invite* abuse.

Every year, the number of "disabled" grows. When Boston University fired a professor for sexually harassing students, he sued, saying he couldn't be fired. He was protected by the ADA because he had a "sexual disability." A police officer in North Carolina sued, saying she couldn't work the night shift because she had a "shift work sleep disorder." When a high school tried to fire a guidance counselor who'd been caught with cocaine, he sued, saying he was protected by the ADA because his drug problem was a disability. When GTE fired a man for carrying a loaded gun to work, he sued, claiming his disability, "chemical imbalance," caused him to carry the gun. Such suits often fail, but they cost enough to terrorize some employers into settling.

Dan Kaiser, a young employment attorney I interviewed, was gleeful about the new, lucrative opportunities the ADA gave him. "Now, you can sue in court for emotional injuries," Kaiser said. "You couldn't before. You can sue for punitive damages; you couldn't before. And you have attorney's fees, which can be enormous. . . . They'll likely be $100,000."

SOCIAL SECURITY DISABILITY

Politicians keep expanding the giveaway, rewarding more victims and thereby creating more victims. Social Security was designed to help the elderly and the severely disabled. But today checks go to young men like those I met waiting in line in San Francisco's Social Security office. Their "disability"? Addiction. A strong-looking man named Clay said he got a check because "I'm an alcoholic—smoke too much rock. Smoke weed every day. And I like my heroin, too."

I think addiction is primarily a bad habit—a lack of self-control. But the government labeled addiction a disease. Since disease isn't your *fault*, the kindly social workers decided addicts are entitled to monthly checks.

Most I interviewed didn't even bother to *pretend* they wanted the check for medicine or housing; they admitted they used it to get high. Clay said, "We should not be getting this money. But since it's there, we're going to take it."

Another man, Carter, made his $602.40 check last longer by investing it in his "business." "I take my money from the government and I deal a couple of drugs to make sure I've got money all month."

Many felt *entitled* to their checks. "Everybody has some sort of an addiction," said Mike. "That's society, man. You know?" He said he was willing to work, "but they won't get me a job." When I asked him how many jobs he'd applied for that week, he said, "Hey, I ain't gonna apply for a job."

If he got a job, he'd lose his check.

Dr. Mark Herbst, who ran a detox center in San Francisco, said Social Security Disability encouraged addicts to stay addicted, "because the government becomes the supplier, the enabler. . . . A check's going to encourage you to keep doing what you're doing. Why should you change?"

Why would America encourage people to act like victims? For a TV special we called "The Blame Game," we interviewed Roger Conner, who'd quit a law practice to start the American Alliance for Rights and Responsibilities, a group encouraging people to take responsibility for themselves. The victims movement "started as a way to defend the people who had been made victims by segregation, discrimination, and oppression," said Conner. "Then other groups began to see the benefits of elevating your interest to the state of civil right. And the temptation now is for people who have problems that they can cope with, with great effort, being convinced to give in and wallow in their fate as a victim."

Then the lawyers make it worse, he said, because they encourage people to sue rather than strive. The big awards make "people think, I'd be a chump if I did otherwise. If I take responsibility for what I do and for what happens to me, I'm a fool. Now, when that idea gets loose, America's in trouble. . . . People start thinking that this is the appropriate way to live. . . . Where we're headed is the notion that I never have to insure myself, protect myself, take responsibility for myself, plan for myself because there'll always be someone there to pick up the pieces. You can make demands upon the society, 'Give me my rights!' And now, everybody has rights. Nobody has responsibilities."

MULTIPLE CHEMICAL SENSITIVITY

What taught me how far things had gone was one small workplace in Ithaca, New York. It was filled with "victims" who said they were being poisoned by the office air. This was odd, since most of the windows opened and the building was in a rural area.

But the workers were furious. They complained chemicals emanating from a new rug gave them a zillion different symptoms—memory loss, headaches, sore throats, "severe mouth infections," a "metal taste in your mouth," "shortness of breath," "burning, itching, tearing eyes."

Four said they were sick *all* the time. They said the building gave them a disease called multiple chemical sensitivity, or MCS. This meant they were hypersensitive; just a whiff of copier fluid could disable them. Their doctors went along, declaring them totally disabled. One of the employees, Jim Ellis, said, "My life's been ruined. My wife can't put on perfume in the house. And my son at times can't play with me."

Jim and the others worked for Tompkins County's Social Services Department, the agency charged with dispensing services to "victims." Is that a coincidence? Or does being in the "victim business" make you susceptible to *becoming* a victim? I think it's the latter.

The Social Services Department went out of its way to accommodate its "sick" employees. Tompkins County hired a self-professed environmental expert to test if there was anything wrong with the building. His tests found no problems, but he did point out that the office photocopiers give off fumes. So the county installed vents to suck any fumes out of the building. One vent cost $3,000.

Not enough! said the workers. We're still sick. The environmental expert said that maybe it was the carbonless paper. This was the same paper restaurants use for credit card receipts. It's not known for "chemically assaulting" diners or waiters. Of course, there were larger amounts of the paper in the county's offices, so the cringing Tompkins County bureaucrats agreed to pay someone to photocopy *every single piece* of paper so these workers never had to touch it.

Not enough! said the workers. You also have to photocopy every single *old* form stored in the basement, and every single form that's *touched* carbonless paper. The county did.

Even that wasn't enough. Margaret Marks said, "I got awful sick." Her co-worker, Claudia Cinquanti, said, "I had to bring her to the emergency room."

So the workers demanded that the county make the photocopies elsewhere offsite and keep them in storage for at least 24 hours. The county agreed, and moved all of the new carbonless paper forms into a separate storage area.

But even this accommodation wasn't sufficient, said the workers. So the county built them their own special room with its own huge ventilation system, bringing in filtered air from the outside. It installed two air purifiers, one to remove fibers, one to remove chemicals.

Were the workers finally satisfied? No. They sued under the ADA, demanding that the county pay them $800 million.

That got the county to propose even more extreme measures. Officials offered to renovate an entire wing of the building, give the new wing to the complaining workers, and move other employees out.

Not enough! the workers told me. "I am going back to work for Tompkins County, whether they like it or not," said Jim Ellis. "I don't care if they have to build a new building. They're going to accommodate me or they are going to pay."

Lonny Dolin, Tompkins County's lawyer, said, "We ripped out all of the carpeting in your rooms. We built you a scientific room. And you won't come back to work because now you say a simple Xerox paper makes you sick. That's not accommodations. They just say, 'Fix the whole building. Make it perfect or blow it up, whatever.'"

The workers' lawsuits were eventually dismissed, but the legal battle cost the county a fortune.

JUROSOMATIC ILLNESSES

Now the "disabled" workers spend their days at home. Jim Ellis and Margaret Marks have applied for permanent disability. Claudia Cinquanti receives $485 a month in disability payments.

Over the years, I have interviewed two dozen people who say they have multiple chemical sensitivity, and it strikes me that their lives *revolve around being sick.* It's as if being a victim is what gives them purpose.

I was once accused of doing that. When I sued the WWF, their lawyers demanded that I see their doctor. Before he examined my eardrums, the doctor told me, "I think this is a *jurosomatic* illness." "What?" I asked. He said, "It means you hold on to your pain because you're involved in a lawsuit."

I was *furious.* I screamed, "You haven't even examined me, and you're making this accusation?"

He backed down. But guess what? After the WWF settled the suit and paid me, the pain slowly went away. Was it "jurosomatic"?

Are the symptoms of the Tompkins County employees jurosomatic? I don't know. Doctors are reluctant to infuriate their patients by suggesting that, but it's odd that the first "sick building" complaints were filed by workers at the U.S. Environmental Protection Agency. If you think terrible chemicals are everywhere, you may *make* yourself sick. My pain was both real and debilitating, but it sure dissipated quickly once I stopped obsessing about my lawsuit.

British psychiatrist Theodore Dalrymple writes the "general rule is this: If you pay people to suffer, they will suffer. . . . Injuries that in the absence of financial reward would be self-limiting become permanently crippling." The Internet, "with its myriad websites established by advocacy and self-help groups," accelerates the problem. "The litigant, formerly healthy, rapidly succumbs to every kind of unprovable ailment: headache, loss of concentration, dizziness, depression, lack of energy, indifference to pleasure, anxiety." This often reduces an active person to "a gibbering wreck, a permanent invalid obsessed by the minor fluctuations of his bodily sensations. When a man says his whole life has been ruined by some . . . accident, I know—without having to ask—that I am in the presence of litigation. . . . It turns hypochondriasis into a way of life."

I think people who say they have multiple chemical sensitivity are highly susceptible to that kind of influence. Some doctors say MCS is psychosomatic. In fact, years of tests at Denver's Allergy Respiratory Institute have shown MCS sufferers' reactions depend not on what chemicals they encounter, but on what chemicals they *think* they've encountered. In blind tests, patients in a sealed chamber couldn't differentiate between chemicals sprayed into the chamber and salt water sprayed in. Nonetheless, your tax money often pays for their "treatment," and has even been used to build them special "odor-free apartments."

Some of those who claim to have MCS may have added to the cost of your medical insurance by going to that doctor in Maryland, Grace Ziem, who calls herself a "clinical ecologist" and regularly decrees that patients have MCS. Made me wonder: What would she diagnose if *healthy* patients came to see her? So I sent her *two*—ABC employee Debbie Colloton and her sister-in-law Julie. They had everyday symptoms—occasional headaches and trouble sleeping; sure enough, Dr. Ziem told both they were "chemically sensitive." Debbie, she said, should walk around with a "smelling buddy" to warn her of dangerous odors! Ziem charged each woman $900.

I wanted to ask Ziem about all this, but that was the confrontation where she never showed up; instead, she accused me of "illegal taping," and got the Maryland's state's attorney to file criminal charges against me. I suspect she didn't want to be interviewed, because "chemical sensitivity" has become a kind of religion, and the priests don't want anyone raising skeptical questions.

MY ACHING BACK

If MCS is psychosomatic, what about other loosely defined illnesses like fibromyalgia, Gulf War syndrome, and even back pain? We spend billions on treatments, but many doctors doubt these are actual diseases. Yes, the patients are suffering, but maybe the pain is in their heads.

I had back pain for 20 years. I did plenty of *20/20* phone interviews lying on my back, and sometimes the spasms were so severe I couldn't even get out of bed to get to work. I went to doctors, chiropractors, and even an acupuncturist, but their treatments didn't help. Then WCBS consumer reporter Arnold Diaz talked me into going to see Dr. John E. Sarno, a professor of rehabilitation medicine at New York University Medical School. Dr. Sarno tells people the pain is in our heads. Well, not exactly; the pain is real, but it's what is going on emotionally that causes it. People tend to blame back pain on physical abnormalities like disk bulges, but now that MRIs are common, doctors have discovered that lots of people who have bulging or herniated disks experience no pain. There turns out to be very little correlation between pain and abnormalities that show up on X rays.

Dr. Sarno got my attention by asking, "How come it was only after medicine discovered a cure for stomach ulcers that so many people got sore backs?" He tells sufferers that we cause our own pain—unconsciously, of course. He says it's the brain's reaction to stress-induced unconscious rage, and to prevent that rage from coming out, the brain redirects our attention by reducing the blood-oxygen flow to our back (or neck or knee). That causes pain, which distracts our mind from the unacceptable feelings. He says focusing on the pain (by seeing chiropractors or taking painkillers) just keeps the syndrome going. It would go away if we ignored it, resumed physical activities, and thought about the stress in our lives.

This sounded totally stupid. My spasms were *very* severe. My brother has similar back pain. The idea that our pain was in our head was insulting, but I was in enough pain that I was willing to try anything, and in short order, Dr. Sarno changed my life. Just talking to him and reading his book, *Healing Back Pain*, cured me.

Today, when I feel the twinges of pain, I just tell my brain to knock it off, that I must be angry at lawyers, or my wife, or something. The pain goes away. Amazing.

Of course, most M.D.'s are skeptical. My brother Tom, now a Harvard Medical School professor, says Sarno's theory is ridiculous. "Sarno was right in challenging the lack of rigor of surgical approaches," says my brother, "but he is dead wrong in promoting dubious science (neural impulses causing back muscles to lack oxygen)."

When I did the *20/20* story on my experience with Dr. Sarno, I put Tom on as the skeptic. He may be right to doubt Dr. Sarno, but I notice Tom too now mostly ignores his back pain, rather than nursing it and focusing on it—and it goes away. If Dr. Sarno is right, and much of the pain is psychogenic, America's culture of victimhood performs a huge disservice. Back pain claims make up the biggest category of lawsuits filed under the ADA. Medicaid, Medicare, workers' compensation, and private insurance plans spend billions on expensive treatments for it, yet results are spotty; the pain tends to come and go regardless of treatment. It may be that all the sympathetic medical ministration actually prolongs the pain. A safety net is a wonderful thing, but American politicians have gone beyond that to build a welfare state that rewards victims. When you reward something, you get more of it. Almost all of us sometimes have a childish wish to feel sorry for ourselves, to be a *victim*. By catering to that, the government exacerbates our illnesses.

"Seeing ourselves as victims," says Roger Conner, is "a disease that's weakening America's moral fiber. *Living* consists of encountering the weaknesses, the failings that we all have as individual human beings, and the problems that inevitably enter our lives. Dealing with those, that's the stuff of life."

THE "STUFF OF LIFE"

Most of the mail I got after "The Blame Game" aired wasn't about the victims. More people wrote about a tiny bit of good news on the program: Marc Simitian's story.

The ADA was designed to help people like Marc. He's blind. Just getting to work was a struggle for Marc. First he had to make his way though the New York City subway system; then he walked for blocks down broken sidewalks to find the right bus. But Marc didn't consider himself a victim, just a guy trying to get to work.

When he applied for jobs, prospective employers sometimes asked how he would get to work. He told them it wasn't their business.

When we videotaped him, Marc had a job taking flight reservations for Northwest Airlines. He used a Braille device to check flight schedules. In just two months, Marc had become one of the office's top ticket sellers.

Marc didn't know whether the ADA had made it harder or easier for him to find work. He didn't care. He just wanted to work, and wanted nothing to do with victimhood.

Sadly, our government and legal system encourage people not to do what Marc Simitian did. They encourage us to wallow in pain.

CHAPTER TWELVE

But What About the Poor?

The policy of the American government is to leave its citizens free, neither restraining them nor aiding them in their pursuits.

—Thomas Jefferson

A few years ago I was in a New York City youth center about to interview a group of foster kids who were upset about their experiences in "the system," when a tall man in khakis, wire-rimmed glasses, and a button-down shirt came up to me and, his voice filled with venom, said, "I know who you are—you are *evil*. I really hope you die soon." When I recovered enough to ask why, he said, "Your TV programs hurt poor people; you don't deserve to live." He turned out to be a lawyer for a public-interest group that claimed to help the poor.

His accusations infuriated me. I wanted to argue with him, but I just walked away. I've learned that people who spew that kind of venom are rarely open to reason. Because I was a TV reporter who defended capitalism, I was simply "evil." It's not surprising people believe that because the mainstream media consistently suggest that capitalism is cruel. It "exploits" the poor. The Reverend Jesse Jackson has been on CNN so often saying, "There is no roof for the wealthy, and no floor for the poor," he could probably trademark the phrase.

I certainly believed that when I started reporting. My Princeton professors had taught me capitalism was a problem and government was the solution. President Johnson's Great Society would tax the rich and use the money for welfare benefits, job training, and programs like Head Start, and this would mark the beginning of the end of American poverty. I wrote college papers on the ways government programs would "level the playing field," if only a serious effort were launched.

Then a serious effort was launched. The War on Poverty doled out more money than was spent on World War II and the Korean and Vietnam Wars combined. Today means tested government spending totals more than $400 billion a year. How much actually gets to poor people still isn't clear. In 2000, the Rockefeller Institute of Government estimated $13,476 per person. The conservative Heritage Foundation says it's about $8,000 per poor child. A liberal Urban Institute study came up with an average of about $10,000 per child. These numbers alone demonstrate the failure of the War. If you simply gave that money to a poor mom with two kids, their income would be well above poverty level (I'm not suggesting we do that).

Politicians can proudly point to people who were helped by the War on Poverty. I would hope they could point to some! When you give away a trillion dollars, some people will be helped. Look at Table 2.

TABLE 2: POVERTY RATE, 1965–2000

Year	US population (in millions)	Number of "poor people" (in millions)	Percentage of population
1965	191.4	33.2	17.3%
1970	202.2	25.4	12.6%
1975	210.9	25.9	12.3%
1980	225.0	29.3	13.0%
1985	236.6	33.1	14.0%
1990	248.6	33.6	13.5%
1995	263.7	36.4	13.8%
2000	275.9	31.1	11.3%

In 1964, the year President Johnson's "war" began, 19 percent of the population lived below the poverty line. In 2002 the number was down to 11.3 percent (of a larger population). That is an impressive achievement, if you don't look (and the media usually didn't) at the poverty data for the years before (Table 3).

TABLE 3: POVERTY RATE, 1959–1964

Year	US population (in millions)	Number of "poor people" (in millions)	Percentage of population
1959	176.6	39.5	22.4%
1960	179.5	39.9	22.2%
1961	181.3	39.6	21.9%
1962	184.3	38.6	21.0%
1963	187.3	36.4	19.5%
1964	189.7	36.1	19.0%

Table 3 shows that the percentage of Americans living in poverty was steadily decreasing *before* President Johnson rushed in to "help." Just living in America gave poor people the opportunity to lift themselves out of poverty. After the war began, there was a surge of progress but then it slowed and stopped. Some years, the percentage of people living in poverty *increased.* Bizarrely, the War on Poverty perpetuated poverty.

How can this be? It happened because government welfare programs teach people to be dependent.

I was clueless about all this when I started work in Portland, Oregon, in 1969, but I soon sensed something was off as I covered the initiatives of the War on Poverty. At the press conferences, the goals were noble, but when I followed up, the promised success was rarely evident. The activists had nicer offices and bigger organizations—lawyers had been hired to sue or lobby for more money. The poor were still poor. And now they were angry, since they'd been told they were "entitled" to a monthly check and more.

This was the time of riots in ghettos, and Portland had its share. Activists I interviewed told me they and their "clients" had a *right* to more of America's wealth. Since America was a racist, classist society, the underclass "deserved" welfare, food stamps, and housing allowances to level the playing field. Reporters I talked to agreed. When Charles Murray wrote *Losing Ground,* which suggested that welfare kept people poor because it rewarded dependency, my colleagues were horrified.

Years later, when welfare reform was proposed, every expert quoted in the mainstream press predicted disaster. "Families will fracture," wrote the *New Republic.* Richard Gephardt predicted, "A million children will be forced into poverty." Daniel Patrick Moynihan predicted "trauma we haven't known since the cholera epidemics."

But the failure of the current system was so obvious that welfare reform passed anyway. We waited for the disaster, but—surprise—it didn't come. Welfare caseloads fell by half. Some people have suffered, but welfare reform inspired millions to better their lives by finding work. Do the doubters admit they were wrong? Never.

TEACHING DEPENDENCY

The left's vision of an America "that exploits the poor" is just a lie, promoted by politicians who thrive by telling people they are helpless "victims." In truth, opportunity abounds for those who are willing to work. The success of immigrants proves it. Children of immigrants typically earn more than the average American.

There is so much opportunity in America that the "poor" people Americans encounter most frequently are often con artists. I'm talking about panhandlers. For a segment of "Freeloaders" we taped people standing on street corners in Denver holding signs that read, "Will Work for Food." The signs moved me—these men didn't want a handout, they wanted work.

But then we asked them what work they would do. One man's answers were particularly telling.

Jeff Hubert: I just can't work for anybody.

ABC: Would you flip burgers at Burger King?

Jeff Hubert: I wouldn't do it. It's a monotonous job.

ABC: Maybe construction?

Jeff Hubert: I can't do it. My back.

ABC: Would you work five days a week?

Jeff Hubert: That I can't do.

ABC: Why not?

Jeff Hubert: Well, why should I? Why does a human have to work every day if he don't want to?

We approached every "work-for-food" guy we saw and offered him a hot meal and a job mowing grass. We gave them bus tokens to get to where the job was. More than a dozen promised they'd come, but only one did. He said he was an alcoholic who wanted the work only to get money for booze.

Later, in Denver "homeless" shelters, men proudly told me how they cleverly work what they called the "circuit" of 21 soup kitchens. There was never a need to *work* for food. "If you got the IQ above an eggplant," said one, "you'll end up with more food than you're going to eat."

The one Denver homeless shelter that actually has a track record for rehabilitating addicts is run by a former homeless alcoholic named Bob Cote. He says government shelters fail to rehabilitate because "they feel comfortable keeping people helpless, telling them, 'Don't even try.'" He said the welfare state has created a "poverty industry"—an army of bureaucrats and social workers—that is reluctant to put itself out of business. "They've made those people dependent, and they keep them there."

A POVERTY INDUSTRY?

I found it hard to believe that a "poverty industry" would want people kept dependent, but the more I watched the professional antipoverty activists work, the more plausible that seemed. They were overtly hostile to ideas that might diminish dependency.

In my hometown, Mayor Rudy Giuliani demanded that welfare recipients clean streets and parks—"workfare," they called it. "Advocates for the poor" were furious. We taped their demonstrations, where they chanted, "Workfare is slavery!"

ACORN (Association of Community Organizations for Reform Now), one of the coalition of 100 nonprofit and religious groups denouncing workfare, assembled a group of "victims" who told us why workfare "is like slavery."

Pierre Simmons: Somebody gets a call somewhere upstairs, "Hey, man, we need 10 workers on some highway." That's not your job, but they can snatch you from your park and put you on a highway.

John Stossel: And that's like slavery?

Pierre Simmons: Yes, it is.

Carrie Tillman: Why not give me a real job?

John Stossel: Because you didn't get a real job on your own.

Pierre Simmons: I'm picking up dog crap all day long, dead animals. I'm tired of it. I don't like it.

Elliott Roseboro: We make less than $5,000 a year.

John Stossel: So quit and get a job. Nobody's making you do this. Most people find work in America. You could. You're well-spoken, smart people. You don't have to be on welfare.

Jose Nicolau: Where are the jobs? Where are the jobs at? Come on. Be real!

I pulled out that day's *New York Post* and started reading from the long list of help-wanted ads.

The ACORN group laughed derisively.

Jose Nicolau: You've got to look at how much the pay is, too.

John Stossel: . . . delivery person, warehouse work . . .

Pierre Simmons: How much is it paying? Four seventy-five an hour?

John Stossel: Not enough?

Pierre Simmons: A minimum-wage job would kill me. I'd be crushed. No
benefits, no medical . . .

I couldn't believe what I was hearing. First jobs don't pay well, but
they are the first rung on the ladder of opportunity. They teach people
how to show up on time, follow instructions, and handle responsibility.
They give them the self-respect that work alone brings. Then the workers
can move into better jobs. ACORN and the rest of the "poverty industry"
hurt poor people by deriding entry-level work.

And calling workfare slavery is an insult to those who suffered real
slavery. Yes, it would be nice if all workers earned more, but the perfect is
the enemy of the good.

"What you're hearing is the absence of vision," said Errol Smith, a
radio host. "I have worked as a waiter. I have worked as a janitor. I've had
some of the most menial jobs that you can imagine. But they were all
means to an end. I learned something."

We featured Smith in "The Blame Game." We chose him because he is
so passionate about opportunity. He grew up poor in Harlem. His first
business, a hot dog stand, failed. But he kept trying, and 10 years later
was a successful business owner.

"If you're looking for opportunity, you'll find it," he says. "What we
should be doing is the same thing that immigrants routinely do. They see
the opportunity and they go about taking advantage of it."

The "we" he was talking about was American blacks.

If anyone has a right to label themselves victims, blacks do. No other
group has had to endure slavery, Jim Crow laws, and continuing discrimination. The question, however, is what does one do with that? Smith said
"so-called black leaders like Jesse Jackson and Al Sharpton" teach a
destructive message: Racism has stacked the deck against blacks. We're victims, and therefore we cannot be expected to compete on an even footing.

"Where can you go at a minimum-wage job?" roared the Reverend Al when I confronted him about that. "You can barely survive. So that is why a lot of people don't even try that, because it doesn't pay their bills."

Give me a break. My father was penniless when he came to America from Germany. He spoke no English, and the only job he could get was cleaning toilets, and later, fixing them. But 20 years later, he was part owner of a business and a member of the "middle class."

Of course, he was white. But "if the door of opportunity in America is closed to blacks" because of racism, it's hard to explain the success of black immigrants. For "The Blame Game" we visited a Caribbean community in Brooklyn. The prosperity was obvious. The streets and stores were bustling with busy people coming home from work. Here were people who had more to complain about than the workfare workers. Their skin is just as dark, and their ancestors were just as cruelly enslaved, but they had an extra disadvantage: Many could hardly speak English. Yet the Census Bureau says in 2000, 66 percent of New York's Caribbean immigrants over the age of 16 held jobs, while only 53 percent of American blacks did. Six percent of Caribbean immigrants received welfare, and 5.7 percent got Supplemental Security Income, but about twice as many American blacks did. Why? Because Caribbean blacks aren't eligible for governmental assistance until they've been in the United States for two years, says Vera Weekes of the Caribbean Research Center at Medgar Evers College. "So they definitely go out and look for jobs."

I interviewed Marco, a Caribbean immigrant, who told us welfare creates dependency. "It makes some people lazy," he said. He should know. He works for the welfare department.

Welfare and government set-asides continue to "make us dependent," said Errol Smith. "It [welfare] doesn't foster self-reliance. As opposed to individuals and communities recognizing what they can do, it leaves us thinking that we're poor and powerless. . . . Can't accept that. My parents taught me to believe that the American dream is real. . . . That belief empowered me. . . . We appreciate the training wheels, but you can take them off now."

GOVERNMENT HELP
HURTS THE POOR

Often, the more the state helps, the worse things get. Look at what government "help" did to American Indians. Rightfully ashamed by what early settlers had done to the Indians, the politicians tried to make amends by "protecting" the remaining tribes. This "protection" wrecked their lives.

For the show "Mr. Stossel Goes to Washington" we visited Shannon County, South Dakota, home of the Lakota Sioux. The Sioux have been herded and controlled by the government for over a hundred years. The result? No county in America is poorer. "Every month they receive some type of handout from the federal government," a Lakota Sioux member named Dale Looks Twice told us. "So our people become lazy and they don't want to work." Unemployment within the tribe is about 80 percent.

With no culture of work, the tribe's members turned to getting drunk.

Indian activist Russell Means points out that today American Indians "have the least life expectancy. Less than Guatemala. Less than Bolivia, Brazil. Hardly anyone reaches 65 anymore." This happened, he says, because the Bureau of Indian Affairs, the government agency that was supposed to make the Indians' life better, instead made it worse.

"There's no Bureau of Jewish Affairs," Means points out. "There's no Bureau of Irish Affairs. There's no Bureau of Black or African Affairs. . . .

We cannot make a plan or a decision without the express consent of the secretary of interior," says Means. "We submit anywhere from two- to five-year economic plans. Does that sound like the Soviet Union? The old Soviet Union in their failed economic plans?!"

"They sit up there in Washington, D.C.," says Dale Looks Twice, "and they legislate laws that affect us when in fact they don't know what the heck's going on here."

Is there something about the American Indians that makes it hard for them to prosper in the United States? Of course not. Look what happens when a tribe manages to get free of government control. In 1944, the BIA put the Choctaw on a reservation in Mississippi. For two decades, they continued to live in poverty, much like the Sioux.

But then the Choctaw persuaded Congress to exempt them from some BIA rules. Members of the tribe were allowed to manage their own lives. In 1969 the tribe opened its first company, Chahta Development, to build housing. Twenty years later, the Choctaw were wealthy. The tribe now has factories that generate hundreds of millions of dollars in sales. Every Indian who wants a job has one, and they even hire non-Indians from off the reservation. They've built their own school and hospital, and a thousand new homes. They are prosperous—because government left them alone.

THE PRIVATE SECTOR DOES IT BETTER

But government keeps trying anyway. The planners always have such good intentions. But again and again, their plans make life worse.

In the name of giving the poor better places to live, the Department of Housing and Urban Development spent billions on public housing. Some people have homes now, but the overall result is not pretty. In housing projects all across America, elevators don't work, repairs aren't made, and crime is rampant. Sometimes the failure is so stunning, the government just gives up and blows up the project. Between 1996 and 2001, HUD demolished 44,089 units in 90 housing authorities in Atlanta, Chicago, Detroit, New Orleans, Philadelphia, Washington, D.C., and other cities.

Yet government keeps promising to "house the needy." An honest press release would say: "HUD will spend a vast amount of your tax money to build a monstrous apartment complex that will quickly deteriorate into a crime-ridden slum and make life worse for the people who live there." Don't think I'll see that release soon.

During the Clinton administration, HUD secretary Andrew Cuomo took the pandering to new lows: He sent out press releases that said, "Andrew Cuomo makes the American dream achievable" and "Cuomo awards $10 million." Cuomo made it sound as if he were giving *his* money away. Cuomo's press releases also promised public housing residents "a safe, clean, decent place to live." Did he deliver? Has any administration? No.

Some housing officials say it's the tenants who are the problem. Many won't pay their rent. They vandalize their own buildings. But if the tenants are the reason public housing is in sorry shape, how do you explain what can happen when government gets out of the way?

We videotaped at an apartment complex in the middle of one of the poorest sections of New York City. It was clean and well maintained. Playgrounds were filled with happy children. It wasn't always this way.

"When this was a public housing project," says resident Dave Burrell, "living here was hell. There were some 4,000 broken windows. The elevators wouldn't work for months at a time. This place was a shambles."

Residents told us the government let the building run down. They said half the place had no heat, and more than a hundred apartments were controlled by drug dealers. "Management just let it happen," said one resident. "People are civil servants. They get paid at the end of the week whether they do their work or not."

But then a private developer took over and did odd things. He brought in musicians to work with the kids, gave karate lessons, built a new playground. "For the first time in a lot of years, they had children running around in that park," says Burrell.

The housing project's new private managers decided little things like karate lessons would send the message that management cared. That attracted new tenants, and encouraged existing ones to treat the project with respect. Under private management, everything changed. The profit motive worked better than government handouts.

CHARITY

Private enterprise won't solve all problems. The sick, the mentally ill, and the truly helpless need direct help. But why is government always the first choice? Why not private charity? The fall of the Soviet Union should have shown us that government doesn't do things very well.

I once thought there was too much poverty for private charity to make much of a difference. Now I realize that private charity would do much more—if government hadn't crowded it out.

In the 1920s, 30 percent of American men belonged to mutual aid societies, groups of people with similar backgrounds who banded together to help members in trouble. They were especially common among minorities.

Mutual aid societies paid for doctors, built orphanages, cooked for the poor. Neighbors knew best what neighbors needed. They helped the helpless but administered tough love to the rest, taught self-sufficiency.

Mutual aid didn't solve every problem, so government stepped in. But government didn't solve every problem, either. Instead, it caused more problems by driving private charity out. Today there are fewer mutual aid societies because people say, "Why do it ourselves when we already have huge welfare bureaucracies? We already pay taxes for HUD, HHS. Let the professionals do it."

I react that way when I talk to Cheech, a "homeless" man who begs outside my apartment building. He tells me about his gambling and family issues, and I encourage him to consult New York City's social services agencies. I could do more, but I say to myself, "Better leave it to the specialists—my city is spending $30 billion on this already—they have a system for dealing with people like Cheech."

For my special on government we visited Delancey Street, a mutual aid charity in San Francisco. It's a collection of society's worst, hundreds of former street people and ex-cons (18 felony convictions is the average) who live and work together and help one another out.

Delancey Street has been hugely successful. Thirteen thousand people have been though the program. The ex-addicts now run a dozen businesses, including a restaurant and a moving company.

But Mimi Silbert, who started Delancey Street, says it almost didn't happen, because government kept getting in the way. "We have had to fight every bureaucracy that exists." Silbert doesn't employ certified teachers and drug counselors; so, she says, welfare workers tried to smother her with red tape. "If Jesus Christ walked in today and wanted to start Christianity, he wouldn't be able to do it because they'd say to him, 'You need two psychiatrists, you need one social worker, somebody has to sign the things.'"

Fortunately, she fought the bureaucrats and won. Others are beaten down. In Houston, a woman named Carol Porter decided she would feed poor people. She founded a charity called Kid Care. Soon, she and her volunteers were serving 20,000 meals a week. She said her charity worked well because it wasn't a government bureaucracy. "We know the people, get involved in their lives, know their names," she told me. "And when someone at Kid Care needs assistance, we don't have to do a form in triplicate. We give them service right then and there."

But then she accepted a government grant, and with that came rules. One demanded that every child be given a full carton of milk. Porter couldn't believe it. "Even though the child may not drink the milk, I had to place it in front of them. So I was throwing sixty and seventy containers of milk in the garbage every day!" Other rules limited what she could serve, when she could serve it, whom she could serve it to. Eventually she gave up.

Later, she started again, but on a smaller scale, without government aid. Big Government tells both the poor and those who would help them, "Don't try."

THE BEST POVERTY FIGHTER, CAPITALISM

At least the fate of most of the poor does not depend on government or private charity. The world's best poverty fighter is capitalism. Capitalism is held in withering contempt in newsrooms, but it has allowed millions of people to lift themselves out of poverty. We're told capitalism serves the rich at the expense of the poor, but in many ways, capitalism is the big equalizer. "It's the people at the bottom who need capitalism most," says David Kelley of the Objectivist Center, a think tank devoted to exploring ideas popularized by Ayn Rand. They need a "system in which everyone is free to trade and free to pursue money, because capitalism opens up opportunities to climb up that economic ladder." Money doesn't care if you're black or white or green.

Free-market capitalism does allow some people to get much richer than others, but *that's okay.* The inequality may seem unfair, but all that the alternative systems accomplish is to ensure that *everyone* is poor. China, North Korea, and Cuba have worked that out pretty well.

Isn't there a middle ground?

President Clinton used to talk about a "third way—something in between socialism and capitalism." I once I asked Czech Republic president Vaclav Klaus what he thought about that. Klaus had helped move the Czech Republic from communism to capitalism, and his country was the most prosperous of the former Soviet states. Klaus answered, "The 'third way' is the fastest route to the Third World."

That might have been hyperbole, but he had a point. You are either free or not free. Either you choose what you do with your money or government does.

America and Europe are now experimenting with a middle ground, increasingly *regulated* capitalism. But every regulation throws sand in the gears of the economic engine. You see the harm more clearly in Europe because it regulates more. France requires that most employees be given six weeks' vacation and paid parental leave, and makes it very hard to fire anyone. The regulations were intended to make life better for workers, but the unintended consequence is that employers fear hiring anyone, because every employee is more expensive—and nearly impossible to fire.

The result? Employers don't hire many people, and the unemployed stay unemployed. The Bureau of Labor Statistics says that from 1982 to 2002, businesses in the United States created 37 million new jobs. The six leading European countries—France, Italy, Germany, Sweden, Netherlands, and the UK—with almost an identical population, created only half as many jobs. Europe's high taxes and strict regulations are driving out entrepreneurs. In the past 10 years, 300,000 people, many of France's best and brightest, have left—often moving to countries with more limited government.

Free-market capitalism is why, even though government poverty programs fail, poor people in America don't suffer the way the poor have suffered in most of the world. A thriving economy means even the people at the bottom of the ladder do pretty well. One of the biggest health problems facing America's poor is obesity. You know you live in a good place when *over*eating is a problem.

Most of the 6 billion people in the world live short, brutal, miserable lives; 1 billion people try to survive on just a dollar a day. They would love to have the lifestyle of America's poor. Ninety-seven percent of American families our government classifies as "poor" have color televisions and half own *two*. Seventy-five percent of poor people have cars and nearly half own their own homes.

ECONOMIC FREEDOM

You may doubt that a relatively free market is the prime reason America is prosperous. Isn't it our natural resources? Or democracy? Something unique about Americans' character?

No. If you look at societies that succeed at bettering the lives of their people, and compare them to those that fail, it's clear that what makes the difference is economic freedom.

India is desperately poor. When we were filming in Calcutta for the ABC special "Is America #1?", I was surrounded by kids begging. Yet India has democracy, and plenty of natural resources. Then why is India poor? The popular answer is overpopulation, but that's totally wrong.

The population density of India is roughly equal to that of New Jersey. New Jersey does pretty well.

If overpopulation or lack of resources created poverty, then Hong Kong should be poor. Hong Kong has 20 times as many people per square mile as India, and no valuable natural resources. Yet Hong Kong is rich; the average income there is higher than in Great Britain or Canada. This is a recent development. In the 1920s, Hong Kong was as poor as India. But in a relatively short time it became rich because of one key ingredient: economic freedom.

Economic freedom prevailed because Hong Kong's British governors provided limited government. They built roads and schools, and enforced simple and understandable laws against murder and theft. But that was about it. Hong Kong thrived because its rulers didn't do too much. After keeping the peace, the British officials basically sat around and drank tea.

No Federal Trade Commission, no OSHA, no labor laws or minimum wage. "When you leave things alone, people just get on with it. It's very simple," said David Tang, who's made lots of money running an elegant club in Hong Kong and selling clothing at a chain of stores called Shanghai Tang.

Bretigne Schaffer, who worked in Hong Kong for the *Asian Wall Street Journal,* told us that without the "crutch" of government handouts, people in Hong Kong are inspired to create things. And thanks to Hong Kong's flat 15 percent tax, they get to keep more of what they create. "It's possible to save enough money that you can start your own business," says Schaffer, "and become very rich." Easier than in America, she says, "with all the different taxes, all the different employee benefits you have to pay out, and all the regulations."

To illustrate that on TV, I decided I would try to open a business in Hong Kong. I found out that I could, without a lawyer, set up a legal business in just one day. All I had to do was wait in one line and fill out one form. The next day I had a booth in a shopping mall selling ABC Frisbees. I failed, of course. ("Is America Number 1?" showed shoppers *not* buying anything from my store.) But the freedom I had to try, and fail, is what allowed Hong Kong to thrive. As Nobel Prize–winning economist Milton Friedman put it, Hong Kong is just a rock, but "on this rock people can produce for themselves a higher standard of living than they can produce in Britain with its centuries of history. Incredible. [It's] because of freedom."

This freedom may not endure. Communist China now runs Hong Kong. So far the island's stunning success has deterred the Communists from imposing their usual rules, but they may yet kill the goose that's been laying golden eggs.

By contrast, I dare you to try to start a business in India. We didn't even try to open one when I was in Calcutta, because the paperwork takes years. If you want to be an entrepreneur, you must submit reams of papers, and then wait for days, months, or even years while bureaucrats debate the merits of your application. When Kentucky Fried Chicken wanted to open outlets in India, Parliament spent months debating whether the request should be allowed. A government minister worried the chicken wasn't healthy enough.

The regulation is all well intended—to make sure the food's clean, the building's safe. But the result is that good ideas die in the piles of paper forms that we saw bundled on regulators' shelves.

WE KNOW WHAT WORKS

When people get free of their repressive governments, they thrive. I interviewed Kanwal Rekhi, who came to California and started a computer company. "India is full of smart people," he said, "but their brains are in the drains because the government doesn't let you blossom them out." One generation after Indian immigrants arrive in the USA, most earn more than the average American.

The Heritage Foundation and the Fraser Institute rank countries by economic freedom. Here are their top 10:

TABLE 4: COUNTRIES WITH THE MOST ECONOMIC FREEDOM

	Heritage Foundation (2003)	Fraser Institute (2002)
1	Hong Kong	Hong Kong
2	Singapore	Singapore
3	Luxembourg	United States
4	New Zealand	United Kingdom
5	Ireland	Switzerland
6	Denmark	New Zealand
7	Estonia	Ireland
8	United States	Canada
9	Australia	Netherlands
10	United Kingdom	Australia

Looking at the lists, you clearly see that places with the greatest economic freedom are also places where even the poor do pretty well. You may be surprised to find countries like Denmark and Canada on the list, since they are often labeled as socialistic welfare states. While they are socialist in some ways, they also protect private property, regulate fairly lightly, and make it relatively easy to open a business. I'm wary of Singapore, where a repressive government stifles speech and other non-economic freedoms. But like Hong Kong it has lifted itself out of the Third World in a relatively short time.

TABLE 5: COUNTRIES WITH THE LEAST ECONOMIC FREEDOM

	Heritage Foundation (2003)	Fraser Institute (2002)
1	North Korea	Myanmar
2	Cuba	Congo
3	Zimbabwe	Guinea-Bissau
4	Laos	Algeria
5	Libya	Malawi

At the bottom of the economic-freedom rankings are countries where government runs the economy. These are the worst places to live—for everyone, but especially for the poor.

Given that we know what works, how can leaders of those poor countries continue to impose policies that perpetuate poverty? *Most* of the people on Earth suffer under governments that limit economic freedom. Billions of people are ruled by leaders who—despite a record of failure, despite the collapse of the Soviet Union, and despite the astonishing success of unplanned places like Hong Kong—sanctimoniously say they know better.

In Calcutta, I visited the local political boss, Hashim Abdul Halim. His Socialist Party had been in charge for years, so it was not surprising that his was the poorest part of a poor country. Still, he smugly said, "Government has to plan the economy."

I couldn't contain myself. "Calcutta is poor because of your stupid policies," I said.

"No," Halim responded confidently. "We have risen on the ladder . . . if America became socialistic, it'd be good."

He's got to be kidding, right?

High school students sometimes watch my interview with Halim in school. (Teachers sometimes asked for copies of my ABC News specials to show to their students, so I created a charity that offers the videos to teachers. You can order the tapes and teaching guides at www.intheclassroom.org.) Some students who watch "Is America Number 1?" complain about the way I talked to Halim.

Deidre Leahy, a teacher at Shawnee Mission South High School, Overland Park, Kansas, wrote, "My students and I were upset that [Stossel] told the leader from India that socialism was stupid—that seemed rude and unnecessary."

I *was* rude. But this man wrecked people's lives. Socialism and central planning consistently wreck people's lives. Anyone paying attention to modern history can see that. Places like Hong Kong and the United States have demonstrated that economic freedom works. Yet Halim persists in pursuing policies we know don't work!

Someone ought to be rude to him.

Don't get me wrong. Economic freedom isn't all that's needed for people to prosper. Rule of law is crucial. It creates the security that makes capitalism possible. Many poor countries are poor because they don't have *enough* government. Entrepreneurs won't create the enterprises that allow people to lift themselves out of poverty if they can't be sure they'll enjoy the fruits of their labor—if they fear their neighbors, the police, or the local dictator might steal what they create. We need government. *Limited* government. No one needs it more than poor people.

CHAPTER THIRTEEN

Greed or Ambition?

Wealth is the product of
man's capacity to think.

—Ayn Rand

The wailing about "corporate greed" goes on endlessly. Protesters sneer at the "selfishness" of capitalism.

From the press, we learn there are two worlds: the nonprofit one, where everything warm, caring, and devoted to the "public good" happens; and the for-profit one, where opportunists cruelly exploit the weak. And in the movies, the person most likely to be portrayed as a murderer, child molester, or destroyer of the environment is not a Nazi, or a member of Al Qaeda; it's a businessman. According to a study by media watchers Lichter, Lichter and Amundson, businesspeople represent 12 percent of all TV characters but commit 32 percent of crimes—and 44 percent of murders.

And reporters equate capitalism with greed. They look down on it as bourgeois, and point out that free markets produce dramatic inequality.

When Ralph Nader says America has "an apartheid economy" where "corporate greed" exposes poor consumers to "frauds and hazardous products," reporters nod in agreement.

Let's calm down here a moment.

I'm repulsed by greed, too. I hate the wretched excess of the avaricious. People whose materialism knows no bounds and those who try to get ahead by stepping on others deserve condemnation. But what do we mean by greed? I make a lot of money and I've never turned down a pay raise. I don't think that makes me greedy.

AFL-CIO president John Sweeney makes more than $200,000 a year. His salary comes out of the pockets of union workers who make much less. So is he greedy? I asked him. He didn't like the question.

He was leading a raucous demonstration on Wall Street, protesting high executive pay. When I approached him with a camera, he was eager to be interviewed. As his union demonstrators chanted anticorporate slogans and waved signs that read "Greed," Sweeney told me, "This is basically about corporate greed."

"But what exactly does 'greed' mean?" I asked him.

"'Greed' means selfishness. It means taking more than you deserve."

But who gets to decide what people deserve? Is $29,101 a year fair pay? That was 2001's average income for a man in America. Would $30,000 then be "more than you deserve"? Sweeney made seven times the national average, so I asked him, "Do you ever turn down a pay raise?"

John Sweeney: No.

John Stossel: You're not greedy?

John Sweeney: No.

John Stossel: But that's wanting more. We could live on less.

John Sweeney: Well, I'm not sure about *you.*

John Stossel: Well, *you* could, couldn't you?

John Sweeney: No.

John Stossel: You need every penny you got? I mean, you could take less, right? Give some to the workers?

John Sweeney: Yeah.

John Stossel: So aren't you greedy?

John Sweeney: No.

His demeanor got colder by the second. But I think my questions were fair.

Railing against greed is a demonstration of lazy thinking by the left. The truth is that greed, when exercised in the private sector, is useful. Yes, the inequality can be gross; some business executives make a hundred times what their subordinates make. But there's usually a reason for it. Those managers' decisions make a huge difference, and they can create more wealth than other workers create. A company's directors don't pay the executive big bucks out of generosity. They pay it because they think he can make shareholders (and them) the most money. If big bucks are what they have to pay to get that executive's services, they'll hand over big bucks.

It's hard to believe a manager's contributions could be worth so much more than the rank and file's, but they often are. Presumably John Sweeney is worth $200,000 to the AFL-CIO. Ford Motor Company wouldn't be worth anything were it not for Henry Ford's innovative use of the assembly line. I envy my boss's compensation. Disney CEO Michael Eisner has taken home over a billion dollars. That seems ridiculous and yet, after Eisner took charge, Disney's net worth climbed from $2 billion to, as I write this, $42 billion. Forty-two billion dollars is $41 billion more than Eisner has been paid. Not every CEO's contributions are valuable—there are clueless and venal boards of directors who shovel money to their friends. But they are the exceptions.

WHO GAVE US MORE— MICHAEL MILKEN OR MOTHER TERESA?

I did a TV special about all this titled "Greed." I wish I'd picked a different title (maybe "Ambition" or "Enlightened Self-Interest"), because calling it "Greed" made it too easy for my critics to smear the content. On the other hand, how many viewers would have tuned in for "Enlightened Self-Interest"? "Greed" was a sexier title.

We began the show by asking: Who did more for the world, Michael Milken or Mother Teresa?

This seems like a no-brainer. Milken is the greedy junk-bond king. One year, his firm paid him $550 million. Then he went to jail for breaking securities laws. Mother Teresa is the nun who spent her lifetime helping the poor and died without a penny. Her good deeds live on even after her death; several thousand sisters now continue the charities she began. At first glance, of course Mother Teresa did more for the world.

But it's not so simple. Milken's selfish pursuit of profit helped a lot of people, too. Think about it: By pioneering a new way for companies to raise money, Milken created million of jobs. The ignorant media sneered at "junk bonds," but Milken's innovative use of them meant exciting new ideas flourished.

We now make calls on a national cellular network established by a company called McCaw Cellular, which Milken financed. And our calls are cheaper because Milken's junk bonds financed MCI. CEO Bill McGowan simply couldn't get the money anywhere else. Without Milken, MCI wouldn't have grown from 11 to 50,000 employees. CNN's 24-hour news and Ted Turner's other left-wing ventures were made possible by Milken's "junk."

The world's biggest toy company, Mattel, the cosmetics company

Revlon, and the supermarket giant Safeway were among many rescued from bankruptcy by Milken's junk bonds. He financed more than 3,000 companies, including what are now Barnes & Noble, AOL Time Warner, Comcast, Mellon Bank, Occidental Petroleum, Jeep Eagle, Calvin Klein, Hasbro, Days Inn, 7-Eleven, and Computer Associates. Millions of people have productive employment today because of Michael Milken. (Millions of jobs is hard to believe, and when "Greed" aired, I just said he created thousands of jobs; but later I met Milken, and he was annoyed with me because he claimed he'd created millions of jobs. I asked him to document that, to name the companies and the jobs, and he did.)

David Kelley of the Objectivist Center appeared on "Greed" to ask, "Shouldn't we value the people who create wealth, by starting companies, offering new products and services—or putting their money at risk to invest in those things, as Milken did? . . . Why isn't that our moral ideal?"

It was Kelley who came up with the idea of comparing Milken and Mother Teresa. "People look at the two, and they say, 'That's absurd. Mother Teresa was a moral hero, and he was a criminal. Michael Milken didn't suffer. He didn't go into the slums.' . . . But I say, what's so good about suffering? Look at the value [these two] people created. And on that scale, I have no trouble—Michael Milken [did more for the world]." Kelley wasn't even counting the hundreds of millions Milken donated to education and medical research. He considered only what Milken created by pursuing profit.

GREED IS GOOD

If pursuit of profit is greed, says economist Walter Williams, then greed is good because it drives us to do many good things. "Those areas where people are motivated the most by greed are the areas that we're the most satisfied with: supermarkets, computers, FedEx." By contrast, "Those areas [such as welfare and public education] where people say we're motivated by 'caring' are the areas of *disaster* in our country. . . . How much would get done," Williams wonders, "if it all depended on human love and kindness?"

Contrary to what you might expect, greed gets people to cooperate. Consider one of the wonders of our age, the supermarket. There are thousands of products on the shelves. How'd they get there? For the "Greed" show, we traced just one product—a piece of beef I bought for my dinner—back to the farm.

We taped David Wiese and his family, farmers in Manning, Iowa, as they put in 14-hour days—fixing fences, digging ditches, harvesting hay, and feeding the cattle. They do this not because they care about me.

"Do you think it's because they love people in New York?" Williams asks. "No, they love themselves. And by promoting their own self-interest, they make sure New Yorkers have beef."

The Wieses are just the first in a long series of people who, by caring about *themselves,* make sure *I* get my steak. For "Greed," we videotaped Virgil Rosanke, who delivers the propane that heats the cattle's water; Wanda Nelson, who keeps the packinghouse clean; the people who slaughter the cattle and butcher the beef; the people who make their knives, their overalls, their protective gear; the people who make the plastic that seals the meat, who run the machines that do the sealing, who pack the meat in boxes, who make the boxes and inspect the boxes, who run the freezer facilities, track orders by bar code, make the bar-code machines. Finally, we videotaped the truck driver, Randall Gilbert, who hauled my steak to New York. It showed that no one person can make me dinner. It takes a village—no, many villages and thousands of people—to get me beef for my dinner. Yet none is doing it for me.

Virgil Rosanke asked, "Who's John Stossel?"

I'm *no one* to Rosanke. He and the others don't particularly care if some TV correspondent gets his steak, yet they cooperate to make it happen, motivated by self-interest. "In a free market, you get more for yourself by serving your fellow man," says economist Williams. "You don't have to care about him, just serve him. I'd feel sorry for New Yorkers in terms of beef. If it all depended on human love and kindness, I doubt whether you would have one cow in New York."

BUT ISN'T NONPROFIT *BETTER?*

Even if pursuit of profit helps bring us some good things, we don't like it. We praise institutions motivated by "selflessness."

Like the Red Cross. It's a charity devoted to saving lives, not making a profit. That may comfort you if your child swims in a pool supervised by Red Cross lifeguards. A private company might be greedy and cut corners.

Yet, in 300 cities, Jeff Ellis Associates, a for-profit company, provides lifeguards, too. When we compared its performance to that of the Red Cross, the for-profit company did better.

To make money, company owner Jeff Ellis has to convince pool managers that his lifeguards are better trained and more vigilant. To make sure they stay focused, he sneaks around and videotapes them to see that they constantly scan the water, rescue tubes always in hand. His camera caught one guard talking to a girl, getting off the chair to sit next to her. Ellis yanked his license. As I sat in Ellis's car, watching him secretly videotape, I said his lifeguards must find his spying creepy. No, says Ellis. "They were given forewarning that in order to be in this lifeguard program, they were going to be held accountable."

Sure enough, lifeguards told me they don't mind his spying. Some who once worked for the Red Cross said they were now proud to work for an organization with higher standards. "With the Red Cross, we never had anybody really come up and check up on us," said one.

More than a thousand pools have switched from Red Cross lifeguards to Ellis's. The city of Orlando switched because, says city pool manager Robert Barrows, Ellis's guards are better, "more alert."

To keep winning business, Ellis has to constantly innovate. He invented the "rear huggie" rescue, which places the weight of the victim on the rescue tube instead of on the lifeguard. He makes guards carry a plastic mouthpiece to help with mouth-to-mouth resuscitation. The Red Cross has since adopted many of Ellis's techniques. Why didn't the Red Cross think of them first? "I think they'd been very complacent," says Ellis.

Saving lives is noble, but even saving lives doesn't motivate the Red Cross the way saving lives *and* the potential for profit motivate Ellis.

We asked the Red Cross about this. Their spokesperson said I was making "an unfair comparison" because neither the red Cross nor other nonprofit programs provide the extra supervision Ellis does. They leave that up to the local pool.

Exactly my point. Ellis lifeguards are better trained and extra vigilant because Ellis wants to make a profit. His pursuit of profit saves lives. Is this greed?

CAPITALISM IS UGLY

Not that capitalism is perfect. Although my brain knows that greed has made America better, the vast inequality in wealth saddens my heart. Sweeney's corporate-greed message resonates. Why should those at the top be paid so much when workers get so much less? T. J. Rodgers, CEO of Cypress Semiconductor, a Silicon Valley computer chip maker, already has more than $30 million. "I can take what I have," he says, "and I'd never have to work another day in my life. As a matter of fact, I'd never have to spend another day in the same city for the rest of my life." Yet he wants still more.

Rodgers was one of very few capitalists willing to appear on my TV show to celebrate capitalism. Most CEOs we asked were unwilling to speak up for the system that had done so many good things for them and for America. Perhaps they were cowed by the antibusiness chanting of the left, or maybe they assumed there was no way they'd get a fair shake in the mainstream media.

Rodgers, however, was candid even about the meanest side of capitalism. He admitted he once fired hundreds of employees to cut costs, but he made no apologies for keeping his vineyard and his big house.

"I have a nice house," he says, pouring another glass of wine from a bottle that cost "probably $500 or $600. . . . I paid $1 million for my house. . . . So what? I earned it."

When *Fortune* magazine wrote about America's toughest bosses, they put Rodgers on the cover.

"You better look to the top guy to be tough," said Rodgers. "Do you want the head guy to be touchy-feely, wear Earth shoes, eat granola, and drive a Volvo?"

In other words, do you want your boss to be someone like Ben or Jerry of Ben & Jerry's ice-cream company? Not long ago, they said they'd practice "caring capitalism"—they'd limit how much their next CEO could make. "How can you possibly justify somebody making $1 million or more a year when their line-level worker can't make enough to afford a house? " said cofounder Ben Cohen.

Ben and Jerry announced that the highest-paid workers would make no more than five times what the lowest-paid workers got. People cheered. Employees sang, "We second that emotion."

But it didn't work. Ben and Jerry weren't satisfied with the people who applied. They ended up hiring someone at a salary of not five times but 14 times more than other workers got. When he didn't work out, Ben and Jerry paid even more to hire another CEO. Then they sold the company.

Cypress Semiconductor is a bigger success. Rodgers turned a one-man business into a billion-dollar chip company. That's why, he says, he thinks of himself as a "good guy."

"Our company was worth zero in 1982," he points out. "It had one employee, me, and it was in debt. Today, it has 2,500 employees. Our company today is worth $1.4 billion. All of that money has been *created*. That is a positive thing that impacts favorably the lives of a lot of people. They buy cars with it. They go to school with it. They retire on it. . . . the world's better off when I make a dollar."

MAKING THE PIE BIGGER

At the union rally on Wall Street, a worker complaining about his pay said, "Forget about the size of their piece of the pie. We don't even get a piece. We get the crumbs."

The protesters assumed that when investors and executives get rich, there's less money left for the workers. In the movie *Wall Street,* the cruel tycoon Gordon Gecko says, "It's a zero-sum game. Somebody wins. Somebody loses. Money itself isn't lost or made, it's simply transferred."

As usual, Hollywood, like the AFL-CIO, got capitalism wrong—it's *not* a zero-sum game. T. J. Rodgers making $10 million and Bill Gates acquiring $40 billion doesn't mean the rest of us have $40,010,000,000 less. People like Gates and Rodgers get rich by making the pie bigger. That's what entrepreneurs do. Gates's and Rodgers's innovations gave the world new ways of saving time and money. Fred Smith creating Federal Express meant more people could get it there overnight. The entrepreneurs all got richer, but they didn't deprive anyone else of money. They baked a whole new pie.

If greed makes that possible, let the greed fly.

JUST DON'T LET GOVERNMENTS DO IT

Governments *don't* enlarge the pie. When government doles out $1 million to a favored group, the rest of us *do* have $1 million less. If a country's rulers can use the power of government to feed their greed, then greed is nasty indeed. In Haiti, Jean-Claude "Baby Doc" Duvalier's tax collectors funded his shopping sprees. His wife had the nerve to tell Barbara Walters, "I don't believe the money was badly spent."

In the Philippines, Imelda Marcos spent her loot on thousands of shoes. She needed them, she said, because she had to change clothes a lot. This kind of greed takes pie away from the poor. But only governments can do that, because only government can use force.

Capitalists like Bill Gates may be just as greedy as Imelda and Baby Doc, but to get rich, they have to do good things for us, because they can't use force. To get our money, they have to persuade us, entice us to buy—willingly. If the transaction doesn't benefit both of us, it doesn't happen. It's why everyone wins under voluntary capitalism. Unless someone cheats.

CHEATING

Greed does lead people to cheat. I spent years reporting on the cheaters. Ever see the ad for the solar-powered clothes dryer? On sale for only $50! When ABC paid, the mail brought us—a clothesline.

I did hundreds of stories on such scams but over the years, I came to realize that in the private sector, the cheaters seldom get very rich. It's not because "consumer fraud investigators" catch them and stop them; most fraud never even gets on the government's radar screens. The cheaters get punished by the market. They make money for a while, but then people wise up and stop buying.

There are exceptions. In a multi-trillion-dollar economy with tens of thousands of businesses, there will always be some successful cheaters and Enron-like scams; but the longer I did consumer reporting, the harder it was for us to find serious rip-offs worthy of national television.

To run a big enterprise, year after year, capitalists have to be honest. They have to give you something you want—a more comfortable car, better-looking clothes, faster food—and they have to price it competitively, deliver it reliably, and do a host of consumer-friendly things better than others do. Greed is useful. It gets people to work very hard at giving us what we want.

THE ROBBER BARONS

I taped the "Greed" show in Asheville, North Carolina, in front of the Vanderbilt Mansion. It's gargantuan. It has 250 rooms, and the dining room alone is as high as a five-story building. The mansion looks like a monument to greed.

Cornelius Vanderbilt and his fellow tycoon John D. Rockefeller were often called "robber barons." Newspapers said they were evil, and ran cartoons showing Vanderbilt as a leech sucking the blood of the poor. Rockefeller was depicted as a snake. What the newspapers printed stuck—we still think of Vanderbilt and Rockefeller as "robber barons." But it was a lie. They were neither robbers nor barons. They weren't robbers, because they didn't steal from anyone, and they weren't barons—they were born poor.

Vanderbilt got rich by pleasing people. He invented ways to make travel and shipping things cheaper. He used bigger ships, faster ships, served food onboard. People liked that. And the extra volume of business he attracted allowed him to lower costs. He cut the New York—Hartford fare from $8 to $1. That gave consumers more than any "consumer group" ever has.

It's telling that the "robber baron" name-calling didn't come from consumers. It was competing businessmen who complained, and persuaded the media to join in.

Rockefeller got rich selling oil. First competitors and then the government called him a monopolist, but he wasn't—he had competitors. No one was forced to buy his oil. Rockefeller enticed people to buy it by selling it for less. *That's* what his competitors hated. He found cheaper ways to get oil from the ground to the gas pump. This made life better for millions. Working-class people, who used to go to bed when it got dark, could suddenly afford fuel for their lanterns, so they could stay up and read at night.

Rockefeller's greed might have even saved the whales, because when he lowered the price of kerosene and gasoline, he eliminated the need for whale oil. The mass slaughter of whales suddenly stopped. Bet your kids won't read "Rockefeller saved the whales" in environmental studies class.

Vanderbilt's and Rockefeller's goal might have been just to get rich. But to achieve that, they had to give us what we wanted.

CHARITY

And then they gave us more. Both "robber barons" donated millions to charity. Rockefeller helped start the University of Chicago, and established the Rockefeller Institute for Medical Research. Vanderbilt built Vanderbilt University. He gave away 1 percent of his money.

One percent, however, is pretty cheap. Ted Turner calls it appalling. Turner was the only billionaire who agreed to be interviewed for "Greed."

He was a hoot. He acknowledged that he was greedy. He said there was competition among his fellow tycoons to get a better ranking on *Forbes* magazine's list of richest people: "You want to be number one.... greedy, greedy, greedy—everybody's greedy."

Turner gives big bucks to charity. Shortly after we interviewed him, he stood up at a UN function and announced that he'd donate *$1 billion* to UN causes. The press cheered—finally, a tycoon was giving something back. Turner said we should shame other rich people into giving more.

Take Warren Buffett, said Turner. "He's going to give all his money away when he dies. But he could live another 20 or 30 years. He should give some away now, because he's already worth $18 billion or $20 billion. You'd have to say that he falls into the Ebenezer Scrooge category."

I thought it was a great interview. But T. J. Rodgers pointed out that Turner's comments about charity showed he doesn't appreciate the gifts capitalism brings. "What he said is patently *stupid*, okay?" said Rodgers. "What he should do is take his money and *invest* it. And he can't help people any other better way than to invest it and to have the companies and buildings and plants that are created with his investment create jobs and wealth and products for other people. So running around giving his money away is a way to maybe make himself feel good. But it sure as hell isn't a good way to help people."

That's counterintuitive: charity not a good way to help people? I guess I disagree, because I give about 10 percent of my income to charity. But Rodgers makes a good point: Entrepreneurs investing money will probably help more people than charity will. Ted Turner's gift to the UN might be put to good use, but there's no guarantee of it. The UN is famous for squandering money on its own bureaucracy. Turner's record of creating jobs is more impressive.

"Why do we think that giving away money is better than making money?" asks David Kelley. "Giving away money is a lot easier than building a new business or a new industry, where you've created something that didn't exist before. I have a lot more respect for Ted Turner for building CNN at a time when no one thought it was possible than I have for any possible good he could do as a philanthropist.... If you create a job, you are giving someone the means to support himself. If you give money away, you're not helping him to be self-supporting."

I asked Kelley, "What's wrong with doing both—creating businesses *and* giving away money?" "People should do what they do best," said Kelley. People like Turner and Bill Gates are so good at creating jobs. If they devote their means to charity, they're depriving people of jobs.

I tried to argue this with Ted Turner, but he would have none of it. I suggested his investing his money in new businesses might help more people than giving it to the UN, and he just gave me a bewildered look.

"What are you beating on me about?" said Turner. "You're just another—this is why people don't like newsmen. I'm a newsman, too. I know your dirty tricks.... There's nothing more to say. Good-bye. I'm walking off the set."

And he did. It was sad. This hugely successful capitalist, whose investments had created so many jobs and given consumers more choices, wouldn't even discuss whether investing might do more good than charity. Capitalism, the system that has lifted more people out of poverty than any other, is so out of favor that even the capitalists won't defend it.

I wish they would.

CHAPTER FOURTEEN

Owning Your Body

*The urge to save humanity is
almost always only a false-face
for the urge to rule it.*
—H. L. Mencken

I'd like to think that since I'm an adult, my body belongs to me. In a free country, I should be allowed to eat as much as I want to, dye my hair red, exercise or not exercise, whatever. If I own my body, can't I do whatever I want with it, as long as I don't hurt anyone else?

Actually, no. There are all kinds of things society forbids us to do with our bodies.

DWARF TOSSING

I interviewed a dwarf named Dave Flood who wants to be tossed. Tossed? Well, yes. Dwarf tossing—usually a barroom contest in which men compete to see who can throw a dwarf the farthest, or bowl him into pins—is a party sport in some parts of the world. The idea repulses me.

But do I get to decide for Dave?

Dave could make money being tossed. In Tampa, Florida, where Dave lives, bars would pay him to be part of the "entertainment." Dave wants to do it. But he may not. A group called Little People of America convinced Florida's legislators that dwarf tossing should be illegal. The vote wasn't close.

"The dwarf is being objectified, dehumanized," says Little People spokeswoman Angela Van Ettan. "And it's dangerous."

It may be, but Dave wondered why the Little People of America and the politicians get to decide for him. "I'm a grown man," Flood says. "I'm thirty-seven years old, you know. I can protect myself. . . . You know, if I was seven feet tall I'd be paid to put a basketball through a hoop. I'm not seven feet tall. I'm three foot two and a dwarf, so [I want to] capitalize on getting tossed."

He makes a good point. Lots of people make money with their bodies. Football players do it. So do actresses. Some wreck their bodies for sport or money. Some enhance their careers by having surgeons change their shape. Is surgery less risky than being tossed? Should breast enlargement be illegal? People make different decisions about what risks they want to take. But if it's your body, shouldn't you have the right to decide?

I asked the Little People spokeswoman about that.

"That is a little different," said Angela Van Ettan. If this is allowed in bars, she said, it could put all dwarfs at risk. "We have to make a stand on something like this," added her husband, Robert Van Ettan, "because of the negative impact it has on our members."

Do activists like him get to decide for everyone?

Often, yes. Because the busybodies who want to run other people's lives have more political clout. They make the rules because they lobby harder than the people who just want to be left alone. And in the political arena, the winners get to tell everyone else what they can do.

SEX AND CONSENTING ADULTS

In most of the world, the busybodies have decided that you should be arrested if you ingest the "wrong" chemicals, have the "wrong" kind of sex, or bet on the wrong thing.

In Iran, they sometimes beat adulterers, or bury them up to their waist in sand and stone them. In Afghanistan, the Taliban crushed homosexuals to death. In America, if you don't get in other people's faces about it, you can have sex pretty much any way you want. Most states do have laws against adultery and fornication, but they're rarely enforced.

You could say that since we don't enforce them, such laws are no big deal, but rarely enforced laws are a threat to freedom because you never know when you might be in trouble. Governments can use selective enforcement to punish their enemies. The politically connected are safe; everyone else has to worry.

In Atlanta in 1995, a zealous prosecutor decided to enforce a law against "devices for the stimulation of human genitals." Police raided a sex shop and carted off vibrators and blow-up dolls. It sounds funny, and I'm sure the cops were chuckling—but if you were in the store, it was frightening. "Fifteen to 20 men in black ski masks entered the store, arrested my whole staff," Sean "Tip" Gagne, store manager, told us. Customers couldn't believe the police cared about what they were buying. One said, "If you come in, you're obviously consenting. . . . If I want to buy a vibrator, I should be able to buy a vibrator."

Not in that part of Atlanta that week. In Minneapolis, you can't buy a vibrator from Ferris Alexander anymore. Alexander sold vibrators, sex magazines, and videotapes—sold them only to adults. Nevertheless, one prosecutor deemed some of his tapes obscene, so authorities closed Alexander's businesses and put him in jail for five years.

The raids had no lasting effect on the supply of sex toys or porn. When we visited Minneapolis one month later, video stores were selling the exact same tapes that got Alexander in trouble. Lots of people must want them, because business was good. The Atlanta sex-toy shop is back in business, too—in fact, now the owner has several sex shops. The prosecutors' raids didn't change anything.

Georgia had a law against sodomy (oral or anal sex). The law was enforced selectively, usually only against homosexuals. When Chris Christiansen was arrested for propositioning another man, he challenged the constitutionality of his arrest. Georgia attorney general Mike Bowers fought that challenge all the way to the state supreme court and won. The law against sodomy was upheld until the U.S. Supreme Court overturned the state court in 2003. But in any case, who was Bowers to tell people what they should do with their sex organs? While he was condemning Christiansen's behavior, Bowers was having an affair with an employee of his law office. Adultery is illegal in Georgia, but Bowers didn't prosecute himself. They never do.

Georgia legislators defended the sodomy law. State Representative Mitchell Kaye complained, "Through some of these acts, you can't propagate the species. They're not morally correct. They say you can't legislate morality, but that's what we do as a legislature every single day: setting curfews for our children. . . . speeding laws, other laws," said Kaye. "We are legislating morality."

This is lazy thinking on the right. Speeding is very different from sex. Speeding is a direct threat to innocent bystanders. Sex isn't. Furthermore, morality is based on choosing the right option among many, not on doing what the law forces. "The problem comes when people come in and say, We're going to put you in jail for your own protection,'" said Peter McWilliams, whom I interviewed for a special about this we titled "Sex, Drugs, and Consenting Adults." McWilliams was a special person. His license plate read, CONSENT. He called himself a modern-day freedom fighter.

Peter McWilliams: There's a lot of stupid things that you can do with your life, and people do them all the time. But there's a difference between what wise people do and what the law should be.

John Stossel: We need these laws to make people behave better—to make society civilized.

Peter McWilliams: No. Civilized society is "You do what you want. I do what I want. I will not harm you or your property. You don't harm me and my property." The government does not need to come in and tell us, "There, there, little children. We'll take care of you. Just do what we say."

But the government does do this all the time. I understand the rationale. Drug abuse, prostitution, gambling, and dwarf tossing can destroy lives. But so can overeating.

What America forbids keeps changing. In colonial days, idleness and cursing got people put in the stocks. Some who had sex outside marriage were whipped. There really was a scarlet letter. Adulterers were forced to wear it, usually for life. The laws didn't stop adultery, cursing, or idleness any more than today's laws stop prostitution.

And I'm confused. Alcohol destroys lives, too. So does watching too much TV. All do tremendous damage to individuals, and impose big costs on society. Why are *they* legal? Because they're popular?

Vice is part of life. I want to discourage immoral behavior, but outlawing it doesn't make it go away; in fact, it makes it worse by driving it underground. The endlessness of the crusade against prostitution shows its pointlessness. Vice squads arrest a tiny percentage of the lawbreakers, put a few of them in jail, and then usually release them the next day. The madams may get longer sentences. Hollywood's Heidi Fleiss was jailed for a year and a half. But Sydney Biddle Barrows, who admitted to running a big New York City call girl operation, got off with a $5,000 fine. Barrows (called the "Mayflower madam" because she's a descendant of a Pilgrim family) appeared on "Sex, Drugs" to point out that prostitution arrests change nothing. "People who are going to do it are going to do it whether it's legal or not. . . . There are a lot of women out there who simply do not feel that it is immoral to sleep with a man for money, and who are we to criminalize their doing something that is okay with them?"

John Stossel: But isn't it better if it is illegal? Aren't we better off protecting ourselves from what you did?

Sydney Biddle Barrows: What are we really protecting people against? We're protecting women from making a living, and we're protecting men from spending their money as they please. I don't think that anyone needs to be protected from that.

I've found it relatively easy to get reports on prostitution on TV news broadcasts. Producers know we'll attract more of those young viewers advertisers want with a story about sex than with one on, say, economic freedom. What's tougher is getting "working girls" to agree to an interview, because flaunting their criminality may get them arrested. So thank goodness for Barrows and Norma Jean Almodovar of COYOTE, the prostitute activist group. COYOTE stands for Call Off Your Old Tired Ethics, and COYOTE can be counted on to assemble a group of working prostitutes for TV interviews.

I ask the usual questions, and they knock them out of the park.

John Stossel: This is degrading for women.

Norma Jean Almodovar: I don't think a lot of women would choose to scrub toilets for a living. Nevertheless, because a lot of people might think that's degrading, we don't put them in jail.

One prostitute, Heather Smith, made an interesting comparison: "It's legal for two men to go into a boxing ring and beat each other bloody for money," she said, "but it's not legal for me to go in and give someone sexual pleasure for money. What kind of sense does that make?"

Not much. If adults want to rent their bodies to other adults, that should be their choice.

In most of America, prostitution is plagued by violence and disease, and often run by thugs—*because* it's illegal. In much of Nevada, the sex business is legal. The sky hasn't fallen. In fact, Las Vegas keeps appearing on those "best cities to live in" lists. The sex business in Nevada is relatively safe and clean.

"It's shameful what we're doing in the name of morality," Peter McWilliams said. "So you have to ask yourself not, Is prostitution a good idea? You have to ask yourself, Is prostitution worth putting people in prison for?"

DRUGS

Still, while it was easy for McWilliams to convince me that adults renting their bodies to other adults should be legal, I once thought some other "consensual crimes" were just too dangerous to allow. Drug use, for example. I was among the majority of Americans who agreed that drug use must be illegal. But then I noticed that when vice laws conflict with supply and demand, the conflict is ugly, and supply and demand usually wins. Government's declaring drugs illegal doesn't mean people can't get them. It just means drug users buy drugs on the black market, where even nastier things happen. It's why, after watching my government conduct its drug war, I have come to think the drug laws are worse than the drugs.

The drug war costs taxpayers more than $30 million a day in federal money alone, and President George W. Bush wants to spend still more. Cities and states spend vast amounts, too. "Up to three quarters of our budget can somehow be traced back to fighting this war on drugs," says Detroit police chief Jerry Oliver. Yet the drugs are as available as ever.

Oliver was once a big believer in the war. Not anymore. "It's insanity to keep doing the same thing over and over again," he says. "If we did not have this drug war going on, we could spend more time going after robbers and rapists and burglars and murderers. That's what we really should be geared up to do. Clearly we're losing the war on drugs in this country."

The last time America engaged in a war of this length was Vietnam. Then, too, government regularly predicted success in the war—the "light at the end of the tunnel." Now we hear Vietnam-style optimism about drugs. We're winning, says the DEA. Prosecutors hold news conferences announcing the "biggest seizure ever." But what they confiscate (maybe 10 percent of the supply) makes little difference.

Even as the drug war fails to reduce the drug supply, many argue that there are still moral reasons to fight the war. "When we fight against drugs, we fight for the souls of our fellow Americans," said President Bush. But the war destroys American souls, too. America locks up a higher percentage of her people than most any other country. Every day, police arrest 4,000 people for selling or using drugs. That's more people than are arrested for aggravated assault, burglary, vandalism, forcible rape, and murder combined. Most of those arrested on drug charges are quickly booked and released, but about half a million are behind bars—*just for drugs,* not for doing anything violent.

In Texas, Will Foster was sentenced to 93 years in jail for growing marijuana plants. "In America," Foster said, "to have committed a crime, there used to have to be a victim. I've never beat up anybody. I've never raped nobody. I haven't molested a child. I haven't killed anybody. I worked. I paid my taxes. I took care of my family."

No longer. Now his computer business is closed, and his wife has left him. His sentence was reduced and he served "just" six years, but what was gained? His arrest turned a productive citizen into a burden on the state.

Authorities say his jailing sent a message—it warned people not to mess with drugs, and that's a critical message to send to America's children. Protecting the children. That's justified many intrusive expansions of government power. It's a debate stopper; no one wants to argue against protecting children. No one wants children to gamble, see prostitutes, drink alcohol, or use drugs; that's why I called my TV special "Sex, Drugs, and *Consenting Adults.*"

I have teenage kids. My first instinct when I thought about the drug laws was to be glad cocaine and heroin are illegal. The law meant my kids couldn't trot down to the local drugstore and buy something that gets them high. Maybe that would deter them.

Or maybe not. The more reporting I did, the more skeptical I got. There's the forbidden-fruit effect. The fact that drugs are illegal may make them *more* desirable to teens. The law certainly doesn't prevent them from getting the drugs. Kids say drugs are no harder to get than alcohol. Authorities can't even keep the stuff out of prisons—why do we think we can keep it out of America?

Perhaps a certain percentage of Americans will use drugs—no matter what the law says. The government says about 5 percent of Americans use regularly. So maybe 5 percent of Americans will use drugs no matter what the law says. Or maybe the law has deterred some people from trying them. It's impossible to know.

UNINTENDED CONSEQUENCES

But I do now know the *unintended* consequences of the law. Because now I can *see* them. The side effects are many, and they are horrible:

First, there's the crime. It's caused *by* the drug laws. Drugs themselves rarely cause crime; few people get high and then run out to commit crimes. Most drugs just make drug users stupid and sleepy.

The crime happens *because* the product is illegal. Since drug sellers can't rely on the police to protect their property, they form gangs and arm themselves. Drug buyers steal—to pay the high black-market prices. The government says alcohol is as addictive as heroin, but no one robs 7-Elevens to get a six-pack of Bud. It's our own laws that cause the crime.

The second unintended consequence is corruption: The drug black market distracts police from pursuing other sorts of crimes, and sometimes corrupts them. We demand that cops who make $25,000 a year turn down $25,000 bribes. Not all do. "With all of the money, with all of the cash, it's easy. . . . to purchase police officers, to purchase prosecutors, to purchase judges," says Detroit's Chief Oliver.

Our drug war even corrupts other countries. Much of our cocaine and heroin comes from Colombia. When I went to the Colombian jungle to tape a show on the drug war, I saw coca plants growing everywhere. It's like a weed. America has spent millions trying to persuade Colombian farmers to cultivate anything else but coca, but drug prohibition makes the coca trade so profitable, they won't stop. So now we spray their fields with herbicide. Of course the dive-bombing planes make the peasants hate Americans. One farmer told me, "First of all, it was the helicopters. Then it was the airplanes. Everything around us was wet. Two days after that, the leaves started to fall off the plants." The herbicide killed the coca, and other plants, too.

The spraying hasn't worked. Prohibition's black markets are more powerful than the law. Constrict supply, and prices and profits are driven up. That lures more poor farmers into the coca business.

While we were in Colombia, the CIA admitted that after the spraying, the amount of coca under cultivation *increased* by 25 percent.

I confronted then DEA director Asa Hutchinson about that.

"We have not had the measure of success in the eradication program in Colombia that we need or that we want to have," he admitted. But "whether you look at it as 10 percent, 20 percent, or 30 percent, there is some teenager out there that will not be able to afford the drug, and it results in saving somebody's life on the streets of the United States."

But there's no evidence of that. Authorities were excited when Pablo Escobar was killed. They said it would stop the supply of drugs. It didn't, because the Cali cartel stepped in. Then the Cali cartel members were arrested. The prosecutors beamed. But within days, other drug dealers took the Cali cartel's place.

Now the CIA claims the spraying is working—less coca is being grown in Colombia. But if that's true, so what? It's as if authorities squeezed a balloon; the coca business just moved across the border to Bolivia and Peru. In the meantime, the vast profits created by drug prohibition have torn Colombia apart. You think we have a problem with crime in the United States? In Colombia there are 80 murders a day, and you're more likely to be kidnapped in Colombia than you are anywhere else in the world.

Drug laws, not drugs, are an enemy of law and order.

The third unintended consequence of the drug war is that it tells kids in poor neighborhoods that work is for suckers. Why take an entry-level job at McDonald's when your little brother can make more as a drug lookout? Why work at all when the role models in the neighborhood—

the coolest people, the ones with the best cars and the best clothes—are criminals?

"We are recruiting children [to be drug dealers] in barrios all over the nation because of drug money," says James Gray, a superior court judge in Orange County, California, who spent years locking up drug dealers. Now he's concluded that prohibition's pointless because it makes the drugs so absurdly valuable. Ounce for ounce, cocaine is now much more valuable than gold. Selling it on the black market brings such huge profits that as soon as cops arrest a dealer, new ones line up to replace him. Judge Gray has concluded, "The money to be made from the sale of the illegal drugs is a bigger problem than the drugs themselves."

The fourth unintended consequence of the drug laws is the creation of unbelievably rich criminal gangs. We forget that alcohol prohibition created Al Capone. The gangs we're creating now are even richer, probably rich enough to buy nuclear weapons. Terrorists like Osama bin Laden have been funded partly by drug money.

So why is America doing this? We do it to protect Americans from *themselves*. But if that's the right thing to do in a free society, maybe we should have exercise police come into our homes and make us run laps and do push-ups. Ridiculous as that might seem, it's the logical next step.

If you accept the idea that it's government's job to protect us from ourselves, government will grow endlessly. As David Boaz of the Cato Institute wrote in *Libertarianism, a Primer,* "The failure of one government intervention leads to pressure for more intervention. Drug prohibition fails to stop the drug trade, so the government points to that very failure as a reason to hire more police, pressure foreign governments, expand its powers of search-and-seizure and civil forfeiture, deprive law-abiding people of public telephones in drug-trade areas, subject all employees to drug testing, and so on."

LEGAL DRUGS?

But the alternative, legal drugs, seems frightening. More people might try them. More might get addicted. At the turn of the last century, drugs *were* legal. Bayer aspirin had heroin in it. Some wine contained coca leaves. Some Americans got addicted, and people didn't like that. So politicians passed drug laws.

But what good have they done? Now we have drug crime, corrupt vice cops, terrible role models for poor children, a vicious underworld that funds terrorists—and people still get addicted. The drug laws made life worse.

If only we could do a test, observe what happens in a society where drugs were legal. Actually, such a test is under way now. Canada has quietly been legalizing drugs. Today, police in most of Europe ignore marijuana use. Spain, Italy, and Luxembourg have decriminalized most drug use, and Portugal has decriminalized all drug use.

In Holland, marijuana has been officially "tolerated" since 1976.

Is everyone getting stoned? No. The Dutch are actually less likely to smoke marijuana than Americans. Thirty-eight percent of American adolescents have smoked pot, while in Holland, only 20 percent have. When we taped in the marijuana shops in Amsterdam, half the people we talked to turned out to be American. Legalization took the mystique away from the drug. The Dutch minister of health said, "We've succeeded in making pot boring."

In America, there's little interest in legalizing any drug. Authorities even discourage debate about it. Willie Williams, Los Angeles's former police chief, said, "It's simply wrong, and it should not be even discussed here in America."

Don't even discuss it? Authorities fear that talking about legalization sends the wrong signal—tells kids we don't think drugs are harmful. But that's shortsighted. Legalizing something doesn't mean we think it's okay. We condemn cruelty and hatred without trying to make them illegal. Let people condemn. But let's not pretend going to war against behaviors millions of people enjoy will make life better. It makes it worse.

The attitude of some of the drug warriors is chilling. I interviewed DEA director Tom Constantine. He said if America "got more serious" about the drug war, we could win it. When I asked him why alcohol was okay, but not marijuana or cocaine, he said people drink liquor for the taste, not to "get high."

This inspired me to provoke him: "I hate to say this, but when I have a glass of gin or vodka, I'm doing it to get a little buzz on. That buzz is bad? Should it be illegal?"

"If you drink for that purpose," said Constantine, "that's not too smart."

"But shouldn't people be allowed to harm themselves if that's what they want to do?" I asked. "Should we outlaw smoking?" His answer had a Taliban-like quality to it: "When we look down the road, I would say 10, 15, 20 years from now, in a gradual fashion, smoking will probably be outlawed in the United States," Constantine said.

Great. The drug warriors want to ban all forms of intoxication? And the president wants to give them still more money and power?

Everything can be abused, but that doesn't mean government can stop it, or should try to stop it. It's the legitimate function of government to protect us from one another—to deter and punish those (like stoned drivers and airline pilots) whose drug use threatens other people. But government goes astray when it tries to protect us from ourselves. As Judge Gray put it, "It makes no more sense to put actor Robert Downey Jr. in jail for drug abuse than to put Betty Ford in jail for her alcohol abuse." Hold people accountable for what they do, but not for what they put into their bodies. "Once the principle is admitted that it is the duty of the government to protect the individual against his own foolishness, no serious objections can be advanced against further encroachments," wrote economist Ludwig von Mises. "Why not prevent him from reading bad books and bad plays, from looking at bad paintings and statues and from hearing bad music? The mischief done by bad ideologies, surely, is more pernicious both for the individual and for the whole society, than that done by narcotic drugs."

When I first reported on this topic, America was in the midst of the crack epidemic. Crack was said to be so powerful—so addictive and destructive—that those who tried it just once were on the road to ruin.

I said to Ed Crane, president of the Cato Institute, "If crack is as bad as they say it is, how can you think legalizing it will be okay?" Crane looked at me as if I were a Martian and said, "I don't know about crack, and I don't know if more people would get hooked, but don't you own your own body?"

That shut me up.

The crack epidemic has since subsided. It turns out crack was not as hopelessly addicting as we'd been told. In fact, most people who've smoked crack have stopped smoking crack. Many were harmed, but people were able to give it up. Others saw the harm it did and stayed clear of it. But that's not the point. Crane made the point: we should own our own bodies.

David Boaz adds, "What right could be more basic, more inherent in human nature, than the right to choose what substances to put in one's own body? Whether we're talking about alcohol, tobacco, laetrile, AZT, saturated fat, or cocaine, this is a decision that should be made by the individual, not the government. If government can tell us what we can put into our own bodies, what can it not tell us? What limits on government action are there?"

MY LIFE

Which brings us to the *ultimate* choice. Since it's my body, shouldn't I have the right to decide if I want to stay alive?

One of my big fears is being afflicted with a painful terminal illness. I would hate to be trapped in my body if I was helplessly in pain. I'd like to have the option to end my life.

When my father was 92, I interviewed him about this for "Sex, Drugs, and Consenting Adults." He was always a good sport about appearing in my stories. (I still get nice comments from people who remember how, at age 83, he agreed to join me in taking a driving test for a story I was doing on dangerous elderly drivers. Dad passed the test; I flunked—I couldn't read the eye chart.) Nine years later I put him on TV again, only to ask, "What if you got cancer or some disease, and you were in pain? Would you want to die? Would you want a doctor to help you?"

He said, "I think I should have the privilege to demand it of my doctor to do something of the sort. . . . I think it still should be my decision what I want to do with my life—not anybody else's, even if it's *you*."

I agree. It's his body. My father died a few years later, of pneumonia, but it seems wrong that if he had been in terrible pain, his death could not legally have been under his control. In Oregon, voters got a chance to vote on that. They passed a ballot initiative that allows doctors to help terminally ill patients who want to commit suicide.

Family physician Dr. Peter Goodwin helped draft the Oregon law. "In Oregon we have publicly acknowledged what people around this country believe," Goodwin says, "and that is that aiding dying is appropriate for some few terminally ill patients who want this, want it desperately."

The law says no, and "should say no," says lawyer Wesley Smith, who frequently writes about this in the *Weekly Standard.*

I asked Smith, "Isn't it my choice? It's my life, isn't it?"

Wesley Smith: The law is not about "I, I, me, me." When we make public policy, it is about "us, us, we, we." There are certain individual conducts that we have a right to stop, and I think having doctors help kill people is one of those.

John Stossel: But what if I'm in terrible pain? I want to be able to end that pain.

Wesley Smith: We're all scared about the end of our lives, and what we need to have is to be ensured that our pain can be ended. But killing isn't ending pain. Killing is killing.

I disagree. If I own my body, the length of my life ought to be my choice. If I need the expertise of a doctor and one is willing to help me, that should be legal, too.

RETHINKING THE RULES

I should be able to do whatever I want to my body, as long as I don't injure anyone else. People who don't like my decisions have every right to complain about my behavior, to boycott, to picket, to embarrass me. God bless the critics. They make America a better place by making us think about what's moral, what's good and evil, perhaps shaming us into being better people. Let them mock and criticize, shame the drunks and drug users into better behavior. Society's influence, wrote John Stuart

Mill, "practices a social tyranny more formidable than any kinds of political persuasion, since it leaves fewer means of escape, penetrating much more deeply into the details of life."

But shaming is one thing, using the force of law another. "The law is a very powerful thing," said McWilliams. "The law means that you send people out with guns to get people when they don't follow it. It's a very, very serious matter."

When I interviewed McWilliams, he smoked marijuana in front of our camera. He didn't think he'd be jailed for it, because we were in California, where "medical use" of marijuana is legal. McWilliams had AIDS and said marijuana relieved the nausea his AIDS medicine gave him.

But shortly after we talked, nine DEA agents showed up at his house and ransacked it, looking for "evidence of marijuana growing." Federal authorities don't much like California's liberal law.

They didn't much care for McWilliams, either. He smoked openly and advocated legalizing the drug. In 1998, federal authorities arrested him, charging him with giving a friend money to grow marijuana.

Authorities took McWilliams to federal court, where, unbelievably, the rules of the trial forbade his even mentioning his medical condition, or the fact that California had legalized medical use of marijuana (state law was inadmissible in federal court). Since he couldn't make the most basic arguments in his own defense, he gave up—pled guilty to a lesser charge, which got him a shorter jail term. A condition of his release was that he not smoke marijuana.

But it was the marijuana that kept him from vomiting up his medication. He took the plea bargain, but then several months later, he died, because he couldn't keep his medicine down. Those of us who revere freedom miss him.

CHAPTER FIFTEEN

Free Speech

He that would make his own liberty secure must guard even his own enemy from oppression.

—Thomas Paine

As I write this, ABC just made me coanchor of *20/20*. This should be an interesting new chapter in my life. Or I could just get fired.

Barbara Walters thinks I'm a little weird, and argues with me about the ideas presented in this book (you may have seen that on the air: "John, I *totally* disagree . . ."). People often assume we have a contentious relationship because she argues with me so forcefully, but that's just part of the job. Actually, we get along very well. Barbara, in fact, is more open to the concept of limited government than many of my colleagues. She even agreed with a piece I did on the virtues of a flat tax, and I once heard her challenge another correspondent, "Come on, we can't have a law for *everything!*" Maybe I'm gradually convincing her.

Probably not.

My boss and the executive producer of *20/20* is now David Sloan, who 20 years ago produced some of my consumer reports for *Good*

Morning America. He doesn't agree with me, either, and we fight about it sometimes, but at least he is open to my ideas. He calls my reporting "a jungle gym for the brain." That's nice. And he puts my libertarian pieces on TV. Sometimes.

I used to have to fight constantly to get my contrarian stuff on the air. It was like pushing string. TV is a collaborative process, and if the producer, editor, and executive producer are not on board, it doesn't get done.

Now that I have my specials and "Give Me a Break," I have outlets for it. I propose some of my stories; producers and researchers propose more. Then we have to get the executive producer's approval. His main concern is whether it can be promoted simply ("Tonight, the breast-examination device you are not allowed to have!") so people will watch.

The fact that I'm *20/20* coanchor says something good about ABC News. Plenty of people at ABC don't like my point of view. Some despise it—after "Boys and Girls Are Different," a well-known correspondent approached one of my producers and accused her of betrayal, saying, "How could you work on that show with that Stossel?" Other correspondents avoid speaking to me, but ABC execs still gave me the job. They believe other viewpoints deserve to be heard.

And many of you apparently agree. It's not only angry viewers who stop me on my neighborhood streets. Many of you actually thank me for "finally telling the truth" about government, or lawyers, or junk science. I get particular satisfaction when people talk enthusiastically about some show I did 10 years ago and remember specific details about it. Yes, there are also all those people who call out, "Hey, Geraldo!," but that happens less lately. Now I'm more likely to get, "Hey! Give me a break!" When we filmed in a prison for my last special on drug laws, I was startled to hear a whole chorus of big, scary cons—they reminded me of the bullies who terrorized me in high school—chanting, "John Stossel! Okay! Give me a break!"

I'm glad they and ABC News think my libertarian ideas deserve to be heard. Not everyone does.

The totalitarian left certainly doesn't.

I got a taste of their wrath a few years ago, when I went to Brown University to do a *20/20* report on a controversy over a student's punishment for "sexual misconduct."

Adam Lack, a senior from Iowa, had sex with a woman he met at a fraternity house. The girl claimed he'd raped her. Adam never physically forced himself on her, she admitted, but she was drunk when she had sex, and therefore she said she could not have given proper consent.

Adam denied any "sexual misconduct." I suspect Adam knew she was drunk. On the other hand, it must have been an odd form of rape because the girl spent the night with him and *gave him her phone number the next morning.* She only made her accusation five weeks after the incident (after talking to feminist activists).

Nevertheless, Brown filed disciplinary charges against Adam, and students put his picture on the front page of the school newspaper.

Adam might have stayed at Brown and fought to clear his reputation, but he couldn't take the pressure. After weeks of snubs from classmates, and hateful anonymous phone calls, Adam quit school, cleaned out his room, and went home to Iowa.

20/20's producers thought this was an interesting controversy, so they asked me to go to Brown. Once there I was surprised to discover that campus activists didn't consider this a controversy that had two sides. There was only one correct side: theirs. Someone who might disagree (like me) was not welcome.

The campus newspaper ran a story saying I was coming to Brown. A "women's studies" professor described me as the "known woman hater" (my show on gender differences [Chapter 10] apparently proved I hate women). When we arrived, 30 students carrying signs that said "Students Against Sexual Violence" were chanting, "Stop sexual violence!"

One young man (perhaps a professional activist, because he was no longer a student—he'd graduated years before) shouted into a microphone, "We don't have to prove beyond a reasonable doubt anything. We just have to say, look, is it likely that a Brown student raped another Brown student? If we think it's probably true, let's kick him off campus!"

The demonstrators cheered, and then their leader asked if anyone else wished to speak. No one did. So I asked, "May a reporter ask a question?"

The demonstrators warily agreed, and I picked up the mike and said, "I'm here to do a report on the Adam Lack case, but I'm not sure I understand the current definition of rape. When I was a student, it meant physical force, maybe with a knife or gun—"

I never got to finish. The crowd *screamed* at me. "Get off campus! Get off this campus!" When one student tried to answer my question, the crowd shrieked, "Don't talk to him!" Then they made it impossible for me to interview anyone by screaming in unison: "Rape is not TV hype! C'mon, everybody, louder! Rape is not TV hype. . . . Rape is not TV hype!"

I've covered race riots in Portland, a birth-control riot in Mexico City, and criminal looting in New York City, yet these privileged students at an Ivy League university were louder, and *more* intense. Some got right in my face, spitting insults, until I foolishly lost my temper and told one to "fuck off." (*That* got coverage in local papers, and earned me a lecture from ABC vice president Richard Wald about "how stupid" I was.) Eventually the demonstrators ended our taping altogether by ripping out our microphone cable.

Why would these students feel entitled to censor me? Because in their world (the smothering cocoon of left-wing academia), any challenge to their thinking must automatically be hate-filled and sexist (or racist, classist, or homophobic). They'd been taught that such comments create a "hostile environment," where women, minorities, and other "victims" cannot learn. Therefore, say the campus activists and the totalitarian left, the opposing viewpoint must not be heard at all.

I understand how they feel. I want people to agree with me. I don't like it when people criticize me. And people constantly say hateful things about me. I cringed when TV critic Tom Shales mocked me in the *Washington Post*, calling me "the long fingernail on the blackboard of television," and when Ralph Nader called me "dishonest." Even on abcnews.com, people publish vicious things. "Stossel is a butt weasel," "a moron . . . a disgrace to journalism." This is on *my own message board*. This is threatening to a reporter—credibility is all we have. I hate the criticism. It hurts my feelings. It creates a "hostile work environment." But too bad for me. We are supposed to have free speech in America, so I just have to take it. The totalitarian left has to take it, too.

YOU CAN'T SAY THAT!

Of course, free speech doesn't mean you can say anything. You may not scream "Fire!" in a crowded theater if there's no fire (though you *should, if* there is one) because your words could cause people to be trampled. "Fighting words" are illegal. If you tell rioters, "Beat that guy up," and they do beat him up, you're in trouble. Creating a "clear and present danger" used to be the Supreme Court standard. Now it's "inciting imminent lawless action."

Fair enough. Words that directly cause injury should be restricted. But "directly cause injury" should be the standard. The founders thought granting us a constitutional right to express opinions is the best way to preserve freedom.

It's why burning an American flag is legal. Congressman Bob Barr, fighting for a constitutional amendment to outlaw flag burning, shouted on the floor of Congress, "We are not limiting free speech, which is what the Bill of Rights talks about, we are limiting offensive conduct!" Bunk. He wanted to limit speech. If politicians like him get to ban "offensive conduct," then they can outlaw not just flag burning but all forms of protest and criticism, even my asking skeptical questions at Brown, where the demonstrators obviously considered my question "offensive conduct." Criticism, even flag burning, must be allowed if we are to be free.

Of course the Bill of Rights says only "*Congress* shall make no law . . . abridging the freedom of speech." Businesses and private universities can set all kinds of speech rules. The founders worried about government censorship because we have only one government. But we have lots of schools and businesses; if I don't like Brown's speech code, or ABC's editorial review, I can go to a different school or pick a different job. If ABC wants to fire me for criticizing ABC or Brown students, they have every right to do that. Brown can have as restrictive a speech code as it wants.

Trouble is, the combination of American's new antiharassment laws and the "victim" politics of the left have frightened schools and businesses into passing suffocatingly restrictive speech rules. Jonathan Rauch says in *Kindly Inquisitors,* his wonderful book about free speech: "There's a new commandment: *Thou shalt not hurt others with words.*"

This is a dangerous idea.

As always, the goal is noble: to create a kinder, more civil society. But who gets to decide how much "hurt" is acceptable? If the victim gets to decide, this invites censorship that will never stop.

A few years ago a "disabilities activist" at a stuttering organization demanded that Porky Pig be taken off the air to "protect children." I used to cringe when Porky cartoons ran, because I feared other boys would mock my stuttering. Sometimes they did. It was cruel. Didn't I have a right not to have my feelings hurt? No. Today, people would argue that since I am "a person with a disability," I have that right.

The National Federation of the Blind demanded that Disney cancel a Mr. Magoo movie because Mr. Magoo "has caused blind children to get into fights." I confronted federation head Marc Mauer for a "Give Me a Break" segment. (I dread such confrontations; I know I won't look good on TV suggesting to a blind person that he should put up with something he says hurts blind children . . . but I plunged ahead.) He answered adamantly, "Our lives are at stake here!"

They are? If you accept his logic, censorship will never end. We should change *Snow White*'s "seven dwarfs" to "seven vertically challenged people," and the "hunchback" of Notre Dame to "the physically challenged bell ringer."

Sadly, we are moving in that direction. The National Alliance for the Mentally Ill demanded that Sears stop selling T-shirts that said, "You should hear the names the voices in my head are calling you," and Sears quickly complied. To be "sensitive to Indians," Berkeley, California, changed Columbus Day to "Indigenous People's Day."

The University of Maryland's speech code restricts "distribution of written or graphic materials that are derogatory." This book would break their rule. So would much of the world's great literature. The university also bans "sexual looks, such as leering and ogling, licking lips or teeth," and "holding or eating food provocatively."

It's as if Americans, instead of trying to be more self-reliant, now compete to be victims, and revel in taking offense. Workers now sue bosses because a co-worker told a dirty joke, colleges punish "insensitive" speech, and bosses ban flirting—all to protect people from "hurt." Some Columbia students complained to ABC when one of my producers called them "kiddo" during his interviews with them for our special on free speech. Is "kiddo" a form of hurtful "insensitive speech"? Some of this grows out of political correctness, but America's new sexual-harassment laws have made some employers feel they must censor, to avoid lawsuits.

Don't get me wrong; I agree that sexual harassment is bad. But speech codes don't really stop it. Sexual-harassment law mostly restricts freedom—while enriching consultants and lawyers. The well-intended rules have unintended consequences.

Terrified employers respond by passing freedom-killing rules.

Even *love*-killing rules. Work has always been a good place to find love. We spend so much time there. It's where Bogie met Bacall. It's where I met *my* wife; she was a writer for *Good Morning America*. But that was before the new rules. Now some companies, in pathetic, cringing attempts to avoid being mangled by lawyers, demand that co-workers who want to date sign "love contracts." Here's a sample of just *part* of one company's contract:

> D. [First employee] and [second employee] each, independently and collectively, desire to undertake and pursue a mutually consensual social and/or amorous relationship ("Social Relationship") with the other.

> E. [First employee's] desire to undertake, pursue, and participate in said Social Relationship is completely and entirely welcome, voluntary, and consensual and is unrelated to the Company, [first employee's] professional or work-related responsibilities or duties, or [first employee's] and [second employee's] respective positions in the Company or business relationship to each other....

> ... [First employee] and [second employee] agree not to engage in such conduct on Company property or when performing work-related tasks in public areas. Such prohibited conduct includes, but is not limited to, the following: holding hands or touching in

an affectionate or sexually suggestive manner; kissing or hugging; romantic or sexually suggestive gestures; romantic or sexually suggestive speech or communications, whether oral or written.…

And so on, for page after page. Just reading it could kill love. Some companies forbid dating in the office altogether. An overreaction to sexual harassment law? Probably. But that's what happens. Given what lawsuits cost, managers must take desperate measures. If workers lose freedom of speech, so what? Better safe than sorry.

Sexual-harassment law requires employers to become speech police, says UCLA law professor Eugene Volokh. "The government is trying to set up a nationwide orthodoxy in all of the nation's workplaces—these are the jokes you can't tell. These are the opinions you can't express. These are the words you can't use. And employers are listening."

THE MOST SENSITIVE SET THE RULES

In hopes they can avoid being punished by lawyers, companies now try to "educate employees." Some pay consultants like Olivet Jones $2,000 a day to run sexual-harassment seminars. We assembled a group of employees and videotaped one. It was frightening. She told us we must make sure we do not engage in even the most basic kinds of friendly, human interaction. "Don't touch a co-worker on the shoulder. And be careful of compliments!"

Olivet Jones: Don't talk about body parts. Don't give people sexual attention of any kind, whether you think they want it or not.

John Stossel: *No* body parts? No "nice eyes"?

Olivet Jones: Your "nice eyes" may be interpreted by somebody else as a totally different thing. So, what does this add up to? Are you becoming a bland person? Yes, you are.

Everyone must become bland? I don't want to! I want to laugh, joke, flirt. One seminar participant complained Jones's rules would make the workplace "cold, unhealthy, less fun." Yet by seminar's end, Jones had convinced most participants that workplace speech *should* be censored.

How easily we give up our freedoms.

WORDS ARE BULLETS

There is no end to how much speech may be censored, because under sexual-harassment law, *the offended get to decide* which speech is offensive.

"What is inappropriate really exists only through the eyes of the person experiencing it," says Olivet Jones.

"So the person who hears it gets to determine if it's offensive?" I asked. "Even if your intention is good?"

"It doesn't matter, John. If I shoot you dead," she asks, "do you care that I didn't mean to?"

Shooting equals speaking? There's a difference between bullets and words.

"No," Jones says. "They have the same power."

That's a dangerous concept. Yes, words can wound, but words are different from bullets. It's important to our freedom that we remember that.

Maybe I'm quick to bristle at the dicta of the Olivet Joneses of the world because I'm a reporter in a city where people revile ideas I value. At least the sensitivity police are not in charge at ABC. I do have plenty of censors, however; we call them editors and lawyers. Everything I put on TV must first be read or watched by three or four producers, a lawyer (or several), and a "news standards" executive.

As long as I work for ABC, those people have every right to censor me, but I still get furious when my bosses tell me I may not say this or that. Other reporters handle it better; they just shrug and make the changes. Maybe I resent the censorship so much because of my stuttering. I spent much of my childhood in a self-imposed silence ghetto, afraid to speak. Now that I can speak, I hate it when people tell me I can't.

A FEW SUGGESTIONS

It was a reason to write this book: In a book, I get to say more. I even get to propose solutions to some of the problems I brought up:

Lawsuit abuse. The party that loses a lawsuit should pay the other side's legal costs. The losing lawyer should pay, too. Lawyers complain "loser pays" would deny some people access to the courtroom. I say, fine; loser pays works well enough in the rest of the world. We deny people access to missiles because missiles are destructive; so are lawsuits.

Other proposed remedies (for example, damage caps on medical malpractice suits, forbidding suits against vaccine and small-plane makers) help one group at the expense of others. That's not fair; we're supposed to be equal under the law. Loser pays is better because it's one simple rule that applies to all.

Some lawsuits are necessary. Loser pays would get rid of some bad ones.

Safety and regulation. We have enough rules; stop making new ones.

No, that's too rigid; obviously, changing conditions require new rules. But let's acknowledge that freedom and wealth are the greatest providers of safety. Affluence allows people to focus on safety. Freedom brings the flexibility that lets people adjust to risks themselves, rather than counting on clumsy big government to do it.

Acknowledge that government has too many rules already. Fifty thousand new pages added to the *Federal Register* every year don't make us safer. Since the unintended consequences of regulation are so harmful, regulators ought to have to make an overwhelming case before passing new rules. At least invoke the Stossel rule: Before you pass a new law, you must repeal two senseless old ones.

Government. Let there be less of it. How much less? I don't want to be greedy; how about we just limit it to 20 percent of the economy, instead of 40 percent? That's hardly starving the state. It still gives more than $1 trillion to the federal government alone. Isn't that enough?

The $1 trillion freed up by cutting government in half would allow people to create all kinds of good new things, and enjoy life a lot more.

Government should stick to what it needs to do: set basic safety and environmental rules and keep the peace. Otherwise government should *leave people alone.*

FREEDOM

Despite my complaints about big government and political censorship, America is still a relatively open society. Thank goodness for that. Openness made America prosperous; our reluctance to censor has given us all kinds of unexpected benefits: better music, better literature, even lifesaving science.

Science has thrived in the United States because no one expert—no "authority"—has the right to decide which ideas are permissible. No one can say, "That's dangerous; you can't say that." Instead, learning progresses though argument. We debate—sometimes viciously—until we reach a consensus. The arguments often hurt people's feelings. Tough. This openness lets us to argue our way to the truth.

The United States was first to split the atom because Einstein left Germany when the Nazis banned "Jewish physics." In France, thousands once died of smallpox because authorities said inoculating people with small amounts of a disease was against God's will, and they had the power to stop the experiments. In the Soviet Union, authorities marginalized gene research because they said it was "bourgeois science." We have vaccines and gene therapy only because in most of the west, speech and ideas were free.

"Free" is the key.

Every presidential election year, reporters ask, "Who will run the country?" Run the country? Hello? A *president* runs the country? What arrogance. The politicians are so important that if they're not in power, America stops? I don't think so.

Fortunately, America is *really* run by millions of free people, entertaining themselves, building spectacular buildings, offering us thousands of wonderful new inventions. Politicians don't run that.

Most of the best of life has nothing to do with government. People falling in love, worshiping, creating things, making families work. Yes, good government can keep the peace and create conditions that allow these good things to flourish, and presidents can do dumb things that make our lives worse. But for the most part, the complex, thriving giant that is the United States runs itself.

The country isn't a jet plane that will fall out of the sky without the Anointed at the helm. Government doesn't create new musicals or the old Latin Quarter, produce miracle drugs, or invent the computer chip.

Government doesn't build the cars, the machines that make them, or the enterprises that supply America with its amazing variety of food, shelter, and clothing.

My epiphany was seeing that we don't need experts to "run the country." We do need limited government, a referee that keeps the peace. But that's all. Then free minds and free markets make good things happen.

ACKNOWLEDGMENTS

I could never do enough to thank those at ABC who work so hard to make my stories accurate and coherent: Roje Augustine, Audrey Baker, Ted Balaker, Joanna Breen, Mike Clemente, Deborah Colloton, Carla Delandri, Brian Ellis, Alan Esner, Nancy Gammerman, Mark Golden, Joel Herson, Colin Hill, Ruth Iwano, Sharon Kaufman, Marika Kelderman, Kristina Kendall, Ryan Kessler, Patrick McMenamin, Frank Mastropolo, Victor Neufeld, Martin Phillips, Bud Proctor, Abby Rockmore, Dori Rosenthal, Neil Sass, Joe Schanzer, Todd Seavey, David Sloan, Steve Trevisan, Richard Wald, David Ward and Hank Weinbloom.

I couldn't get it done without my brilliant student interns: Laura Cantera, Mackenzie Chambers, Jeff Corn, Marie Davies, Edward Ehrber, Joy Jia, Greg Newburn, Michael Pucci, David Rochelson, Rena Silverman, Gehna Singh, and Dustin Stephens. If you want to work for me as an intern, please email us at JohnStossel@abc.com.

I am grateful to those who exposed my small brain to the grand benefits of liberty: Virginia Postrel and the other writers at *Reason* magazine; Charles Murray, for *In Pursuit of Happiness and Good Government*; Jonathan Rauch, for *Kindly Inquisitors*; political scientist Aaron Wildavsky for *Searching for Safety*; Frederick Hayek, for *The Constitution of*

Liberty; biochemist Bruce Ames; Elizabeth Whelan of the American Council on Science and Health; economists Walter Williams, Steven Landsburg, Don Boudreaux, and others from George Mason University; scholars of the Cato Institute, particularly Pat Michaels, Michael Tanner, José Piñera, Tom Palmer, Jerry Taylor, and David Boaz; those from the Manhattan Institute, especially Walter Olsen and Peter Huber; physicist Bernard Cohen; Andrea Rich of Laissez Faire Books; David Kelley of the Objectivist Center; science writer Michael Fumento; John Graham and Kimberly Thompson of the Harvard Center of Risk Analysis; law professors Eugene Volokh and John Langbein; and great thinkers John Kramer; Bob Poole of the Reason Foundation; and Bob Chitester and Rick Platt, of intheclassroom.org, which offers my ABC tapes to high schools and colleges.

I thank my liberal, Marxist, and socialist (although most deny that they are) friends for patiently arguing with me: Miriam Cukier, Dan Danser, Jim Floyd, Alan Meyers, Joe Sibilia, Joe Simonetti, Mark Smith and Michael Steinhardt.

This book was improved by the excellent editing I got from David Hirshey, Nick Trautwein, Tom, Ellen, Lauren, and Max. Finally, for editorial, financial, emotional, and mechanical guidance, I'm indebted to Bob Asahina; Richard Leibner; Joni Evans; my mother-in-law, Ruth; Eric Strauss and Jennifer C. Cohen.

INDEX